Expanding Possibilities for Inclusive Learning

While many teachers articulate a strong commitment to the values of equity and excellence underpinning inclusive education, they are often anxious about teaching increasingly diverse classes of children. This book, co-authored by researchers and practitioners, offers a strong foundation in the key principles, theories and debates that underpin current understandings of inclusive education and their implications for the development of inclusive learning for all members of a school's community.

Drawing on a wide range of recent research and practice, *Expanding Possibilities for Inclusive Learning* offers perspectives on inclusion from teachers, school leaders, other practitioners, children and parents. Readers are encouraged to reflect on their own beliefs, knowledge and practices as they plan to expand possibilities for inclusive learning in their own context. Each chapter provides reflective and practical activities to support practitioners to try out ideas in classrooms and schools.

As part of the Unlocking Research series, the book draws on recent research to enrich the professional development of student and practising teachers, teaching assistants and school leaders. The examples of practice and reflective activities that run throughout offer authentic opportunities to challenge existing practices and policies and bring about meaningful change.

Kristine Black-Hawkins is Professor of Inclusive Education at the University of Cambridge. She is internationally recognised for her research on working with teachers to develop inclusive pedagogical approaches that support the achievements of all learners, including those most vulnerable to educational marginalisation. She began her career teaching in schools and working for local government in the area of inclusive and special education.

Ashley Grinham-Smith is currently training to be an Educational Psychologist. Before this he was assistant head teacher at the University of Cambridge Primary School. He has a special interest in working systemically to endorse and promote trauma-informed inclusive practices within schools. He is passionate about inclusion and pastoral care in education, championing children at risk of marginalisation and exclusion.

Unlocking Research

Series Editors: James Biddulph and Julia Flutter

Unlocking Research offers support and ideas for students and practising teachers, enriching their knowledge of research and its application in primary school contexts. Packed with imaginative ideas and practical suggestions, the series aims to empower teachers, teaching assistants and school leaders to take research-informed and principled approaches to making necessary changes in schools so that teaching and learning ignites the social imagination for 21st century educators and learners.

Expanding Possibilities for Inclusive Learning
Edited by Kristine Black-Hawkins and Ashley Grinham-Smith

Unleashing Children's Voices in New Democratic Primary Education
Edited by James Biddulph, Luke Rolls and Julia Flutter

Sculpting New Creativities in Primary Education
Edited by Pam Burnard and Michelle Loughrey

Reimagining Professional Development in Schools
Edited by Eleanore Hargreaves and Luke Rolls

Inspiring Primary Curriculum Design
Edited by James Biddulph and Julia Flutter

For more information about this series, please visit: https://www.routledge.com/Unlocking-Research/book-series/URS

Expanding Possibilities for Inclusive Learning

Edited by Kristine Black-Hawkins and Ashley Grinham-Smith

Routledge
Taylor & Francis Group

LONDON AND NEW YORK

Cover image: Art by the Children of University of Cambridge Primary School and Linda Culverwell of Artbash www.artbash.co.uk

First published 2023
by Routledge
4 Park Square, Milton Park, Abingdon, Oxon OX14 4RN

and by Routledge
605 Third Avenue, New York, NY 10158

Routledge is an imprint of the Taylor & Francis Group, an informa business

© 2023 selection and editorial matter, Kristine Black-Hawkins and Ashley Grinham-Smith; individual chapters, the contributors

The right of Kristine Black-Hawkins and Ashley Grinham-Smith to be identified as the authors of the editorial material, and of the authors for their individual chapters, has been asserted in accordance with sections 77 and 78 of the Copyright, Designs and Patents Act 1988.

All rights reserved. No part of this book may be reprinted or reproduced or utilised in any form or by any electronic, mechanical, or other means, now known or hereafter invented, including photocopying and recording, or in any information storage or retrieval system, without permission in writing from the publishers.

Trademark notice: Product or corporate names may be trademarks or registered trademarks, and are used only for identification and explanation without intent to infringe.

British Library Cataloguing-in-Publication Data
A catalogue record for this book is available from the British Library

Library of Congress Cataloging-in-Publication Data
Names: Black-Hawkins, Kristine, 1957- editor. | Grinham-Smith, Ashley, editor.
Title: Expanding possibilities for inclusive learning/edited by Kristine Black-Hawkins and Ashley Grinham-Smith.
Description: Abingdon, Oxon; New York, NY: Routledge, 2023. | Includes bibliographical references and index.
Identifiers: LCCN 2022014393 | ISBN 9780367684600 (hardback) | ISBN 9780367684624 (paperback) | ISBN 9781003137634 (ebook)
Subjects: LCSH: Inclusive education–Great Britain. | Education, Primary–Great Britain.
Classification: LCC LC1203.G7 E96 2023 |
DDC 371.9/0460941–dc23/eng/20220708
LC record available at https://lccn.loc.gov/2022014393

ISBN: 978-0-367-68460-0 (hbk)
ISBN: 978-0-367-68462-4 (pbk)
ISBN: 978-1-003-13763-4 (ebk)

DOI: 10.4324/9781003137634

Typeset in Bembo
by Deanta Global Publishing Services, Chennai, India

Contents

List of contributors　　　　　　　　　　　　　　　　　　　　　　vii

1　Expanding inclusive learning in primary classrooms and schools　　1
　　Kristine Black-Hawkins and Ashley Grinham-Smith

2　Language matters　　　　　　　　　　　　　　　　　　　　　14
　　Elizabeth Walton and Catherine Marais

3　Developing inclusive practices: the role of student–teacher dialogues　30
　　Kyriaki Messiou and Leanne Galbally

4　Taking account of neurodiverse learners in the classroom:
　　supporting inclusive classroom practices　　　　　　　　　　45
　　Craig Goodall and James Ward-Sinclair

5　Exploring LGBT+ identities and their relationship to inclusive
　　practice in the primary school　　　　　　　　　　　　　　61
　　Max Biddulph and Sarah Hewitt-Clarkson

6　Developing inclusive school communities through parental
　　engagement in their children's learning　　　　　　　　　　77
　　Janet Goodall and Sam Greasley

Contents

7   Doing art, (un)colonised bodies: immersing curricula in our acts
    of living   91
    John Baldacchino and Faisal Abdu'Allah

8   Inclusive approaches for children at risk of exclusion: supporting
    mental health in primary schools   108
    Lysandra Sinclaire-Harding and Ashley Grinham-Smith

9   Maximising the work of teaching assistants: building an inclusive
    community of research-led practice   125
    Paula Bosanquet and Aimee Durning

10 Leading inclusive practice   141
    Pete Dudley and Bavaani Nanthabalan

11 Promoting inclusion and equity in schools through practitioner–
    researcher partnerships   160
    Mel Ainscow

    Afterword: why inclusion matters beyond primary school:
    University … a space for all?   177
    Graham Virgo

Index   181

List of contributors

Faisal Abdu'Allah
Department of Art History
University of Wisconsin-Madison
Madison, Wisconsin
and
Research Institute For Media, Arts and Performance
University of Bedfordshire
Luton, England

Mel Ainscow
Manchester Institute of Education
University of Manchester
Manchester, England
and
School of Education
University of Glasgow
Glasgow, Scotland

John Baldacchino
Division of the Arts
University of Wisconsin-Madison
Madison, Wisconsin

Max Biddulph
School of Education
University of Nottingham
Nottingham, England

Kristine Black-Hawkins
Faculty of Education
University of Cambridge
Cambridge, England

Paula Bosanquet
Department of Psychology and Human Development
UCL Institute of Education
London, England

Peter Dudley
Faculty of Education
University of Cambridge
Cambridge, England

Aimee Durning
University of Cambridge Primary School
Cambridge, England

Leanne Galbally
Wordsworth Primary School
Southampton, England

Craig Goodall
St Mary's University College
Belfast, Northern Island

Janet Goodall
School of Education
University of Swansea
Swansea, Wales

Sam Greasley
Awel y Môr Primary School
Port Talbot, Wales

Ashley Grinham-Smith
University of Cambridge Primary School
Cambridge, England

Sarah Hewitt-Clarkson
Anderton Park Primary School
Birmingham, England

Catherine Marais
The King's School Robin Hills
Randburg, South Africa

Kyriaki Messiou
School of Education
University of Southampton
Southampton, England

Bavaani Nanthabalan
Netley Primary School and Campus, Camden
London, England

Lysandra Sinclaire-Harding
Cambridgeshire Virtual School for Looked After Children
Cambridge, England
and
Tavistock and Portman NHS Foundation Trust
London, England

Graham Virgo
University of Cambridge
Cambridge, England

Elizabeth Walton
School of Education
University of Nottingham
Nottingham, England

James Ward-Sinclair
Founder, Autistic & Unapologetic
https://autisticandunapologetic.com/

Expanding inclusive learning in primary classrooms and schools

Kristine Black-Hawkins and Ashley Grinham-Smith

In this introductory chapter we set out our overall rationale and purposes for the book. In so doing we highlight some key principles, theories and debates that underpin current understandings of inclusive education. In particular, we consider how a range of views and perspectives emerge from and are shaped by differing political, social, cultural and historical contexts. These in turn raise a number of complex questions about the nature of inclusive learning. Throughout the chapter, and indeed the book itself, readers are encouraged to reflect on their professional values and beliefs, knowledge and practices, and to consider what next steps they might take to expand possibilities for inclusive learning in their own context.

What is this book about?

One gloriously sunny day in January 2020, just before the pandemic established its grip, we were invited to a meeting to discuss whether we would like to co-edit a book contributing to the Unlocking Research series. Its focus was to bring together research and practice around the theme of inclusive education in primary schools. Beyond that, the book was ours to create. Whilst we agreed that it should be useful and interesting for practitioners, and that it should focus on children's learning, we had a number of matters to resolve:

- What were our fundamental aims and purposes?
- Who would be our audiences?
- Which key topics should it cover?

DOI: 10.4324/9781003137634-1

During the course of that meeting we decided that the book should:

- Be underpinned by a principled approach to inclusive education, which values all members of a school's community (children and adults) and recognises everyone's right to participate and make progress in learning.
- Focus on the professional needs of all practitioners in primary schools and classrooms, offering support for readers who want to develop more inclusive approaches to children's learning.
- Bring together research and practice in inclusive education in order to identify and illuminate key issues for 21st-century primary teaching and learning.

So far, so good!

However, our conversation then took a less straightforward turn, revealing some significant differences in our views, and specifically around which learners (who) and what barriers to learning (why and how) we understood to be the focus of inclusive education. This is, perhaps, not surprising. Over the last few decades it has become something of a truism to note the contested nature of inclusive education. Conceptually, it can hold very different meanings for different people and for different purposes, which then shape how it is enacted in practice in classrooms and schools (see Ainscow, 2020, and Thomas, 2012, for discussions on this topic). Therefore, it was likely that we, as the co-editors, would also have distinct views from each other, based on our individual professional and personal knowledge, ways of working, and our beliefs about education more generally. Rouse (2008) has described this as the 'knowing', 'doing' and 'believing' of inclusive practice (see Figure 1.1).

In many ways, the dialogue between us as co-editors, starting on that day in January, represents a microcosm of the kinds of theoretical and practical discussions about the nature of inclusive education that have challenged educational researchers, policymakers and practitioners over many decades and continue to do so. Does inclusive education concern all children or only some? And if the latter, which children in particular? Historically, the connection between inclusive and special education is deep-rooted, and for some educationalists the terms *special educational needs* (*SEN*) and *inclusion* are used as if synonymous. Whereas for others, SEN is, in itself, an exclusionary term that draws on deficit models of learning. That is, it separates *some* children, whose educational needs are deemed to be 'special' (not 'normal'), from *most* children, whose educational needs are, by default, 'not special' (are 'normal'). (See Florian, 2019, for further discussion.)

For others, again, whilst inclusion is concerned with all children, it has a clear focus on those most at risk of educational marginalisation, because of a range of often systemic barriers to their learning: for example, in relationship to economic status, family circumstances, ethnicity, gender, disability, sexual orientation or religion. Finally, for many educationalists, this broader understanding of inclusive education must also take careful account of all members of a school's community. That is, processes of educational inclusion and exclusion affect not only children

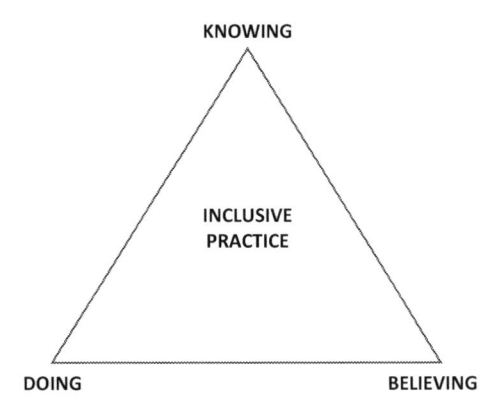

Figure 1.1 Inclusive practice (adapted from Rouse, 2008)

but also their parents/carers, as well as teachers and all other adults who work in or visit a school (Florian, Black-Hawkins and Rouse, 2017).

The questions in Box 1.1 not only illustrate some of the commonalities, variations and tensions in our discussions, they also represent the range of views and interests in the book as a whole. We believe it is important both to acknowledge and to respect the diversity of approaches to inclusive education of our contributing authors, by recognising that, like us, they too are shaped by their particular knowledge, practices and beliefs (Figure 1.1). We also invite you to reflect on these questions and how your responses are informed by your own personal and professional experiences.

Box 1.1 Reflecting on understandings of inclusive education

1. Who is the focus of inclusive education?
   - Individual children identified with special educational needs and/or disabilities
   - Particular groups of children at risk of marginalisation or exclusion from education
   - All children
   - Children and their families
   - Children and colleagues in schools
   - All members of a school's community

2. Is the inclusion of some learners more (or less) highly valued than others?
   - If so, who, why and by whom?

3. What really matters in inclusive education to …?
   - You as an education professional
   - The children in your school
   - Their families

- Your colleagues
- Other education professionals who support your school
- Your broader school community

4. Which factors promote or impede educational inclusion and exclusion?
   - Within individual children
   - Their peers
   - Practitioners and other education professionals
   - A school as an institution
   - Children's families
   - Their local community

5. What is the relationship between inclusive education and …?
   - Inclusive practice
   - Inclusive teaching
   - Inclusive learning

The final question in Box 1.1 was particularly useful for deciding the title of this book. We chose *Expanding Possibilities for Inclusive Learning*, because every chapter, albeit in a variety of ways, examines educational barriers that exclude children from making progress in their learning, and suggests very practical possibilities for breaking down those barriers to enable learning to be inclusive and to flourish. Furthermore, we wanted to emphasise that all practitioners must be given opportunities to be learners too (whether beginning or experienced teachers, other educational practitioners and support colleagues, or school leaders), if they are to develop the professional skills and knowledge they need to engage in the kinds of inclusive practices that support the learning of all children.

Returning to Figure 1.1, Rouse's triangle shows how the three elements of inclusive practice are not separate but closely interconnected. Over time, they influence and shape one another to enable professional learning to take place.

> [D]eveloping effective inclusive practice is not only about extending teachers' knowledge, but it is also about encouraging them to do things differently and getting them to reconsider their attitudes and beliefs. In other words, it should be about 'knowing', 'doing', and 'believing'.
>
> *(Rouse, 2008, p. 12)*

When teachers have opportunities to expand their knowledge in ways that enable them to develop their inclusive classroom practices, then their beliefs about educational inclusion will shift too. This in turn will encourage them to seek new knowledge. Likewise, when a school leader formulates a clear set of values around inclusive education, which they encourage colleagues and other members of the school community to draw on to underpin their daily practices, then not only will professional knowledge grow across the community, but also shape its collective and individual beliefs about inclusive education. This continual process of professional inclusive learning is at the heart of this book. Each chapter presents and examines knowledge about inclusive learning: for example, by interrogating theoretical perspectives, drawing on empirical studies, listening to parents' concerns and asking children what helps them to learn. Each chapter also challenges readers to reflect on their often taken-for-granted beliefs about learner diversity, as well as how, and why, children do and do not learn. Suggestions for thinking differently about classroom and school practices are given throughout.

Finally, as co-editors we needed to select a dozen or so topics on inclusive learning to form the chapters, which would then comprise the book. What should we include? And what might we leave out? In addressing these questions, further insights into different understandings of inclusive learning are provided and particularly with regard to who, why and how. Now that the book is published, we find it interesting to speculate what readers expect as they scan the contents page. Which topics are you pleased, surprised or, perhaps, even disappointed to see? Box 1.2 encourages you to imagine your own contents page. Or, put another way, what do you consider to be the essential who, why and how of inclusive learning?

Box 1.2 The who, why and how of inclusive learning

1. Which topics do you consider to be essential in a book focusing on expanding possibilities for inclusive learning?
2. How would you justify your choices?
3. Looking at the contents page of this book, in your view:
    *   Which topics most closely match your choices?
    *   Are there topics that you think are missing? Why?
    *   Are there others that seem unnecessary? Why?
    *   Are there any surprises? Why?

How is inclusive education understood by others?

The previous section invited readers to reflect on their understanding of inclusive education, drawing on personal and professional beliefs, experiences and knowledge. This section explores some of the ways in which inclusive education is understood by others by presenting, albeit briefly, a selection of four different perspectives from research and policy. The first introduces a global view from the United Nations Sustainable Development Goals (SDGs), and specifically Goal 4 concerning 'inclusive and equitable quality education' (United Nations, 2021). The second examines core values for all teachers in inclusive education by drawing on a multinational research study into Initial Teacher Education (ITE) from the European Agency for Special Needs and Inclusive Education (EASNE,

2012). The third offers a national government's policy perspective on inclusive education, regarding individual teacher's professional responsibilities. This focuses on the Department for Education's (DfE, 2013) Inclusion Statement, embedded in the English National Curriculum. The section ends with children's views on inclusive classroom communities, illustrated with findings from research undertaken by Kristine Black-Hawkins in collaboration with colleagues (Black-Hawkins, Maguire and Kershner, 2021). As already discussed, inclusive education, and its enactment in practice, has different meanings in different contexts, for different people and purposes. Certainly, the four perspectives presented here do not aim to provide a comprehensive understanding of the field; rather, they illustrate some of its complexity and provide further opportunities for reflection.

United Nations' Sustainable Development Goals (SDGs): A global perspective

A recent report from UNESCO (2020, p. 39) states: 'The world has committed to inclusive education not by chance but because it is the foundation of an education system of good quality that enables every child, youth and adult to learn and fulfil their potential.' This view of inclusive education is embedded in the UN's SDGs. Established in 2015, with the expressed aim of being achieved by 2030, a number of the SDGs 'refer directly to equity, inclusion, diversity, equal opportunity or non-discrimination' (UNESCO, 2020). In particular, SDG 4 sets out to 'ensure inclusive and equitable quality education and promote lifelong learning opportunities for all' (UNESCO, 2020). This goal emphasises three interrelated themes:

1. Inclusive education is for everyone.
2. Inclusive education is of high quality.
3. Inclusive education is for life.

However, it also recognises that how these are developed in practice must take into account local, regional and national contexts.

Despite this stated commitment from the international community, the UN acknowledge that it is highly unlikely that SDG 4 will be achieved by 2030. Notably, in 2020 an estimated 258 million children and young people (17% of the global total) were not in any form of education at all (UNESCO, 2020, p. 258). For very many others, the quality and quantity of provision was woefully inadequate. Furthermore, although the SDG 4 focuses on the rights and needs of all learners, UNESCO (2020) also highlights how certain groups of learners are far more at risk of educational exclusion because of 'gender, remoteness, wealth, disability, ethnicity, language, migration, displacement, incarceration, sexual orientation, gender identity and expression, religion and other beliefs and attitudes' (p. v). Significantly, UNESCO notes the impact of what it describe as 'layers of discrimination': for example, a girl living in relative poverty in a remote rural location; or a migrant, who has a disability and is experiencing prejudice because of their sexual orientation.

Most recently, the impact of the Covid pandemic on achieving SDG 4 has been devastating. According to the United Nations (2021), the pandemic has 'wiped out 20 years of education gains', and in so doing exacerbated long-standing barriers to 'equitable quality education' for all:

> COVID–19 has wreaked havoc worldwide on children's learning and well-being. Before the pandemic, progress in education was already too slow to achieve Goal 4 by 2030. One year into the crisis, two in three students were still affected by full or partial school closures. One hundred million more children than before fail to demonstrate basic reading skills. The poorest and most vulnerable children are bearing the brunt of the crisis, exacerbating longstanding inequalities. Many risk never returning to school; some are forced into child marriage or child labour.

Box 1.3 Mitigating the impact of the pandemic on children's learning

The preceding quotation highlights how the pandemic has affected children's learning and well-being worldwide, albeit it very different ways in different contexts. Reflecting on the experiences of the children with whom you work:

- What barriers to inclusive learning has the pandemic exacerbated?
- What might be the longer-term consequences of these?
- What steps might you take to mitigate their impact?

European Agency for Special Needs and Inclusive Education (EASNIE): Initial teacher education for inclusive learning

EASNIE, established in 1996, is an independent organisation comprising 31 European countries, including the UK, which undertakes, coordinates and disseminates research on the development of more inclusive education systems. It is concerned with how this can be achieved at different levels – individual teachers, classrooms and schools, as well as local and national policies – and the interplay between them. The agency describes its 'ultimate vision' as being:

> To ensure that all learners of any age are provided with meaningful, high-quality educational opportunities in their local community, alongside their friends and peers.

(EASNIE, 2017, p. 2)

There are strong parallels here with the three themes from the UN's SDG 4 that emphasise inclusive education as being about everyone, high-quality provision, and lifelong learning. Likewise, the EASNIE also stresses how different countries will achieve these in different ways, depending on their past and current political, social and cultural contexts (2017, p. 1). (For further information about the agency, plus access to a wide range of its resources, see https://www.european-agency.org/.)

The European Agency for Development in Special Needs Education (EADSNE, 2012) undertook a three-year study, across 25 European countries, which examined the kinds of practices undertaken in ITE programmes that enable student and early career teachers to support all learners in inclusive classrooms. The research posed two overarching questions (p. 10):

- What kind of teachers are needed for an inclusive society in a 21st century school?
- What are the essential teacher competences for inclusive education?

From this work (EADSNE, 2012), a *Profile of Inclusive Teachers* was developed, providing stimulus material to guide the design and implementation of ITE programmes. Whilst the profile is comprehensive in nature, it is not mechanistic or prescriptive, because it recognises the complex nature of day-to-day teaching and learning. Although its primary target audience comprises teacher educators and policymakers, the materials are well worth exploring by all education professionals interested in developing more inclusive practices. The Profile highlights two interrelated key areas. These concern teachers' attitudes and beliefs and the importance of a values-led approach to inclusive education.

Teachers' attitudes and beliefs and a values-led approach to inclusive education

First, findings from the research indicate that the following attitudes and beliefs are necessary for all teachers if inclusive education is to develop and thrive (EADSNE, 2012, p. 11):

- Education is based upon a belief in equality, human rights and democracy for all learners.
- Inclusive education is about societal reform and is non-negotiable.
- Inclusive education and quality in education cannot be viewed as separate issues.
- Access to mainstream education alone is not enough.
- Participation means that all learners are engaged in learning activities that are meaningful for them.

> ## Box 1.4 Attitudes and beliefs underpinning conceptions of inclusive education
>
> Considering each of the aforementioned attitudes and beliefs:
>
> 1. What do you understand each one to mean?
> 2. How far do you concur with the ideas embedded in them?
> 3. What are their implications for you as a professional?

Second, the research findings highlight the importance of a values-led approach to ITE. At the heart of the profile, and shaping all associated materials and guidance, are four core values that form the basis for the work of all teachers, regardless of the settings in which they work (EADSNE, 2012, p. 7).

1. *Valuing learner diversity*: Learner difference is considered as a resource and an asset to education.
2. *Supporting all learners*: Teachers have high expectations for all learners' achievements.
3. *Working with others*: Collaboration and teamwork are essential approaches for all teachers.
4. *Continuing personal professional development*: Teaching is a learning activity and teachers take responsibility for their own lifelong learning.

Collectively, these core values seem particularly useful in exploring understandings of inclusive learning. Notably, they focus on high-quality learning for everyone: not only for all children, but for teachers too. They also recognise and value diversity across a school's community: again not only in terms of children learning with and from each other, but also teachers learning with and from children and, of course, colleagues and parents and other community members. Finally, achievement is understood to be about all forms of personal, social and academic attainments, rather than simply in terms of test or examination results. There is also a strong focus on taking careful account of the kinds of learning and achievements that are valued by children and their families, as well as the broader society.

> ## Box 1.5 Four core values for all teachers in inclusive education (EADSNE, 2012)
>
> 1. Focusing on each core value, how far does it resonate with your understanding of teaching and learning for inclusive education?
> 2. How is it enacted currently in your daily practice?
> 3. What steps could you take to embed it further in your work?

The English National Curriculum Framework Inclusion Statement: Requirements for teachers

The current statutory National Curriculum Framework, implemented by the DfE in 2014, provides an 'Inclusion Statement' (DfE, 2013, p. 8). It is very brief (a single side in a document of 200-plus pages). Nevertheless, because it sets out the government's expectations and requirements for teachers in all state-funded schools in England, it provides insights into national policy perspectives and their implications for practice. Like both the UN and EASNIE documents already considered, the DfE statement expects teachers to have a very clear focus on the achievements of all children. Notably, it refers to the importance of 'set[ting] targets which are deliberately ambitious' and having 'high expectations for every pupil'.

Alongside this concern with the inclusion of all learners, the DfE 'Inclusion Statement' also requires teachers to take particular account of 'individuals and groups of pupils' more likely to encounter 'potential barriers' to learning and achievement; for example, in relationship to the protected characteristics of 'race, disability, sex, religion or belief, sexual orientation, pregnancy and maternity, and gender reassignment' as enshrined in the Equality Act (2010). In addition, the statement highlights the following learners:

- Low levels of prior attainment
- Attainment is significantly above the expected standard
- Disadvantaged backgrounds
- Special educational needs
- Disabilities
- English as an additional language

In some ways this shifting focus between *all* learners and *some* learners (i.e. those more vulnerable to educational marginalisation) reflects the earlier discussion arising from the UNESCO materials, regarding groups of learners at risk of educational exclusion. Even though the identified vulnerable groups are clearly rather different – highlighting again the need to take account of the context in which learning occurs – there are parallels. UNESCO's reference to 'layers of discrimination' also has relevance here too: for example, a child may be attaining significantly above the expected standard, have a disability and come from a disadvantaged background. Furthermore, however 'potential barriers' and 'layers of discrimination' are characterised, they never exist in isolation from all other aspects of what it is to be that individual child now and in the future. All children's lived experiences, both in and outside school, are multifaceted, complex and changeable (Alexander, 2010, p. 115).

> ## Box 1.6 Layers of discrimination
>
> Reflecting on the children in your class, how might the idea of 'layers of discrimination' help you to develop your inclusive practices?

Children's perspectives on developing inclusive classroom communities

The study 'Developing Inclusive Classroom Communities' (Black-Hawkins et al., 2021) addressed the question: What matters to children in the development of inclusive classroom communities? Groups of children (aged 4–11 years, from seven different schools) participated in peer group discussions on two related areas – belonging and learner diversity – to explore how these might matter to their classroom learning.

Four key interconnecting themes emerged from analysis of the findings (Table 1.1); these were consistent across all groups and regardless of children's ages or particular classroom and school contexts. Furthermore, as the summary in Table 1.1 indicates, in the children's daily classroom experiences, all four themes are closely connected to each other. That is, securing classroom communities as

Table 1.1 What matters to children in inclusive classroom communities

1. *Feeling comfortable and being safe*: Feeling comfortable and being safe were fundamental to the children's experiences of belonging to their classroom communities and were highly valued by them. This theme is also closely linked to the feelings expressed in number 4 below.
2. *Learning as the main activity*: All groups referred to learning as the main activity, or purpose, for being in their classes, and engaging in this collective enterprise seemed to strengthen their feelings of membership. Some (older) children brought together themes (1) and (2) to articulate how being at ease supported their capacity to learn.
3. *Having friends and working together*: A range of classroom relationships contributed to the children's experiences of inclusive classroom learning. Positive peer friendships were crucial to feeling comfortable; some described feelings of discomfort when friendships did not go well and the detrimental effect on their learning. Some children liked to work with their friends, but many also valued the communal and varied resource brought by peers more generally, to support their own and others' learning.
4. *Sharing values and behaviours*: All groups emphasised how sharing values and behaviours contributed to their sense of community: from younger children's views on 'being good' and 'not being naughty', to older children's articulation of the importance of sharing, being kind and being willing to contribute. These understandings were also explained in terms of loyalty, attachment and pride in being members of their particular class, often expressed as being 'special' in comparison to other classes.

Source: Adapted from Black-Hawkins et al. (2021).

places where children feel comfortable and safe, is likely to be enhanced through mutually supportive relationships, which in turn encourages children's individual and collective learning. Meanwhile, engaging in collective learning not only promotes shared values and behaviours but also nurtures mutually supportive relationships, which then underpin children's sense of feeling comfortable and being safe.

Box 1.7 Developing an inclusive classroom community: Listening to children

- What steps could you take to develop one or more of the themes outlined in Table 1.1?
- How might you draw on informal group discussions amongst children in your class to inform your planning? For example, you might choose to adapt the following questions that were used as prompts with the children who participated in this study.

  - What does it mean to belong to your class?
  - Does belonging matter to your learning?
  - How are children similar to each other in your class and how are they different?
  - Does being similar or different matter to your learning?

What are the possibilities for expanding inclusive learning?

In this chapter we have presented a number of ways in which inclusive education can be understood. We have also drawn attention to how these variations are shaped by particular contexts, perspectives and purposes. Indeed, we began the chapter by describing how, as co-editors, we held rather different views about the potential content of this book, which we then explored in terms of the who, why and how of inclusive education. Nevertheless, throughout our discussions we were always clear that we shared fundamental principles regarding the rights of all learners to be respected and valued for who they are. We also agreed that all learners must be able to participate in high-quality learning experiences which are meaningful to them. Indeed, these principles can be seen to underpin the arguments and ideas raised in every chapter of the book, even though the focus of each one is different. In this way, our intention has been to provide readers with a rich range of possibilities to expand inclusive learning in their own classrooms and schools.

References

Ainscow, M. (2020). Inclusion and equity in education: Making sense of global challenges, *Prospects* 49:123–134.

Alexander, R. (2010). *Children, Their World, Their Education: Final Report and Recommendations of the Cambridge Primary Review*, London: Routledge.

Black-Hawkins, K., Maguire, L., & Kershner, R. (2021). Developing inclusive classroom communities: what matters to children? *Education 3-13*, https://doi.org/10.1080 /03004279.2021.1873398.

DfE (2013). The national curriculum in England key stages 1 and 2 framework. Available at: www.gov.uk/government/uploads/system/uploads/attachment_data/file/335133/ PRIMARY_national_curriculum_220714.pdf.

EADSNE (2012). *Teacher Education for Inclusion: Profile of Inclusive Teachers*, Odense, Denmark: EADSNE. Available at: https://www.european-agency.org/sites/default/files/Profile -of-Inclusive-Teachers.pdf.

EASNIE (2017). https://www.european-agency.org/sites/default/files/agencyflyer2017-en _a4_electronic.pdf.

Florian, L. (2019). On the necessary co-existence of special and inclusive education, *International Journal of Inclusive Education* 23(7–8):691–704.

Florian, L., Black-Hawkins, K., & Rouse, M. (2017). *Achievement and Inclusion in Schools* (2nd edition), London: Routledge.

Rouse, M. (2008). Developing inclusive practice, *Education in the North* 16:6–13.

Thomas, G. (2012). A review of thinking and research about inclusive education policy, with suggestions for a new kind of inclusive thinking, *British Educational Research Journal* 38:1–18.

UNESCO (2020). *Global Education Monitoring Report 2020: Inclusion and Education: All Means All*, Paris: UNESCO. Available at: unesdoc.unesco.org/ark:/48223/pf0000373718/PD F/373718eng.pdf.multi.

United Nations (2021). https://sdgs.un.org/goals/goal4.

2

Language matters

Elizabeth Walton and Catherine Marais

Introduction: R-words

Barak Obama signed Rosa's law in the USA in 2010. Rosa Marcellino is a young woman with an intellectual disability and this law makes it illegal to use the 'R-word' (R stands for 'retarded'). The campaign by Rosa's family was launched in recognition that the R-word had been used widely in society to degrade and insult people with intellectual disabilities. Obama quoted Rosa's brother, saying, 'The way you speak about people is the way you treat them' (The White House, 2010). This statement shows that choice of words is an important indicator of our beliefs and attitudes, which then result in actions.

It is not uncommon for people, like Rosa Marcellino's family, to become activists once their own lives have been personally impacted by disability. One of the aims of this chapter is to help jump-start this process for all educational practitioners. Awareness, starting with self-awareness, is an important first step to real change. The goal is to become more reflective of the language that we use, given that 'overt action without insight is likely to lead to temporary change' (Prochaska and Norcross, 2018, p. 426). We need to have greater awareness and insight into the impact that our language has on those around us.

Language is an important consideration in the quest for more inclusive classrooms, which expect the 'Full and effective participation, accessibility, attendance and achievement of all students, especially those who, for different reasons, are excluded or at risk of being marginalized' (UN, 2016, p. 3). Those who are vulnerable to exclusion or marginalisation are often those who experience discriminatory and offensive language used about them by those who are privileged and powerful in society. The main focus in this chapter is the language used to speak about disability, but the authors acknowledge others who are vulnerable to

DOI: 10.4324/9781003137634-2

exclusion or marginalisation including ethnic and religious minorities, women, and LGBTIQA+ people. In this chapter, we aim to show how language helps to construct people as 'others', and creates, sustains and legitimises their exclusion or marginalisation. We consider some R-words as we explore inclusive and exclusionary language, and note that for the purposes of clarity and illustration we will use some words associated with disability that we acknowledge are offensive.

Recognising what language does

Language is used in policy and other discourses of those in power to describe and categorise children and young people, which in turn has a material effect on their educational experiences and life outcomes.

> Rebecca Hulbert is Arthur's mother. Arthur has Down syndrome. In an open letter, Hulbert wrote, 'With my son's arrival, I have witnessed my world through a new lens. Not only as a mother but as a mother to a little boy with Down Syndrome. I have suddenly felt first-hand the importance of considerate and appropriate language.' Convinced that language creates reality, Hulbert created a series of flashcards to prompt medical professionals to use less stigmatising language. These include saying to parents that there is 'unexpected' rather than 'bad' news and that there is a 'chance' that the baby has Down syndrome rather than a 'risk'.

The power of language is seen in the way it creates 'normal' and 'other' children and young people. In so doing, language encodes ableism. Like racism and sexism, which build a world based on the assumption of the superiority of a particular race or sex, ableism assumes that particular expressions of ability define normal and affords privilege to those who are not disabled.

> Ableism is the belief, or underlying assumption, that an 'able' body or mind is the expected standard of being human. Campbell (2001, p. 44) explains ableism as
>
> > A network of beliefs, processes and practices that produces a particular kind of self and body (the corporeal standard) that is projected as the perfect, species-typical and therefore essential and fully human. Disability then is cast as a diminished state of being human.

The construction of the normal and deviant pupil

The 'normal' child sets the standard for development and achievement, necessarily casting those who do not meet the criteria of normal as 'abnormal', 'deviant' or 'defective' in some way. In England, for example, the determination of 'special educational needs' is made in a judgement against 'the majority of others of the same age' (Department for Education, 2015, p. 16). Special educational provision is provision that is 'different from or additional to that normally available to pupils or students of the same age' (Department for Education, 2015, p. 16). There is no inventory of what the majority can learn or do, but this policy, and other similar policies around the world, takes for granted a general recognition of the 'normal' as a plumb line against which 'non-normal' can be measured.

Binary opposites

Ableist language constructs disabled pupils as being a binary opposite of non-disabled pupils. On 14 October 2019, *The Times* published a report in its online newspaper. It was subsequently and rightly amended, but the headlines and first few paragraphs of the original stated:

> **Pupils lose out as £400m schools funding diverted to special needs**
> Children have been losing out because millions of pounds earmarked for their education has been siphoned off to pay for special needs education, an investigation by (sic) has found.
>
> A surge in pupils categorised as having special needs has led schools to lay off staff, increase class sizes and cut back on subjects as councils raid mainstream education budgets to fund support for them.

The article creates a clear distinction between 'pupils' and those with 'special needs'. 'Pupils' are presented as being disadvantaged by a system that allocates funds for support for those who need it. Words like 'diverted', 'syphoned off' and 'raid' makes it sound like this spending is excessive, unnecessary and even illegitimate. The word 'surge' creates the impression that pupils with special needs are a threat to the educational experience of those in the 'mainstream'. The language contributes to what Ryan (2019) calls the 'demonisation' of disabled people. Contrary to what the article claims, funding cuts have disproportionately negatively affected disabled children (Ryan, 2019).

The boundaries of normal

Language narrows the boundaries of 'normal' by describing more and more ways in which pupils might deviate from the norm. The proliferation of diagnostic categories over the decades has been recognised (Wakefield, 2016) with

Table 2.1 Advantages and disadvantages of labels

Advantages of labels	Disadvantages of labels
■ A diagnosis and the label that is associated with the diagnosis can open the door for resources to be directed to support the child. ■ Labels can lead to greater awareness of diagnoses and can help with understanding the difficulties that some children experience. ■ Labels can aid communication among professionals, as they provide unambiguous information relevant to assisting and supporting the child. ■ Some children and families find comfort in labels as they 'explain' why they experience difficulties with learning. ■ Labels can provide a sense of social identity and belonging to a group of others with a similar identity.	■ Labels may be given, but no actual support or intervention follows. ■ Labels can be stigmatising and associated with negative bias and prejudice, bullying and teasing towards those who are labelled. Low self-esteem may result. ■ Many diagnostic labels rely on clinical judgement, and diagnostic criteria and thresholds can change and be interpreted differently. ■ There is evidence that labels are applied differently to children according to their race, gender and class (Harry, 2014). ■ Labels can lead to generalisations about children, with the assumption that all children with a particular diagnosis are similar. This can lead to a neglect of individual profiles that reflect a range of factors beyond the diagnosis that impact a child's learning. ■ Teachers may have lowered expectations of children with particular labels.

the language of 'disorders' clearly signalling not only difference but deficit. This raises the question of whether diagnostic labels are helpful. This question has been debated by scholars and practitioners (e.g. Graham et al., 2020; Lauchlan and Boyle, 2007) who note a number of advantages and disadvantages of labels (see Table 2.1). These can be helpful when reflecting on the use of labels in classrooms.

Given these advantages and disadvantages, language users need to be alert to the affordances and limitations of descriptions of difference, particularly where these descriptions encode biases and negative stereotypes.

The language of exceptionality

Ableist language creates insiders and outsiders – those who belong by right, and those who do not and must be 'included'. One way this occurs is through presenting disabled pupils as a very different type of pupil from those who are not disabled. This language emphasises difference rather than commonality, and draws attention to features and behaviours that are deemed 'exceptional' or 'extraordinary'. This language of exceptionality contributes to an understanding of disability as an individual aberration, as if the problem lies with the disabled pupil and their family. The schooling system is exempt from any examination of how it contributes to learning difficulties and failure where the fault can be attributed to the individual.

Difference and deviance are reinforced through popular media and fiction that portrays disabled characters (Walton, 2016). The result is a (voyeuristic) preoccupation with the peculiarities of difference, reminiscent of the freak shows of the past. Textbooks are also complicit in creating exceptionality through descriptions of different types of disability, often in discrete chapters or sections (Brantlinger, 2006; Walton, 2016). These chapters suggest ways in which disabled pupils differ from the norm and their requirements of different pedagogical approaches by specialists or experts.

The language of superiority

Concern has been raised about the unchallenged power of professionals claiming expertise about the lives of disabled children and their families (Veck, 2014). This power can be wielded through language in the use of jargon, abbreviations and complex diagnostic terminology. This reinforces professional status, often at the expense of parents and pupils who do not have access to these linguistic resources. It can also be wielded to show disrespect, where professionals use their own names and titles but then refer to a pupil's mother as 'Mum' rather than her name and title. Disrespect is also present when practitioners do not recognise parents and caregivers as experts in their children's lives. The importance of speaking to parents and caregivers as equal partners in their child's education is illustrated next in the story of Becki.

Who is the expert in this scenario?

A newly qualified teacher said to a parent, 'I know all about epilepsy and epileptics, so I know how to deal with Becki.' The teacher could be advised to reconsider who has expert knowledge in this situation. Epilepsy affects different children differently, and the epilepsy diagnosis tells the teacher very little about Becki's learning profile. The teacher could have said to her parent, 'I know Becki has epilepsy, and I know about some of the ways epilepsy might affect children. But I don't know about Becki's experience and how epilepsy impacts her learning. Please tell me about Becki so I can teach her effectively.'

It is clear that language does things. It does not only reflect our understanding of the world, it also creates that understanding. Language is a powerful force in shaping how we see the world. Recognising the power of language and the language of power are crucial in the development of inclusive practice. Slee (2011, p. 156) says, 'Thinking about language should not be dismissed as an academic indulgence, or as the fixation of political correctness. The stakes are high and we need to exercise care.'

> ## Reminder: Recognise that language …
>
> - Encodes ableism.
> - Divides people into those who are normal and those who are deviant or defective.
> - Narrows the boundaries of who is regarded as normal.
> - Presents disabled and non-disabled people as being binary opposites.
> - Emphasises difference rather than commonalities.

Rejecting the language of insult and deficit

Language reveals and perpetuates society's negative views of disability. Insults are used against disabled people and appropriated as a means of denigrating others. The language of deficit might be more subtle, but is no less problematic in the quest for more equitable and just education.

The language of insult

There are many negative and offensive words about disability. The R-word mentioned in the introduction to this chapter is one such word. This word and others[1] are used in disability hate speech to bully and demean disabled people in actual and virtual spaces. These words are also used regularly as insults on the playground and on social media. Even people who are sensitive to other oppressions, such as racism or sexism, use these terms, revealing deeply held ableist views. It is possible that people have not thought of the origins of these words, and how these are associated with long-held beliefs and stereotypes about the abnormality and inferiority of disabled people. These are highly offensive terms, which, like other terms associated with racism and sexism, should be rejected.

The language of deficit

The language of deficit is more difficult to identify because it doesn't seem as offensive. But, in subtle ways, it reflects disability as deficient, needy or pitiful. This is a patronising way of referring to disabled people, as it portrays disability as a tragedy. Words like 'suffer from' or 'victim of' reveal this kind of charity discourse. It is also found in 'despite' expressions (see Figure 2.1).

These sentiments are ableist in that they assume a disability makes a person unable to contribute to society or to have a satisfying personal life. They presume lowered expectations of disabled people and diminish their accomplishments. Nick Hodge (2019) produced a video about the words that 'swirl around'

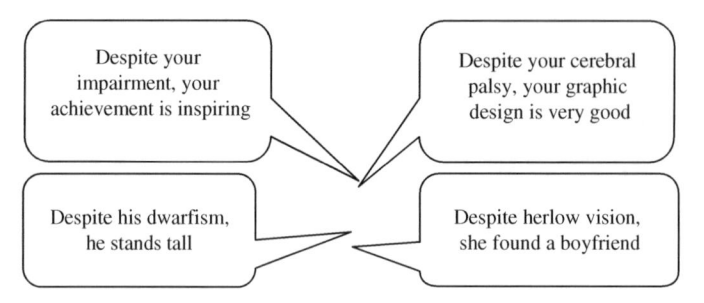

Figure 2.1 'Despite' language

children and impact how they come to see themselves as disordered and 'made wrong'. Harnessing the power of visual communication, Hodge shows how phrases like 'He's one of our special needs', 'She can't do humour', 'He needs more help than we can give him', and 'I worry about his future' are heard by pupils. Through hearing these and other similar words every day, children learn, 'So that's who I am'. Over time this external narrative – said by those adults and peers in a child's life – becomes the child's inner voice. The language of deficit erodes confidence and esteem in pupils.

The language of deficit does not only negatively affect pupils. It legitimises exclusionary practices, as repeated negative discussions about pupils build the case for their unsuitability for their current provision. It normalises ableism because it perpetuates the idea of the normal pupil against whom others are described as deficient. Deficit talk deprofessionalises teachers and allied staff who should be holding high expectations of all pupils and enabling them to meet these expectations. Finally, deficit talk loses the trust of parents who assume school personnel will do the best for their children, including not denigrating them by using disparaging language.

Reminder: *Reject* the language of …

- Insult that uses current and historical terms with negative associations about disability.
- Deficit that makes disabled pupils appear needy and pitiful, erodes their self-esteem, legitimises exclusion and deprofessionalises staff.

Revisiting some terms

There are terms that might have positive origins or intentions, but together they potentially construct pupils in ways that work against the aims of inclusive education. Terms like 'special', 'needs', 'support', 'welcome' and 'diversity' are terms that should be used with critique and caution. These examples remind us of how language use changes and evolves over time, and also that words that may be well-received in one environment or place in time may be offensive in another environment or place or time. Ensuring appropriate language use in the inclusive classroom is thus nuanced and complex, and defies simple rules or generic formulations.

Special needs or special educational needs (often abbreviated as SEN) is used in many places across the world, sometimes in conjunction with disability (like special educational needs and disabilities, or SEND), and sometimes to signal disability. It is a term that is embedded in national policy and practice, and is often used uncritically. The term 'special needs' is attributed to Baroness Warnock in England in 1978. The intention was to focus on the inadequacies of the schooling system rather than blaming individuals for difficulties in learning (Thomas and Vaughn, 2004). But, as we know, the system has not changed much, and 'special needs' has become another label that signals individual deficit and suggests the need for segregated or 'special' provision. There are good reasons for revisiting the term.

The first reason is that it is not very useful as a label. It is so broad that it tells nothing about the particular adjustments and access arrangements that people require. The second reason is that many disability activists reject the term and argue against its use. Malaquais (n.d.) sees the term as damaging and offensive and wants it consigned to the 'scrapheap'. She says,

> The label of 'special needs', serving by definition to segregate or exception-alise people with disability, is inconsistent with recognition of disability as part of human diversity. In that social framework, none of us are 'special' as we are all equal siblings in our diverse family of humanity.

A video[2] was produced for World Down Syndrome Day in 2017, titled 'Not Special Needs'. Actors show that 'special needs' are things like needing to wear a suit of armour or to be woken up by a celebrity. People with Down syndrome and other disabilities have human needs like education, jobs, opportunities and friends, just like everyone else. These needs are not special. A third reason is that research shows that the term 'special needs' should be avoided, as it is an ineffective euphemism, and it is regarded more negatively than the term 'disability' (Gernsbacher et al., 2016). Finally, it is worth resisting the term because it is associated with segregated learning and living. Malaquais (n.d.) says that the 'special story' is as follows:

> A child with 'special needs' catches the 'special bus' to receive 'special assistance' in a 'special school' from 'special education teachers' to prepare them for a 'special' future living in a 'special home' and working in a 'special workshop'.

She asks, 'Does that sound "special" to you?' Clearly it does not.

Sometimes 'special' is omitted from special needs, given its criticism. Instead, certain pupils are described as having learning or diverse *needs*. But the echo of 'special' remains and to have needs is still associated with lack or deficit. It unhelpfully divides the world into those who have needs and those who meet needs. To have needs is to be needy, which elicits pity or scorn in an ableist society that valorises independence. The discourse needs to shift from 'meeting needs' to 'realising rights'. Ensuring access to educational opportunities is not a benevolent response to a needy group, it is realising the fundamental right to education by all.

The term *support* is used often but it can also indicate deficit assumptions about others. 'Support' and 'needs' are often put together, and then 'additional' is added to give the phrase 'additional support needs'. This suggests that pupils with 'additional support needs' require something extra that is not usually provided by the education system. They are different from their peers for whom the schooling provision is sufficient. This is an indication of a 'most' and 'some' approach to education (Black-Hawkins and Florian, 2012) with a system designed for most pupils, with additions required for some pupils. When pupils are repeatedly described as having 'additional support needs' we should not be surprised to hear that some teachers view inclusive teaching as an 'additional stressor' or an extra burden on their professional practice.

The word *welcome* is often used to describe the culture that is needed in an inclusive school. All children should feel that they belong and can participate in the life of the school. But when welcome is used about disabled or 'other' children in mainstream schools, it is a way of signalling that they are guests in the school. The hospitality metaphor for inclusion (Walton, 2016) is problematic in that it positions some pupils as belonging to the school by right, and others as being there at the invitation and pleasure of the host. Guests have to conform to the preferences of the host, and their stay is dependent on the goodwill of the host. Guests don't belong and can be asked to leave any time they outstay their welcome. McLaughlin, Coleman-Fountain and Clavering (2016, p. 59) use another hospitality term in explaining that 'disabled children get "integrated" by schools looking to *accommodate* them in structures intended for non-disabled children' (emphasis ours). 'Accommodation' speaks of shifting things around to make room, but not of the fundamental reform needed for all children to participate in schools.

Diversity is a term that is usually viewed positively. It should refer to the fact that humans are different in various ways, and that difference should be seen as both positive and natural. But, like other words whose meanings have drifted, diversity has often become a marker for 'others'. It refers to those who do not conform to the norm. It has become a euphemistic term to signify 'people not like me or us'. People seldom think of themselves as being diverse, but that those of different races, religions and cultures as being diverse. It is usually 'diverse' people who are seen to be in need of inclusion. In institutional spaces, diversity is often portrayed as a fantasy world in which everyone is equally different. This use of the term 'diversity' obscures the deep and systemic inequalities that lead to the oppression of some groups by others. It is a word that should be used with critique and caution.

Reminder: *R*evisit some language …

- Special needs may signal individual deficit and suggests the need for segregated or 'special' provision.
- Support can indicate deficit assumptions about others and diverts attention from realising rights.
- Welcome can suggest that some pupils belong to the school by right, but others have to be invited; they have to be accommodated and their stay is conditional.
- Diversity can be a euphemistic term to signify 'people not like me or us'.

Respectful language and communication

This section identifies language that shows respect for individual experience and preference, and affirms the dignity and worth of everyone.

Identity-first and person-first language

Most people, we think, want to use respectful language when talking about disability. But there can be confusion and concern not to cause offence. One debate is whether to use person–first language (e.g. person with a disability, pupil with epilepsy, child with visual impairment) or identify–first language (e.g. disabled person, blind pupil, autistic child). There are valid reasons for each of these options (see Table 2.2).

Table 2.2 Reasons for preferring person-first or identity-first language

Reasons for preferring person-first language	Reasons for preferring identity-first language
■ Person-first language keeps the individual at the forefront, showing that the person is more than their disabled identity. ■ It serves as a reminder not to generalise or stereotype people because of a disability, or assume that because their disability is known, they can be known. ■ Person-first language recognises that humans are intersectional beings and have multiple identities assigned by their gender, sexuality, ethnicity and nationality, as well as their disability. ■ The use of person-first language in schools might prevent the tendency to pre-judge, sort and separate pupils based on low expectations that might be associated with certain disability labels.	■ Many people in the disability community prefer identity-first language. ■ Disability is regarded as integral to a person's identity; it is not incidental or an add-on and separating disability from identity in person-first language only happens because of the negativity associated with disability. ■ Other aspects of identity, like race, gender, sexuality and ethnicity, are never expressed in terms of a person 'with' something. We don't talk about 'a person with blackness' or 'a person with Jewishness', so this position would question why we would talk about 'a person with disabilities'.

Neither identity-first nor person-first language is inherently right or wrong. It is important, though, to ask people what their preference is and respect that in interactions, discussions and any documentation.

Respecting individual worth and human dignity

Teachers and allied professionals can show respect to disabled pupils by refusing to refer to them by acronyms or abbreviations like SENDs (UK term for special educational needs and disabilities); CPs (for cerebral palsy); or IMs, IOs or ISs (Australian terms to refer to classification of intellectual impairment). The diminutive term 'Downsie' for a person with Down syndrome is highly disrespectful and should not be used. Pupils should not be referred to in terms of the assistive devices or communication tools they use, like 'Makaton girl', or by official documentation that prescribes services or support like EHCP pupil (EHCP stands for Education, Health and Social Care Plan in England) or IEP student (IEP refers to an individual education or support plan). Those who use wheelchairs for mobility should not be said to be 'wheelchair bound' or 'confined to a wheelchair'. Finally, people, as individuals in their own right, should not be erased from groups, by talking of 'the blind', 'the disabled' etc.

Confidentiality matters. All professionals interacting with a child need to ensure that they have permission from the child (and in the case of minors, their parents or caregivers) to share any personal information pertaining to the child. Many schools will have a form of handover at the beginning of an academic school year in which the previous year's teachers will provide the current teachers with relevant background information on a pupil. It can be helpful for teachers to ask the pupil, 'What information about you would you like me to share with your new teacher?' and clarifying with the pupil what specific wording and detail should be disclosed. For example, some pupils might want a formal label such as 'autism' to be used, whereas others might want a descriptive phrase such as 'struggles with social interactions and change in routine' to be used instead. These same cautions apply also to any written documentation about pupils.

The language teachers use affects how children see themselves and others. Research shows that teachers' words are 'very influential for children's constructions of meanings about other children' (Messiou, 2008, p. 31). Negative and demeaning comments, put-downs, sarcasm, ignoring and shouting at pupils all offer tacit permission for children to marginalise, bully and exclude their peers.

To demonstrate affirmation, teachers can

- Praise the pupil for qualities like effort, creativity, courage and diligence, using the second person 'you', as in 'You have put in a lot of effort and have some very creative ideas.'

> - Where necessary, critique the work or the task using the third person, as in 'This essay would be improved with more planning and it needs careful proofreading to correct spelling errors.'
> - Monitor their actions, facial expressions and other non-verbal communications that convey attitude.
> - Praise in public but reprimand in private.
> - Use the sandwich technique – an indication of a concern sandwiched between affirmations of potential and dignity.

Acknowledging the reality and impact of disability in pupils' lives

In an attempt to show that they are not racist, some people claim that they 'do not see colour'. Similarly, there are those who claim not to 'see' someone's disability or not to regard them as disabled if they are disabled. Examples of this are phrases like 'When I see you I don't see a disabled person' or 'I don't think of you as disabled'. Claiming not to 'see' or acknowledge disability is disrespectful. It means a refusal to recognise a part of someone's identity and implicitly conveys the idea that disability is regarded negatively. It is not a compliment to render someone invisible. 'Differently-abled' is another way disability is invisibilised. At best this is an unhelpful euphemism for disability, and at worst, it denies the specific oppressions experienced by disabled people. It is as problematic as the 'all lives matter' response to the Black Lives Matter movement. It may be true that there is a continuum of ability and disability across the population. But refusing to recognise disability means that the structural inequalities that disabled people experience will be ignored and people's specific access needs will not be met. These terms may be used by teachers who want to show that they treat all their pupils equally. The problem, as the saying reminds us, is that there is nothing more unequal than the equal treatment of unequal people.

Strength- or asset-based language

An asset-based approach seeks to highlight the strengths, resources and capabilities found within pupils, teachers, and the broader school, family, and community context (Ebersöhn and Eloff, 2006). Teachers and professionals using this approach (rather than a needs or deficit approach) look first at talents and capabilities (what a pupil can do). They recognise that the strengths of courage and creativity that pupils use on a daily basis are often overlooked, but can be harnessed to promote learning success. This change in perspective, and resulting change in language used to describe a child, can mean a shift from 'he never sits still' to 'he has lots of energy'. This second phrasing lends itself far more to affirming the dignity of the child and is already a step closer to a solution-focused approach of finding ways to channel this energy for positive learning.

Parent/caregiver–teacher conferences are an important opportunity to build mutual understanding and to look together for solutions. Here are some ideas of sample wording to include in such a meeting:

- What are you hoping to get out of this meeting?
- What would you like us to concentrate this discussion on?
- What are some of your child's strengths and things they love to do?
- What have you noticed are some of your child's biggest challenges at the moment?
- Please can you share any strategies that are working well at home that we could look at implementing in the classroom?

Communication beyond the spoken or written word

Although this chapter has focused primarily on language, both spoken and written, it would be remiss not to mention other non-verbal aspects of communication, such as body language, tone, eye contact and facial expression. A teacher could say to a pupil 'well done on finally grasping that concept', which at face value could seem to be an encouraging remark, but if it is accompanied by a big sigh and eye roll, could be interpreted as disparaging and even mocking in tone. Non-verbal cues such as the enthusiasm with which teachers answer some pupils' questions versus others can all subtly convey whom the teacher favours. Other aspects of body language that are offensive include mimicking or caricaturing a person with a difference or disability. Many times, individuals are not even aware of their non-verbal communication, as much of it is habitual and often occurs on a subconscious level. It can be helpful for teachers to ask colleagues and mentors for honest feedback on their style of communication. Teachers can also utilise anonymous surveys to glean how pupils experience their classes with statements such as: 'I'd like my teacher to start …', 'I'd like my teacher to stop …', 'I'd like my teacher to …'. Video recording a teaching session or a parent meeting (with the appropriate permissions of course) can also be a beneficial tool for self-reflection (Hollingsworth and Clarke, 2017).

> ### Reminder: *Respectful language…*
> - Asks about preferences for person-first or identity-first language.
> - Honours individuality and personhood, and maintains confidentiality.
> - Demonstrates affirmation, because teachers' words matter.
> - Acknowledges the impact of disability.
> - Uses strength or asset-based language.
> - Includes non-verbal communication, such as gestures and expressions.

Conclusion: Reminders

At the time of writing this chapter, former US President Donald Trump's speech to his supporters had come under scrutiny for inciting the violent storming of the Capitol Building. It serves as a reminder of the power of language. But the events of 6 January 2021 were not only triggered by one speech. They were the culmination of repeated inflammatory slogans, remarks and tacit condoning of extremist views. In the same vein, the effect of exclusionary language is cumulative. As we advocate for inclusive language, we need to caution against teachers being too scared to say anything for fear of offending. We do need to be careful in what we say, but we should also recognise that we will make mistakes, be willing to learn, apologise and move on. We can use the power of our language to bring about the change that 'will be the start of a new attitude towards people with disabilities' (Obama, The White House, 2010).

> ### Changes teachers can make to individual, classroom and staffroom talk
>
> * Refusing to use negative or deficit language about pupils, and calling out others who do.
> * Challenging jokes and insulting language.
> * Staying alert to exclusionary language and abreast of changes in language use.
> * Accepting and making adjustments when familiar terms and terminology are identified as unwelcome, problematic and offensive.
> * Modelling respectful ways of speaking and interacting.

The R-words in this chapter serve as a *reminder* of the power of language in developing inclusive classrooms and more socially just education systems. The first step towards change is a *recognition* of what language does in entrenching ableism. A conscious effort must be made to *reject* offensive and deficit language, and *revisit* some terms that should be used with caution. *Respectful* language in all communication should be used by teachers and other professionals, and ongoing learning is needed as language changes over time and place. Ultimately, language matters in 'the development of inclusive, peaceful and fair societies' (UN, 2016, section 2).

Notes

1 For example, spastic, dumb, idiot, crippled, lunatic, lame, midget, crazy, moron, freak, insane, handicapped, imbecile.
2 See https://www.youtube.com/watch?v=kNMJaXuFuWQ.

References

Black-Hawkins, K., & Florian, L. (2012). Classroom teachers' craft knowledge of their inclusive practice. *Teachers and Teaching, Theory and Practice*, 18(5), 567–584. https://doi.org/10.1080/13540602.2012.709732.

Brantlinger, E. (2006). The big glossies: How textbooks structure (special) education. In E. Brantlinger (Ed.), *Who benefits from special education? Remediating (fixing) other people's children* (pp. 45–76). Mahwah, New Jersey: Lawrence Erlbaum Associates Inc.

Campbell, F. (2001). Inciting legal fictions: 'Disability's' date with ontology and the ableist body of the law. *Griffith Law Review*, 2, 42–62.

Department for Education. (2015). Special educational needs and disability code of practice: 0 to 25 years. Accessed from https://www.gov.uk/government/publications/send-code-of-practice-0-to-25.

Ebersöhn, L., & Eloff, I. (2006). Identifying asset-based trends in sustainable programmes which support vulnerable children. *South African Journal of Education*, 26(3), 457–472. https://www.ajol.info/index.php/saje/article/view/25082.

Gernsbacher, M. A., Raimond, A. R., & Balinghasay, M. T. (2016). "Special needs" is an ineffective euphemism. *Cognitive Research*, 1, 29. https://doi.org/10.1186/s41235-016-0025-4.

Graham, L., Medhurst, M., Tancredi, H., Spandagou, I., & Walton, E. (2020). Fundamental concepts of inclusive education. In L. Graham (Ed.), *Inclusive education for the 21st century: Theory, policy and practice* (pp. 27–54). Crows Nest: A&U Academic.

Harry, B. (2014). The disproportionate placement of ethnic minorities in special education. In L. Florian (Ed.), *The Sage handbook of special education* (pp. 73–95). London: Sage.

Hodge, N. (2019). 'So that's who I am'! Careless classroom talk that damages autistic children. Accessed from https://www.youtube.com/watch?v=Lvn6ZfKX-Ls.

Hollingsworth, H., & Clarke, D. (2017). Video as a tool for focusing teacher self-reflection: Supporting and provoking teacher learning. *Journal of Mathematics Teacher Education*, 20, 457–475. https://doi.org/10.1007/s10857-017-9380-4.

Lauchlan, F., & Boyle, C. (2007). Is the use of labels in special education helpful? *Support for Learning*, 22(1), 36–42.

Malaquais, C. (n.d.). "He ain't special, he's my brother" – Time to ditch the phrase "special needs". Accessed from http://www.startingwithjulius.org.au/he-aint-special-hes-my-brother-time-to-ditch-the-phrase-special-needs/.

McLaughlin, J., Coleman-Fountain, E., & Clavering, E. (2016). *Disabled childhoods: Monitoring differences and emerging identities*. London: Routledge.

Messiou, K. (2008). Understanding children's constructions of meanings about other children: Implications for inclusive education. *Journal of Research in Special Educational Needs*, 8(1), 27–36. https://doi.org/10.1111/j.1471-3802.2008.00099.x.

Prochaska, J. O., & Norcross, J. C. (2018). *Systems of psychotherapy: A transtheoretical analysis*. Oxford: Oxford University Press.

Ryan, F. (2019). *Crippled*. London: Verso.

Slee, R. (2011). *The irregular school*. London: Routledge.

The White House. (2010). Remarks by the president at the signing of the 21st century communications and video accessibility act of 2010. Accessed from https://obamawhitehouse.archives.gov/the-press-office/2010/10/08/remarks-president-signing-21st-century-communications-and-video-accessib.

Thomas, G., & Vaughn, M. (2004). *Inclusive education: Readings and reflections*. Maidenhead: Open University Press.

United Nations (UN). (2016). General comment no. 4 on the right to inclusive education. Accessed from https://tbinternet.ohchr.org/_layouts/treatybodyexternal/Download .aspx?symbolno=CRPD/C/GC/4&Lang=en.

Veck, W. (2014). Disability and inclusive education in times of austerity. *British Journal of Sociology of Education*, 35(5), 777–799. https://doi.org/10.1080/01425692.2014 .919845.

Wakefield, J. (2016). Diagnostic issues and controversies in DSM-5: Return of the false positives problem. *Annual Review of Clinical Psychology*, 12(1), 105–132.

Walton, E. (2016). *The language of inclusive education*. London: Routledge.

Developing inclusive practices: the role of student–teacher dialogues

Kyriaki Messiou and Leanne Galbally

Introduction

A focus on students' voices in schools has gained growing interest internationally, particularly since the United Nations Convention on the Rights of the Child (1989). In England, this interest grew stronger through the influential study of Jean Rudduck (2006). Despite this research, a review carried out by Robinson (2014), focusing on studies carried out since 2007 in the UK on children's experiences of schooling, argues for more research into 'the ways in which primary pupils and teachers can work together to co-produce and co-research teaching and learning within schools' (p. 24).

This chapter focuses on efforts to address this gap by describing collaborative action research between the University of Southampton and Wordsworth Primary School. Researchers, teachers and children collaborated in implementing Inclusive Inquiry (Messiou and Ainscow, 2020), an approach that has been developed as a result of two interconnected studies (Messiou, 2019; Messiou and Ainscow, 2015; Messiou et al., 2016). The approach focuses on the power of students' voices, and the creation of dialogues between children and teachers in order to develop inclusive practices. The study was funded by the European Union between 2017 and 2020 and involved 30 primary schools in five European countries (Austria, Denmark, England, Portugal, Spain).

Inclusive Inquiry involves teachers and children collaborating to co-design lessons that are inclusive. As part of this process, all children are actively involved in facilitating the development of inclusive practices in schools; some students take the role of co-researchers who collect and analyse their classmates' views about learning and teaching, and observe and refine lessons in collaboration with their teachers.

 DOI: 10.4324/9781003137634-3

In this chapter we use an example from the work in Wordsworth Primary School, over a period of four years, to illustrate how a small pilot with a trio of teachers in the first year was then expanded across the whole school. Impacts on the school's practices will be shown through the use of illustrative examples. At the same time, how the study had an influence within a network of schools in England and the development of their practices will also be explored.

Developing inclusive practices

Inclusive education has been described as a process for reaching out to all learners (Ainscow, 1999; UNESCO, 2020). At the same time, inclusion is concerned with all learners' presence, participation and achievement (Ainscow, 2007).

The notion of inclusion has been strongly linked to the concept of students' voices (Messiou, 2012, 2019). This ranges from simple expressions of views, either through verbal or non-verbal means (Thomson, 2008), as well as to active participation and having an active role in decision-making processes (Cook-Sather, 2006). Black-Hawkins, Maguire and Kershner (2021) have demonstrated how listening to children's views can lead to the development of more inclusive classroom communities.

The movement of students' voices gained particular prominence in the early nineties, following the United Nations Convention on the Rights of the Child (1989) ratified by almost every country in the world. However, as Thiessen (2007) rightly points out, a range of much earlier educators and scholars had set the foundations for such a focus on students' experiences, such as Pestalozzi in 1912, Dewey in 1916 and Montessori in 1966. At the same time, Thiessen describes the focus on students' experiences in research as falling into one of three orientations: how students participate and make sense of life in classrooms and school; who students are and how they develop in classrooms and schools; and how students are actively involved in shaping their own learning opportunities and in the improvement of what happens in classrooms and schools. This last orientation has been mostly associated with the student voice movement.

Despite this growing interest in students' voices with educational research and development, Michael Fielding (2001) raised some excellent questions in relation to such approaches, which are still valid today (see Box 3.1).

Box 3.1 Fielding's questions in relation to student voice approaches in research and in schools

- Who is allowed to speak?
- To whom?
- What are they allowed to speak about?

> - What language is encouraged or allowed?
> - Who decides the answers to these questions?
> - Who is listening?
> - How and why?
> - How are those decisions made?
> - How, when, where, to whom and how often are these decisions communicated?

In this chapter, we explore this idea of students having an active role in decision-making in schools. We do this through our experiences using an innovative approach, Inclusive Inquiry. The approach can be seen as a way of addressing Fielding's questions in a number of ways, as we will explain.

Inclusive Inquiry

Inclusive Inquiry involves a set of interconnected processes (Figure 3.1). Central to these processes are dialogues between teachers and their students about how to make lessons more inclusive. These dialogues are focused on learning and teaching aspects. By the term *dialogue* we adopt Lodge's (2005) definition, which, she argues, 'is more than conversation, it is the building of shared narrative'. She goes on to explain: 'Dialogue is about engagement with others through talk to arrive at a point one would not get to alone' (p. 134).

Inclusive Inquiry involves three phases – plan, teach and analyse – carried out by trios of teachers. The three phases each involve a series of steps (12 in total) explaining the actions that are essential to the successful use of Inclusive Inquiry. Together these constitute the Levels of Use Framework (Figure 3.2) that can be used by teachers to determine how far they have implemented the approach.

Each of the three teachers has to choose three or more students from their class who are seen in some way as being 'hard to reach' to become researchers. These may

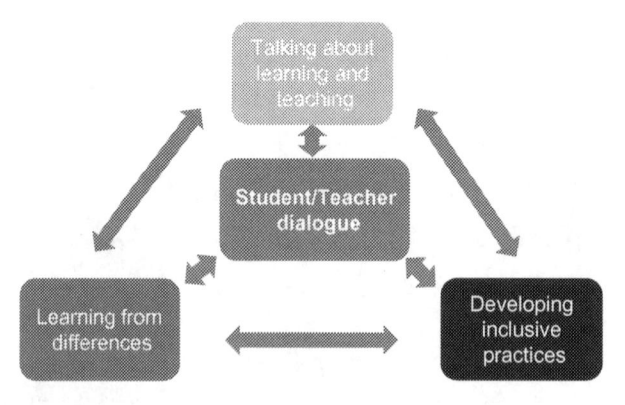

Figure 3.1 Inclusive Inquiry

The Levels of Use Framework	Rating
Phase 1: Plan	
1.1 A trio of teachers has been formed to carry out action research	
1.2 The trio has agreed about which will be their research lesson	
1.3 The trio has involved a group of student researchers in collecting evidence to support the design of the research lesson	
1.4 A lesson plan has been developed that sets out to ensure that all members of the class are engaged in all the activities	
1.5 The three teachers and the student researchers have all contributed to the design of the lesson plan	
Phase 2: Teach	
2.1 Each teacher has used the lesson plan with their class	
2.2 On each occasion, the two colleagues and student researchers observed the responses of class members	
2.3 The views of all students about the lesson were gathered	
2.4 After each lesson, teachers and student researchers met to review what has happened, focusing on the engagement of all members of the class	
2.5 The trio refined the lesson plan before it was used by the next member of the trio	
Phase 3: Analyse	
3.1 After completing all three lesson plans, the trio and student researchers discussed their impact on the engagement of all members of the classes	
3.2 The trio and student researchers drew conclusions regarding what was been learned about making lessons inclusive	

Figure 3.2 The Levels of Use Framework

be children who have been defined as having special educational needs, refugees, children from disadvantaged backgrounds or others who lack confidence in school. These students are then trained by their teachers to collect their classmates' views about learning and teaching on the one hand, and on the other hand about how to carry out observations of lessons. The information collected is analysed by the student researchers to inform the co-planning of a lesson. This lesson is then taught in the classrooms of the three teachers. The lessons are observed by the other two teachers and by student researchers from the other two classes. At the end of each lesson, student researchers analyse with their teachers what they observed, in order to make modifications for the next time the lesson will be taught. The focus of the observations and of the discussions that follow the lesson is on ensuring that all learners are included in the learning process. In what follows, we describe the school context and how Inclusive Inquiry was introduced to the school.

The school

Wordsworth Primary School is a fast-expanding primary school, with 630 children on roll in 21 classes, in the city of Southampton. It occupies a new building, which opened in September 2013, with extensive grounds, a committed and professional staff team, and has a vibrant school community. The school serves a diverse population and is committed to identifying ways of making sure that all children are included in the learning process. Most of the pupils live in the immediate area, where there is a mixture of private and social housing. About two-thirds of the pupils are White British and the remainder are from a wide range of minority ethnic backgrounds, with the largest group being of Polish heritage. The proportion of pupils for whom English is an additional language is 38%, which is well above the national average. There are a few pupils who are still at an early stage of learning to speak the language and the school has a comprehensive 'Language Journey' for the children needing language support. The proportion known to be eligible for free school meals (an indication of family poverty) is above the national average. The number of pupils identified as having special educational needs and/or disabilities is above average.

Wordsworth is passionate about treating all of its pupils as individuals. It is also aspirational regarding the progress of all children, whilst also valuing the creativity and difference in every child, which is why it is developing an ever-broadening curriculum and school clubs programme. This includes specialist music and instrument teaching, environmental studies and a range of sports activities in curriculum time, together with school clubs such as art, drama, French, taekwondo and dance. In taking this agenda forward, Wordsworth is committed to the professional learning of all staff and has a well-developed programme of school-based staff development activities. Given the emphases of the school, the then head teacher was very willing and enthusiastic to take part in this study when he was approached to do so.

Introducing the approach to the school

As part of the European Union study, during the first cycle, the pilot phase, a trio of teachers from Wordsworth school were trained, alongside other teachers from the five participating countries, on how to use Inclusive Inquiry. The training was offered by university researchers. During this time, the trio were given support in carrying out a cycle of research, including how to train student researchers effectively, particularly focusing on supporting students to carry out observations, collecting and then analysing data to inform their discussions with their teachers.

The pilot study at Wordsworth Primary School was carried out between January 2018 and June 2018, using a trio of teachers working across Key Stage 2. The same happened in all the five participating countries. At the end of this cycle, an analysis of the lessons learnt was made that led to refinements of the approach.

In the following academic year, in October 2018, the use of Inclusive Inquiry was expanded across Years Four, Five and Six, with the original teaching trio used to train the teachers working within their year group. Students and teachers were given the rare opportunity to design lessons together, to discuss their ideas collaboratively, and to share expertise to adapt and analyse the success of their ideas. At this stage the new trio of teachers found that their student researchers were becoming much more confident in their abilities to share ideas, were more willing to engage in their learning, and were starting to show a much higher level of respect towards their teachers and peers, both within the classroom and during collaborative discussions.

In September 2019, the project findings were disseminated across the school, from Year 1 to Year 6. Each class had completed at least one cycle of research by the end of the summer term and had started to use their research findings to embed new practice within the classroom. During this final year of the project the reception class became involved. At the same time, the project was also used as a way to drive forward progress linked to whole-school priorities. Across all year groups, examples of positive outcomes were noticed. These included children being given more choice over their lesson outcomes; more freedom given regarding buddies/learning partners; learning environments rearranged to offer more choice to work individually, as part of a pair or in groups; and, most important, (across the majority of classes) an emerging sense of respect and trust developing between the teachers and children.

In what follows, an example from Year 1 is used to illustrate the process, as well as highlight the benefits and some of the challenges involved.

Inclusive Inquiry in practice

The example is from a trio of teachers in Year 1 in the school who worked together on a literacy lesson. It was a phonics lesson dealing with tricky words, i.e. those that cannot be sounded out easily. One of the three teachers led the children researchers' training, which took part in the school's dance studio.

Student researchers were selected based on the fact that they were seen by the teachers as 'hard to reach' in some way, such as children who were not confident or who have recently joined the country. These were all Year 1 children, age 5–6. During the training, the children were provided with various pictures and asked to think about learning based on the pictures presented, as can been seen on the picture in Figure 3.3.

Figure 3.3 Pictures used at the student researcher training to think about learning

The focus of the discussion was on whether children presented in the pictures are learning and how we can tell whether this is the case. In essence, the purpose was to make children think critically about observing lessons. These discussions were followed by practising observing in one of the classrooms. Finally, they discussed different ideas about gathering their classmates' views about learning and teaching, such as interviews and asking them to suggest ideas about lessons and asking them to vote about specific ideas. The student researchers from the three classes decided that they would ask their classmates to vote on two ideas: 'doing things with their hands' and 'working together'.

The fact that the children decided to focus on these two ideas by asking their classmates to vote for their preferred one highlighted tensions that existed between differences in opinions and the narrowing of options that were given to these particular groups of students. Ideally, children in the class should have opportunities to express more freely their own suggestions, as opposed to be given only two ideas to choose from. However, respecting the student researchers' decisions, and taking into account the fact that the children were of a young age, this may have made the process more manageable.

Following this training, the children researchers gathered all their classmates' views during sessions held in each of the participating classes. The teachers explained the role of the student researchers to the class and asked them to tell everyone what they had done in the training session. Then the teachers asked the three student researchers to tell the class the two things that they would want to include in the phonics lesson. These ideas had been decided during the training between the student researchers. The teacher then explained that the student researchers would ask them to vote between two ideas and they would have to vote for one of the two statements – 'doing things with their hands' and 'working together' – by standing next to their preferred statement.

One student researcher held a picture illustrating 'doing', whilst another student held one that illustrated 'working together'. The third student researcher counted the votes for each statement. The teacher explained to the whole class that the student researchers would take the scores of all three classes to plan the lesson with the teachers. Having gathered the views of all students from the three classes, the most favourite idea that had emerged was 'doing things with our hands'.

The teachers went on to discuss with the student researchers different ways in which the key ideas that emerged could be incorporated into the lesson. These were use of play dough and sand, writing outside and a washing line hung with word cards. These ideas were included in the first lesson activities, as explained in what follows.

The first lesson

The children were sitting on the carpet and the teacher explained that they were going to have a lesson that was different from normal, in that some additional activities had been designed, based on the views of the student researchers after they collected their classmates' ideas.

The lesson started with the teacher showing the whole class some cards with tricky words that the students already knew. The teacher explained the differences between this lesson and the previous lessons, where the children had learnt phonics with only the use of the whiteboard. In this lesson, as the teacher explained, there would be hands-on activities in which the children were going to practise writing their tricky words (the ones they had just looked at) on play dough using spoons. Then the teacher showed the tricky words that the children had learnt before and they all read them out loud (i.e. bee, me, we, she, he). Following this introduction, the following activities occurred:

- Play dough and whiteboards – Children were divided into two groups. One group were asked to use spoons and play dough to write the words that they chose from word cards, whereas the other group wrote the words on their whiteboards. After ten minutes, the two groups swapped.

- The washing line outside – The children went outside to look at different new tricky words that were hung on the washing line. When they chose a tricky word, they had to show it to a partner and see if they could read the words. After a few minutes finding words and working with their partners, each student had one word with them and then they lined up to come back to their class. The children then sat on the carpet and the teacher asked them to show the words they found and read them aloud.

- Sand trays – Children were again divided in two groups. The teacher asked children in one group to go to a table where sand, glitter and earbuds were already set up. Then they practised writing the words that they had picked from the washing line, using sand and glitter and earbuds. Those who had finished writing on sand could pick up other tricky words and practise writing them with the play dough again. There were also pasta strings that children could use for writing their words. The children in the other group practised writing the new words with play dough.

- Practice writing sentences – All children went back to the carpet and the teacher asked them to read out the words that they had just practised writing with the sand, play dough and pasta. They were then asked to make sentences using the tricky words that each one of them had. The teacher then explained that they were going to go outside again to practise writing sentences. They were asked to think about the sentence before going out. They went out with paper and chalk, and the children either sat at tables outside or on the ground and worked in pairs, groups or individually to write their sentences and then read them aloud to their partners.

Discussions after the lesson and changes to the other lessons

During this first lesson the two partner teachers who had observed the lesson, alongside the six student researchers from the two classes, used a grid to record

Figure 3.4 The observation grid used by Year 1 children

their thoughts. The grid was focused on the various activities that were used during the lessons (Figure 3.4).

Following the first lesson, the three teachers and the six children researchers discussed what had happened. For example, the teacher who taught the lesson asked the children:

> *Teacher 1:* So, what did you put on your sheet? Can I have a look?
> *Student 1 (Girl):* I've got a lot.
> *Teacher 1:* And you have got a lot on your sheet. Let's have a look. What did you write in yours, K.? Do you remember?
> *Student 2 (Girl):* I am cold.
> *Teacher 1:* 'I am cold', well it was a bit chilly so wasn't it, it's cold outside but some people also wanted to go outside.
> *Student 2 (Girl):* Some of them actually like the lesson but some of them didn't.
> *Teacher 1:* Yeah, some of them like the lesson.
> *Student 2 (Girl):* The people on play dough liked it; the people on the floor that were on the whiteboard didn't like it.
> *Teacher 1:* Yes, did they not like it? Maybe we probably should have more play dough do you think? So that everyone could have done play dough, is that what you think? Rather than swapping?
> *Student 2 (Girl):* Yeah …

> *Teacher 2:* And what we were saying about play dough? Do you remember?
> *Student 3 (Girl):* I think they all like play dough.
> *Student 2 (Girl):* So, all of them like play dough.
> *Teacher 1:* So, play dough was a good idea then. Yeah. You want to keep the play dough in tomorrow. Maybe have more of it so that we don't have half out and half with play dough. Yeah? So, do you want me to write it down so we put [in] the play dough bit?

Interestingly enough, though the grid was focusing on particular activities, the first girl mentioned being cold when they went outside for the activity. It was indeed very cold on that day. Also, it is interesting to note that children were not quick to say that everything was positive in the lesson because it was their ideas. On the contrary, in the light of their observations, they spoke critically about the activities and whether or not they promoted children's participation.

The second lesson

Moving to the second lesson, one of the changes made, based on the observations of student researchers, was to give opportunities for all the groups to do all the activities (i.e. writing on the board, practising their writing on the play dough and the sand). Following the lesson, the teacher who led it highlighted how she noticed that children working on the play dough were more productive rather than those working with the sand:

> *Teacher 1:* I think I did see a lot [more] work on play dough than I saw in the sand. I saw a lot of people just play in sand, whereas in the play dough though I did see more and more actual work. So, it might be easier tomorrow for them just to have the play dough. So maybe tomorrow, they can still have the play dough, they can still do the outside bit but then they can come back in. We can always have the play dough to sit out for those of you but not go to the sand. Do you think that would be alright? You have play dough and not the sand tomorrow? What do you want to do? Would you like the play dough and not the sand?
> *Student 1 (Girl):* Play dough.
> *Teacher 1:* You want play dough.
> *Student 2 (Boy):* I want sand and play dough.
> *Teacher 2:* So, do you think there will be something to write more? When you are writing on the big sheet R. Or when you're right on your own whiteboard? Do you think you …

> *Student 1 (Girl):* Big sheet.
> *Teacher 1:* So, you like doing on the big sheet.
> *Teacher 3:* Do you think children learn more and write more when they are sharing the big sheet? Do you think that was a good idea?
> *(Children nodding)*

Two issues are discussed here. First, whether they should keep both the sand and the play dough in the lesson plan or just the play dough, and, second, whether they should keep the writing of the sentences on big sheets or not. The final decision was to use only play dough for the third lesson and keeping the big sheets.

It is worth noting here how the two student researchers had different views: one wanted the play dough, whilst the other one wanted to retain both the play dough and the sand. The teacher seemed not to pay attention to the second's child suggestion and tried to divert the discussion by bringing in another issue. Having said this, it is interesting that this had stayed in the teachers' mind and they returned to it later, when the children left the room:

> *Teacher 3:* What else? Ah yes. The fact that they love playing with the sand.
> *Teacher 1:* Yeah I put all on there. They were playing it probably more than … is because we never let them play with sand so when they see it, they just think that's a novel idea isn't it. Yes. Would you play, should you see what D. did with the sand? The first thing you did is to take the whole sand pot on the floor. Lovely. But they love they do [love] that a lot. But we use it that's not such a fascination.
> *Teacher 1:* We do use more play dough than sand.
> *Teacher 2:* The sand is a massive fascination.

Following the second lesson, the decision was to give paper to all children individually and to write the sentences inside the classroom. In the final lesson, they decided to only use play dough for the first activity, but also to return to it if they wished to continue. In addition, instead of using the big sheets of paper, they were all given whiteboards to write their sentences.

Some of the changes made to the three lessons were not only as a result of the student researchers' observations but from discussions that took place after the children left, focusing on other things that the teachers noticed that were not picked up by the children. For example, one teacher said: 'I thought with the washing line, the words were quite close together. So, someone had to wait. It is a minor thing.' This illustrates how the process opened up opportunities for teachers to discuss other issues that they noticed, in addition to those brought up by the children. These all related to matters of detail that with relevant modifications could help facilitate children to participate during lessons.

At the end of this year, and having completed a number of rounds of Inclusive Inquiry, the key ideas that emerged from these activities that teachers tried to include in future lessons were:

- Giving children more choice when they're writing and during literacy lessons.
- Including more 'doing things' in a lesson, with at least one active learning activity per lesson.

This led us to conclude that Inclusive Inquiry had an impact on teachers' practices longer term. We also had evidence that this had a positive impact on students' engagement in lessons, particularly amongst those children who took the role of researchers.

Expanding the work to a network of schools

In the second year of the project, parallel to the expansion of the approach within Wordsworth, the approach was expanded across networks in each of the five participating countries, leading to a total of 30 schools. In Southampton, the network of schools all belonged to the same multi-academy trust.

Teachers from the new schools were trained together by university researchers and teachers in Wordsworth who had taken part in the pilot phase. Following the training, they implemented the approach within their schools. There were also occasional network meetings that offered opportunities for teachers to hear about the progress in each of the schools, as well as to exchange ideas about the process and learn from one another's experiences.

The following year, the network carried on its work, with occasional meetings to discuss the developments in each school. Each school focused on areas that they wanted to explore more, such as spelling, times tables in maths, reading for pleasure etc. In each of these examples, children offered a range of ideas in relation to activities to support their learning. For example, in a trio of Year 5 classes the children suggested the following activities for a spelling lesson: spelling bee competition, treasure hunt and Pictionary. In another trio of Year 3 classes, for a reading for pleasure lesson, the children suggested the following activities: to use videos to help with predicting what follows in a story and to introduce games in the lesson. These suggestions facilitated discussions between children and teachers to design lessons that were more inclusive.

Developing inclusive lessons, creating inclusive environments

As we have illustrated in the example presented in this chapter, the teachers and students involved listened to one another with respect and tried to identify ways for ensuring that all children participated in lessons through focusing on joint planning to develop lessons. In this way, the approach addresses the questions that were posed by Michael Fielding (Box 3.1) that we mentioned at the start of this chapter. In particular, all children in the classes were asked their views about learning and teaching, their views were taken into consideration in designing the lessons and making changes in order to make them more inclusive and those decisions were taken jointly by teachers and students. Even though the student researchers were in a more prominent position, all of their classmates had opportunities to contribute their ideas. Finally, children and teachers entered into dialogues about learning and teaching in a way that they had not experienced before. Furthermore, these dialogues often led teachers to concentrate on details of lessons, in ways that may have been overlooked before.

For teachers new to this approach, the set of steps in Figure 3.2 must be followed in order to implement Inclusive Inquiry. However, it has to be pointed out that ahead of following the steps outlined in Figure 3.2, teachers need to be aware that the approach requires different roles on their part, as well as on children's part. Children must be seen by teachers as collaborators who will offer a different perspective to theirs for promoting inclusion in lessons. These perspectives may be ones that teachers do not necessarily agree with, based on their professional expertise. However, they need to allow themselves to hear these different perspectives and discuss with children the different dimensions of their ideas and the implications they may have on their learning. This has to be done in respectful ways, to demonstrate in practice that children's ideas are indeed taken into account. The main question that teachers should ask themselves before embarking on the use of Inclusive Inquiry is: How can children's perspectives allow us to see practices in a different way, from their point of view, and allow us to make possible changes in collaboration with them, in order to develop more inclusive practices?

Our experiences of using the approach lead us to argue that Inclusive Inquiry has the potential to strengthen efforts to realise the concept of inclusion in schools by facilitating the development of more inclusive practices. At the same time, it creates the conditions for the formation of more inclusive and democratic environments in schools. As Fielding (2004) suggests, 'the potential for transformation is more likely to reside in arrangements which require the active engagement of students and teachers working in partnership' (p. 306). We argue that Inclusive Inquiry allows for such an engagement and partnerships that can lead to transformation in schools, as we have illustrated in the example that we described.

> ## Box 3.2 Summary
>
> - Inclusive education is an ongoing process that requires an analysis of existing ways of working that may be presenting barriers to the engagement of some students.
> - Engaging with the views of students can lead to a better understanding of inclusive practices.
> - Inclusive Inquiry, an approach that focuses on dialogues between children and teachers, can facilitate the development of inclusive lessons and the creation of more inclusive environments in schools.

Note: A set of materials for practitioners who wish to use Inclusive Inquiry can be found in five languages at https://reachingthehardtoreach.eu/publication/, including a video that can be used for teacher professional development sessions as an introduction to the approach at https://reachingthehardtoreach.eu/video/.

References

Ainscow, M. (1999). *Understanding the Development of Inclusive Schools*. London: Falmer Press.

Ainscow, M. (2007). From special education to effective schools for all: A review of progress so far. In *The SAGE Handbook of Special Education*, edited by L. Florian, 146–159. London: SAGE.

Black-Hawkins, K., Maguire, L., & Kershner, R. (2021). Developing inclusive classroom communities: What matters to children? *Education 3-13*. https://doi.org/10.1080/03004279.2021.1873398.

Cook-Sather, A. (2006). Sound, presence, and power: "Student Voice" in educational research and reform. *Curriculum Inquiry* 36 (4): 359–390.

Fielding, M. (2001). Students as radical agents of change. *Journal of Educational Change* 2(2): 123–141.

Fielding, M. (2004). Transformative approaches to student voice: Theoretical underpinnings, recalcitrant realities. *British Educational Research Journal* 30 (2): 295–311.

Lodge, C. (2005). From hearing voices to engaging in dialogue: Problematising student participation in school improvement. *Journal of Educational Change* 6 (2): 125–146.

Messiou, K. (2012). *Confronting Marginalisation in Education: A Framework for Promoting Inclusion*. London: Routledge.

Messiou, K. (2019). The missing voices: Students as a catalyst for promoting inclusive education. *International Journal of Inclusive Education*. https://doi.org/10.1080/13603116.2019.1623326.

Messiou, K., & Ainscow, M. (2015). Responding to learner diversity: Student views as a catalyst for powerful teacher development? *Teaching and Teacher Education* 51: 246–255. https://doi.org/10.1016/j.tate.2015.07.002.

Messiou, K., & Ainscow, M. (2020). Inclusive inquiry: Student-teacher dialogue as a means of promoting inclusion in schools. *British Educational Research Journal* 46 (3): 670–687. https://doi.org/10.1002/berj.3602.

Messiou, K., Ainscow, M., Echeita, G., Goldrick, S., Hope, M., Paes, I., Sandoval, M., Simon, C., & Vitorino, T. (2016). Learning from differences: A strategy for teacher development in respect to student diversity. *School Effectiveness and School Improvement* 27 (1): 45–61.

Robinson, C. (2014). *Children, Their Voices and Their Experiences of School: What Does the Evidence Tell Us?* York: Cambridge Primary Review Trust.

Rudduck, J. (2006). The past, the papers and the project. *Educational Review* 58 (2): 131–143. https://doi.org/10.1080/00131910600583993.

Thiessen, D. (2007). Researching student experiences in elementary and secondary school: An emerging field of study. In *International Handbook of Student Experience in Elementary and Secondary School*, edited by D. Thiessen, and A. Cook-Sather, 1–77. Dordrecht Netherlands: Springer.

Thomson, P. (Ed.) (2008). *Doing Visual Research with Children and Young People*. London: Routledge.

United Nations (1989). *The UN Convention on the Rights of the Child*. New York: UN.

UNESCO (2020). *Towards Inclusion in Education: Status, Trends and Challenges: The UNESCO Salamanca Statement 25 Years On*. Paris: UNESCO.

Taking account of neurodiverse learners in the classroom: supporting inclusive classroom practices

Craig Goodall and James Ward-Sinclair

Introduction

How can we, as educators, begin to understand, empathise with, and then include and educate neurodiverse learners in our primary school classrooms? First, we must recognise neurodiverse children and young people as experts of their own experiences. Their narratives should be sought, listened to, engaged with and, in turn, acted upon to develop an educational culture in every school that strives to ensure all young people thrive. We, the authors (Craig Goodall, an autism advisory teacher, and James Ward-Sinclair, an autistic autism activist), discuss how using autism research as an illustrative lens to create positive responses to neurodiversity can inform the development of inclusive classroom practices. This chapter includes the voices, experiences and perspectives of autistic young people, researchers and scholars. It also provides examples of how emphasising positive language and awareness can challenge often deeply held, and sometimes negative, assumptions. James also offers his autistic perspective on autism, research development and neurodiversity. Neurodiversity in this chapter refers to autism, ADHD, dyslexia, dyspraxia and other neurodiverse ways of being. Practical suggestions are presented throughout to enhance inclusive classroom practice.

Neurodiversity and autism

Neurodiversity, coined by Singer (1998), applies to many diagnoses or differences. However, despite not being the same, neurodiversity has been, and continues to be, discussed in relation to autism. Neurodiversity challenges the pathologising

DOI: 10.4324/9781003137634-4

and medicalisation of 'natural human variants' and posits that disablement occurs when the structures and norms of society impede the person. This paradigm seeks to remove stigma from autism, recognising autism as inseparable from identity. Neurodiversity exponents consider autism as both a natural variation (a difference with strengths to be celebrated, not a disorder to be cured) and as a disability (den Houting, 2019). Therefore, neurodiversity does not expunge the word 'disability' from our lexicon, just reframes it. Importantly, considering neurodiversities – whether autism, dyslexia, dyspraxia or ADHD (attention deficit hyperactivity disorder) – does not mean we ignore the challenges children face, nor should we withhold the support required, whether that be adjustments to the classroom environment or the pedagogy.

Happé and Frith (2020) discuss several major changes in how autism is perceived. Box 4.1 provides a useful snapshot for mapping this paradigm shift.

Box 4.1 Changing perceptions of autism (from Happé and Frith, 2020)

1. From a narrow definition to wide diagnostic criteria
2. From a rare to a relatively common condition (probably still under-recognised in females)
3. From something affecting children to a lifelong condition
4. From something discrete and distinct to a dimensional view
5. From one thing to many 'autisms'
6. From a focus on 'pure autism' to the recognition that complexity and comorbidity is the norm
7. From conceptualising autism purely as a 'developmental disorder' (distinct from typical development and usually accompanied by intellectual and language disabilities) to recognising a neurodiversity perspective, operationalised in participatory research models

Reflective questions

* Do any of these changes or shifts surprise you? How and why?
* How might these paradigm shifts and different understandings of autism affect your classroom practice?

Despite these developments, there is still a wide range of understandings of autism across society, which militate against finding ways of being more inclusive. This is hampered further by vastly changing diagnostic criteria; for example, the fifth edition of the *Diagnostic Statistical Manual* (known as *DSM5*), focuses on the 'levels of support' a person requires (see Weitlauf et al., 2014). This approach to greater equality does not consider other circumstances outside of being autistic, such as socio-economic background and other co-occurring diagnoses. Furthermore, focusing on levels of support can present challenges in the long term. Autistic people change across their lifetime: someone may require a lot of support in one area or situation, but not another. This is underscored by the following autism definition offered by Leatherland (2018, p. 359), an autistic person:

> Autistic individuals share a neurological type, which is qualitatively different from that of non-autistics, and which will necessarily impact, both positively and negatively, on: aspects of their thinking and learning; sensory processing; social relational experiences; and communicative style, abilities, and preferences. An autistic person's experience of and ability to be successful in the world, will be dependent on the closeness of compatibility between their individual profile of skills and difficulties and their physical and social environment. Levels of sensitivity to environmental factors vary between individuals, and within the same individual over time, so that the presentation of autism is ever changing. A person's neurological type, however, remains constant, and being autistic is a lifelong identity.

Autistic reflection on neurodiversity: Representations in research

As definitions of the autism spectrum seem to become broader by the year, questions arise regarding the role of neurodiversity within education. Should autism be understood as a condition (reverting to past research in order to better understand a diagnosis)? Or is it preferable to understand the individual (that is, seeking to understand motivations, triggers and potential which are unique to them)? Most existing bodies of research come from accounts in which authors aim to cure or separate autism from the individual (Kapp et al., 2013), in direct contrast to the core beliefs of neurodiversity, which are to understand differences and see the value in encouraging them.

Moreover, there are findings from autism research that still contain derogatory terms when referencing people on the spectrum, such as 'sufferers' or even 'retards'. Doing so contributes to inherently negative perceptions of autistic people, in which the condition is viewed as debilitating. Furthermore, while still medically accurate, many published reports continue to describe autism as a mental disorder, a description which organisations such as the UK National Autistic Society (2021) are campaigning to change. Amongst other reasons, this is because of potential legal consequences of using this category, most notably the improper sectioning of autistic people under the Mental Health Act (1983). Ann Memmott, an autist, writes (in personal correspondence with Craig Goodall):

> The relentless othering, negativity, false beliefs and potentially harmful normalization approaches of such research add further burden to autistic lives. I wade through such things with despair, and at great personal cost. Surely we can do better than this?

Problematic perceptions in research are not limited to language; complications also arise when considering other references to, for example, contested theories like theory of mind, weak central coherence, executive dysfunction and also extreme male brain. Despite consistent criticism of extreme male brain theory (McCarthy, 2019), it continues to shape perceptions regarding the gender imbalance in autism. A caricature of an autistic person as young, white and male is often portrayed. This, in turn, reinforces unfair assumptions about autism representation in a classroom, and potentially leads to the needs of some children, who do not fit this image of autism, being ignored or overlooked. For example, because education professionals may perceive the spectrum as more masculine, an autistic female who develops masking strategies to fit in with school expectations might not be identified as autistic and be given the support she needs.

Additionally, misrepresentation of autistic people can also damage those outside assumed cultural demographics, creating a bias in the diagnostic profile. For example, Black, Asian and minority ethnic (BAME) communities are often largely underrepresented in autism research (Tung, 2019). So too are factors such as social or economic status. This could lead to a number of people not only avoiding assessment but not considering assessment at all. This may then also have an impact on how children are (or are not) supported in the classroom.

Many autistic people who themselves have become researchers in the field have found that these kinds of biases may not be accidental. Anecdotal reports suggest that autistic researchers, who try to interject by including their personal experiences, can be dismissed with claims that they are 'not autistic enough' for their voices to be included in research. This highlights the narrow approach that some researchers may take when selecting participants for their studies, indicating again the need for neurodiverse people to be fully represented in all aspects of research.

Autistic presence and representation are important, as many fields have benefited from the involvement of autistic researchers. Drawing on alternative perspectives can lead to new interpretations of results (Nuwer, 2020) and even different hypotheses. Autistic traits that may be misunderstood can be challenged. For example, Steven Kapp, a lecturer in psychology who, after reflecting upon his own reason for stimulated behaviour, produced research which demonstrated that stimming is not *dis*tressing but *de*stressing, and should be encouraged in students (Kapp et al., 2019), a point returned to later.

James also recalls an event in which he was to speak to an audience comprising neurodiverse and neurotypical members. In what is becoming customary practice, to reduce sensory disruption, he requested that, in place of clapping the 'flappause' was to be used. However, an autistic member of the audience requested that this did not happen as they found silence and rapid hand motions caused the very effect which the flappause aimed to avoid. This demonstrates that, while putting in place neurodivergent practices can be helpful, blanket approaches aimed at wide demographics can inadvertently cause distress to some even when supportive of others. A similar example comes from Craig's experience in the classroom, in which he found that some autistic children do not respond well to obvious visual supports such as visual schedules, even though this approach is widely advocated to support autistic learners. This again emphasises the need to take account of individuals: drifting from 'a one size fits all' to 'a one size fits all autistic pupils' approach is inappropriate. Just because several children share the same diagnostic label, whether autism or ADHD, does not mean that the same approaches (such as using visual schedules) will bring benefit to all children. An adaptive approach is required in order to find which strategies best support each individual child's needs. Having autists involved and represented in research provides lived experiences to support this work.

Autistic people have contributed other benefits to research that subsequently filter down to support autistic people in education. These include being able to create a better environment for research participants, due to their perceived ability to relate to the subject (Nuwer, 2020). However, relying on a neurodiverse input is not always to the benefit of individuals. This is especially true in cases where an individual is not being supported to present their neurodiverse mindset. For example, it may be that an autistic person has previously been informed that their mind is alternatively wired (or another common mechanic-based metaphor such as 'their engine runs too fast'). However, in cases where this positive language tries to communicate the message of different and not disability, an autistic person can involuntarily assume that, like a machine, they are broken or not working (Armstrong, 2017). Students are now being encouraged to view their minds not as wholly different from others but using more natural points of reference, for example, 'the brain forest' and that each will grow differently to others (Armstrong, 2017). This has produced better research results in some instances and demonstrates again that it is not enough to use a general neurodiverse approach, but that it needs to be nuanced for individuals.

A possible note of caution

Creating a focus on difference rather than disability is not without its shortcomings in the classroom. While advocates may wish to celebrate the spectrum for all the strengths and situation weaknesses it may contain, in an education setting it is an unfortunate truth that classrooms are generally more suited to neurotypical children, and that additional support is required for many autistic pupils. Framing autism as an advantage in a situation where it is a disadvantage can therefore undermine the need for teacher training and understanding where there is currently a high demand. Furthermore, while knowledge of neurodiversity does create positive attitudes to and awareness of what someone on the spectrum may accomplish, in practice it can see performance drop and have the inverse effect on an autistic pupil who questions, 'Why can I not meet the standard of my peers?'

However, this should not be perceived as a critique of the neurodivergent stance. Given that much of the support available to families with autistic children is finance based (including disabled student's allowance), continuing to perceive autism as a disability does not diminish their achievements in a classroom. Indeed, it may help restore a more equal footing between peers in the class, where financial struggles and other external factors at home may limit performance. These two concepts are not mutually exclusive.

In conclusion, before neurodiverse approaches can be successful in education, it is crucial that the research behind these techniques is viewed as neurodiverse too. This can benefit finding ways to use the strengths that autism provides to see a pupil excel, and also encourage educators to see the full spectrum and not inadvertently create plans which just target one overrepresented subsection. Conversely, it is important not to let previous knowledge or experiences about teaching autistic children lead to a blanket approach to all such learners; best intentions aside, some support may hinder where previous attempts have succeeded.

Terminology and language

Terminology has the potential not only to influence perceptions of what autism is – or is not – but also to impact on how educators support autistic children and position them, and other neurodiverse children, against their 'neurotypical' peers in classrooms. Language can be stigmatising and lead to misconceptions, particularly when different constructions are used to describe children with or without a disability. Fletcher-Watson and Happé (2019, p. xi) note that the phrases 'neurotypical' or 'typically developing child' and 'a child with autism' place the latter as 'less than', not typical and, perhaps, not as able. Thus, exploring terminology is not only an academic, theoretical or philosophical discussion: it underpins and characterises the ethos in which a teacher, researcher, school and society operate. Language has the potential to influence how autistic children recognise themselves, whether they feel supported and safe to embrace being autistic – to be themselves – or whether they feel pressured to mask who they are due to the ongoing stigmatisation of autism. In short, the terminology we use as educators, and the ethos we establish, may create a situation whereby we emphasise the social construct of 'normal' and assume that a child not classed as (neuro)typical is somehow abnormal and thus they fail to measure up to their 'normal' peers.

Throughout this chapter, identity-first language has been used: 'autistic child' instead of 'child with autism' because the latter describes a person as marred with autism and suggests that autism is separate from who they are. Yet, it is also important to acknowledge that the autistic community does not universally adopt identity-first language; some members prefer person-first language to reflect that autism is a large part of who they are, but not their entire being.

As a middle ground, 'on the spectrum' can be seen as least offensive (see Bury et al., 2020).

Furthermore, although autism, for members of the autism community, is not their entire person, autism is nonetheless intrinsic and not separate from who they are as a person; that is, it is not a condition that changes a pre-existing person. Autism, as with other neurodiversities, such as ADHD, dyslexia and dyspraxia, is simply a different way of being. For Sinclair (1993), an autistic self-advocate, autism 'isn't a "shell" that a person is trapped inside. It is pervasive; it colours every experience, perception, thought, emotion, and encounter, every aspect of existence'. Autistic young people in Goodall's study (2020), all of whom prefer identity-first language, do offer a range of perspectives on how they conceptualise autism: as a difference, as a deficit and as a mix of both.

However, if autism is perceived as a discreet, distinct 'bolt-on' – separate from a person and not part of their makeup – a deficit path may be followed by which an autistic person is viewed as needing to be fixed by way of treatment to reduce so-called 'autistic behaviours', or attempts made to eradicate 'the autism' from the individual. For example, a child's need for stimming, by hand flapping, spinning objects or pacing, may not get the understanding and acceptance needed to enable a child to support their own sensory processing and emotional well-being (to soothe and regulate). Some educators seek to minimise a child's stimming because they believe it will help to 'normalise' their behaviour. However, doing so may impede the development of a child's sense of self as 'autistically normal' (see Beardon, 2019). Educators should support all children (autistic or not) to develop an armoury of supportive strategies, to enable them to be their authentic selves. Therefore, a first step is to recognise the positive function of stimming for autistic learners and try not to reduce their behaviours, unless dangerous, in which case further support may be required to introduce replacement stims which provide the same outcome for the child.

Further, if educators draw understanding solely from the diagnostic criteria and view characteristics such as 'restricted and repetitive behaviours' as symptoms, there may be a failure to appreciate such behaviours as coping strategies. As a consequence, the path followed by some practitioners seeks to reduce or prevent these – changing a child – rather than supporting and working with them: for example, looking to the environment to reduce stressors and unpredictability which underpin a child's need for 'restricted and repetitive behaviours'.

By not embracing who a child is, there is less likelihood that there will be understanding of how a child processes and experiences the world, and how a child responds to the environment they are in, such as the primary classroom. Being in an environment that is not designed with a child in mind, and in an ethos that reiterates (sometimes unintentionally) that autistic children need to change themselves to fit in, perhaps underpins the growing evidence highlighting a high incidence of mental health and emotional well-being difficulties experienced by autistic people (see, for example, Crane et al., 2019). This repeated cycle of a child's (autistic) self being rejected, and having to negotiate reasonable adjustment time and time again to access support and gain understanding, can add to the perception of self as pathologised. This in turn may minimise or deny a child's capacity, as 'expert', to give adult stakeholders advice on how best to support them and influence positive change.

Function-based terminology can also be misleading. For instance, the term 'autism spectrum' can lead to linear assumptions about autism. That is, it suggests an undeviating scale ranging from a 'little autistic' to 'very autistic' and not a multidirectional concept whereby autistic people's sensory, social and communication experiences are changeable. In addition, the use of terms such as 'low functioning' and 'high functioning' serves to create a 'one-or-other' concept of autism and of a person's capabilities and intelligence. Beardon (2019, p. 4) reminds us that 'being autistic does not tell you anything about an individual's intellectual ability', while Woods and Waldock (2020, p. 5) question the accuracy of functioning-based labels and the negative effects they have for 'underestimating the challenges faced by all autistic persons'. These could be the sensory and social challenges posed by the school environment, or the increased risk of bullying and stigma they face.

In reality, 'high functioning' may simply mean a greater ability to camouflage consciously and unconsciously to appear non-autistic. Masking, or developing compensatory techniques (such as using rehearsed conversation scripts), to assimilate, fit in and survive with others is commonplace in classrooms. This therefore means that others may be unaware of the difficulties a child experiences. Camouflaging, which includes masking, compensation and assimilation, is taxing, often sustained over time and is at the expense of physical and mental well-being. Female autists, in particular, may expend considerable cognitive effort to camouflage or compensate for social difficulties to gain social capital. This can lead to poorer mental health, including increased anxiety and depression. Being aware of such aspects of neurodiversity in the classroom is crucial to inclusive practice.

Creating inclusive classrooms

The required effort to maintain a façade of being 'normal', or neurotypical, can be exhausting and might result in support needs being underestimated in educational settings. From Craig's professional experience, many children develop a veneer of coping in school and, when they return home, express the anxiety that has built up from trying to keep up with academic and social demands of the day by way of shutdown or meltdown. Thus, young people may to some degree be making progress academically, but at the cost of 'inner turmoil', demonstrating again the misnomer of the term 'high functioning'. Without appreciating this exertion – not taking into account the neurodiversities of the classroom – and making allowances or adapting practice based on each child's experiences, children can, and do, flounder (see Goodall, 2020). Box 4.2

provides some suggestions for first steps to help educators reduce anxiety for autistic learners.

Box 4.2 First steps to reduce anxiety for autistic learners

- Build routine and structure proactively to counteract unpredictability and help reduce anxiety by giving the child some control in a world that feels chaotic or overwhelming.
- Ensure autistic children have alternative means to communicate their feelings (e.g. setting a red pen on my work means 'I need help').
- Reduce anxiety levels through calm breaks (down time), movement opportunities (as a whole class so as not to single out the child) and being flexible in terms of the demands placed on the child. For example:
  - reduced group work;
  - providing visual instructions;
  - allowing more word processing (or alternative means of representing and presenting their work); and
  - providing time for interest-based focus within their curriculum (as discussed later).
- Have scheduled opportunities to offload and explore any worries with a trusted adult.

Teachers should also be mindful when saying to parents/carers, 'But s/he was fine all day in school …' Instead, it may be more helpful to recognise that stressors may be impacting on the child and that anxiety levels may be building as the day progresses. The suggestions set out in Box 4.2 can also help to reduce this build-up for home.

Limiting understanding to the broad functions (high and low) may lead to not acknowledging, understanding or supporting the uneven profile autistic young people often have. In essence, the term 'low functioning' can be seen to ignore a child's strengths. The term 'high functioning' can underplay the (often internal and hidden) difficulties experienced and the need for support with, for example, sensory and social aspects of the school environment, such as accessing the school canteen or whole-school assemblies. Alternative provision could include, for example, attending assemblies virtually or having a quiet space set up. Both of these slight adjustments may reduce the sensory and social demands placed on an autistic child. Adaptions like this could both attend to a child's needs while still providing opportunities to build friendship with similar peers while eating lunch.

While both authors are advocates of seeing the positives in autism, we are also entirely aware that if we start promoting the idea that every autist will grow up to be Greta Thunberg or Sir Anthony Hopkins then we may increase the chances that children who are limited by their abilities will be ignored or seen as not trying hard enough; thus, opposing the central message of this chapter. For instance, the majority of autistic young people Craig has taught could be dually described as high and low functioning depending on their circumstances. The ability to communicate and interact with others depends on many variables, such as

- *the school environment*, including the understanding of others;
- *the social situation*, including how their day has progressed up to that point, how the child's transitions from home to school and from one activity or lesson to another have been facilitated, could impact on their emotional state and their functioning at that time; and
- *physiological needs*, including amount of sleep and nutrition.

An understanding, flexible, autism-aware, autism-accepting and caring teacher can support a child from being low to high functioning in a given situation, as autistic young people in Goodall (2020) attest. The determining factor, arguably, is whether a young person is in an autism-friendly environment. Here we should heed the advice of Sarah-Jane, an autistic teenager, presented in Goodall (2020, p. 104), and shown in Box 4.3.

> ### Box 4.3 'A good teacher' by Sarah-Jane (in Goodall, 2020)
>
> A good teacher:
>
> - Realises that a person with ASD has sensory issues with noise, crowds etc. and provides support and help when necessary.
> - Realises that it can be difficult for someone with ASD to make friends and understands how to provide social activities to try to help the person with ASD to be an accepted member of the class/year group.
> - Provides an alternative to playground activities such as a quiet reading/games room.
> - Understands that planned activities might need changing to meet the particular needs of someone with ASD.
> - Provides a quiet area in class for those with ASD who need some time out and takes time to explain activities.
> - Listens (to pupils and parents), is patient, kind, understanding, helpful, considerate, calm and above all doesn't shout a lot.

These words highlight the importance of an equation from Beardon (2019, p. 11): 'autism + environment = outcome'. As such, Beardon (2019, p. 5) contends that 'being autistic need not be a problem, being autistic in a society that doesn't understand, however, that most certainly can be a problem'. This is also true for other areas of neurodiversity.

By not appreciating a child's experiences, or not finding out from a child directly what may be of support, or indeed by relying solely on the adult's own interactions with the classroom environment, educators may also misunderstand the behaviour they see. This misunderstanding can again reinforce the child's perception that they need to change to fit in. However, co-constructing understanding with neurodivergent children in the classroom, perhaps engaging in a sensory audit to appreciate the experience of the sensory aspects of the classroom (and, for example, involving a child in developing the calm area and a calm box) may improve the inclusivity of the learning environment. A teacher may be proud of having every part of the classroom walls covered in dazzling displays and laminated (light reflecting) sheets, all adorned with various strings of bunting hanging near to the class focal point, the interactive whiteboard. Whereas, an autistic child, or a child with ADHD, may be bothered by this, it may be an assault on their senses and an increase in cognitive load. It is likely a neurodiverse child processes aspects of the environment more and may be less effective at filtering irrelevant stimuli than their peers. This should not be underplayed or dismissed. What a teacher sees as challenging behaviour may be stress–induced behaviours due to these stressors: sensory overload outweighing the coping strategies a child has available.

Expanding on the 'first steps' noted earlier in Box 4.2, the following approaches can support teachers to develop more inclusive neurodiverse classroom practices. We refer to these as RIPE (reducing, increasing, preparing and embedding) strategies (see Table 4.1).

Table 4.1 RIPE strategies for inclusive neurodiverse practice

Reduce	■ Number of instructions given verbally (chunk and visually support). ■ Rushed endings, provide transitioning time. ■ Extraneous detail in presentations, in worksheets and in the classroom environment.
Increase	■ Time given for processing. ■ Demarcation of classroom areas/zones – coloured spot per child for carpet time. ■ Use of a child's interests (in curriculum and to help with emotional regulation; see Wood, 2019). ■ Pupil preparedness for change – visually show these on the class timetable and involve the child in making this change.
Prepare	■ Inform children of upcoming transitions – use a signifier, e.g. a song ('tidy up time'), phrase (clap, clap, clap '3, 2, 1 quiet lips, listening ears', then give the instruction) or 54321 countdown timer. ■ Worksheets that chunk information into sections or steps and highlight key points to support executive functioning skills, reduce overwhelming and too much visual stimuli.
Embed	■ Keep routines so they become predictable and automatic (e.g. finished work is placed in the green tray, unfinished in the red tray). ■ Expectations of giving instruction when class is quiet. ■ Strengths-based focus to activities by allowing the child to present their learning on a given topic how they feel they can best (this may be a poster, a poem, a play, a 3D model, a rap, a video of them discussing the topic).

Utilising interests: Flipping the narrative

Despite changing concepts and understanding of neurodiversity, and autism in particular, there remains a pervasive pathologising of autism. For instance, Kieran Rose, an autistic autism advocate outlines (in personal correspondence) how the passions, hobbies, interests and focuses of autistic people are still described in 'othering', pathologised terms, such as 'special' interests or obsessions. He explains, just because something seems different it does not need to be pathologised; there are not 'special' pathologised names for things non-autistics do. He flips the deficit narrative by describing 'self-directed learning by a monotropic mind exploring a passion, plus a way to find safety and control through something you love, in a world where safety and control don't exist'.

Autistic young people's passions are now more widely celebrated than they have been historically. This is seen in individuals such as Greta Thunberg and her passion for environmental activism or the love of conservationism espoused by Northern Ireland's acclaimed teenage author of *Diary of a Young Naturalist*, Dara McAnulty. The benefits of supporting such interests are clear. Based on research with autistic young people (and adult stakeholders), Wood (2019) reports that intense interests and a tendency to focus in-depth, in a flow optimal state, to the exclusion of other inputs, is associated with autistic cognition, sometimes framed as monotropism, which is viewed by many neurodiversity advocates as the strongest autism theory (see Wood, 2019). Wood (2019) emphasises the importance of utilising monotropism research and of facilitating children's interests in the classroom. This not only benefits children in accessing the curriculum and learning but can reduce school-based anxiety and, as demonstrated by the earlier examples, promote a possible future career pathway. Further,

> enabling autistic children to focus on areas that interest them could have a significant, positive influence on how they express themselves, also resulting in an important shift in the power dynamic, with the child taking a more confident and assertive role in communication exchanges.
>
> *(Wood, 2019, p. 152)*

This reflects the importance of considering neurodiversity in the classroom and how autistic voice research, such as Goodall (2020), can be used as an illustrative lens for how neurodiverse children experience classrooms and schools. Moreover, it highlights why flipping the narrative from a deficit viewpoint to that of a strengths-based approach is key to developing inclusive practice. The practical strategies outlined in Box 4.2 and Table 4.1 are intended to support practitioners to enhance their own practice in ways that promote wider inclusivity of neurodiverse learners in their classrooms.

Communication, interaction and empathy

When considering social communication and interaction, areas in which autists are often framed as lacking, educators are encouraged to remember that social interaction is not the sole responsibility of the autistic child. Communication is a multidirectional process which involves understanding from both the non-autistic and autistic person. Milton's (2012) 'double empathy' model helps us understand this. Milton recognises that autistic people often lack empathy or insight into non-autistic perceptions and culture, but, equally, non-autistics also lack empathy into the minds and culture of autistic people. This can create a mismatch in communication or interaction styles, suggesting that non-autistic parties can adapt their style to match that of the autistic person. A first step could include matching communication to the child who may, for example, prefer and be able to process concise, one-step-at-a-time instruction using unambiguous language. For instance, ambiguous language such as 'get your books out' may mean 'get your books out and begin working where you left off yesterday', but an autistic child may simply get their books out and sit waiting for the next explicit instruction.

Reflective questions

- Can you think of examples of ambiguous language that you might use in your classroom?
- How might you go about making these more unambiguous?

Research suggests autistic young people better understand other autistic young people and their experiences. Crompton et al. (2020) indicate that autistic people are motivated to engage in social interaction but find greater comfort and ease in building friendships with other autistic people because they are more able to be themselves and feel safer to remove the mask they often wear effortfully when interacting with non-autistic peers. This mask is often reinforced when autistic children are engaged in a programme of non-autistic social skilling to ensure they can become more adept at a neurotypical way of interacting to fit in. Arguably, autistic and, by extension, neurodiverse children are part of a system that encourages camouflaging and fitting in by putting on and communicating in a non-autistic manner.

Lawson, an autist, states that 'language is considered the traditional normal currency of communication. Therefore, if you don't use language as your communication tool, you may be considered disabled, disordered or dysfunctional' (2008, p. 74). These communication differences may underpin why non-autistic peers are found to be less willing to interact with autistic classmates (Sasson et al., 2017). Similarly, limited autism voice research may be a result of an unwillingness to involve autistic children because of (perceived) methodological challenges arising from associated difficulties with social communication (see Goodall, 2020).

Unfortunately, these lived experiences can be more insidious than autism bullying research widely reports. The impact and experiences that social communication differences have on young people have been described in Goodall (2020, p. 90). Sarah-Jane, aged 17, discussed how she wanted friendship but experienced loneliness and was ostracised and bullied by peers for being autistic: 'If you have a disability they don't want to know, they look down at you I think. I was called a geek or weirdo.'

Ro, another girl, aged 16, stated: 'It was like I had germs and they [peers] weren't to go near me.'

Attempts were made by teachers to try and support Ro in making friends, but no true friendships developed. 'He [teacher she liked] tried to get other girls to play with me but once that year ended they would stop playing with me. I thought I had made friends.'

Finally, Wade, a boy aged 13, was told regularly to kill himself by peers. He stated that he would change who he was, exchange some of his intelligence to be able to develop his social skills to fit in more. What these examples demonstrate is that the differences autistic children may have with social interaction ought to be separated from the (misconceived) notion that there is a lack of interest in developing friendship. The importance of listening to neurodiverse learners in our classrooms cannot and should not be underestimated.

Conclusion

This chapter has highlighted that neurodivergent people live in a world that is not always adapted to meet their needs. This leaves many having to cope with the exhaustion of trying to fit in, deal with challenging social and sensory environments, and navigate misunderstandings and stereotypes about what autism is. The research and narratives of autists, as referenced throughout this chapter, including those of James, demonstrate that by seeking, supporting and championing neurodiverse perspectives, educators can understand and take better account of neurodiversity, such as autism, in classrooms. This will start the journey towards greater inclusive practice. The recommendations highlighted in this chapter are intended to help practitioners take some important first steps.

References

Armstrong, T. (2017). Neurodiversity: The future of special education? *Educational Leadership*, 74 (7): 10–17.

Beardon, L. (2019). *Autism and Asperger Syndrome in Children*. London: Hachette.

Bury, S. M., Jellett, R., Spoor, J. R., & Hedley, D. (2020). "It defines who I am" or "It's something I have": What language do [autistic] Australian adults [on the autism spectrum] prefer? *Journal of Autism and Developmental Disorders.* https://doi.org/10.1007/s10803-020-04425-3.

Crane, L., Adams, F., Harper, G., Welch, J., & Pellicano, E. (2019). 'Something needs to change': Mental health experiences of young autistic adults in England. *Autism*, 23 (2): 477–493.

Crompton, C. J., Hallett, S., Ropar, D., Flynn, E., & Fletcher-Watson, S. (2020). 'I never realised everybody felt as happy as I do when I am around autistic people': A thematic analysis of autistic adults' relationships with autistic and neurotypical friends and family. *Autism.* https://doi.org/10.1177/1362361320908976.

den Houting, J. (2019). Neurodiversity: An insider's perspective. *Autism*, 23 (2): 271–273.

Fletcher-Watson, S., & Happé, F. (2019). *Autism: A New Introduction to Psychological Theory and Current Debate.* Oxon and New York: Routledge.

Goodall, C. (2020). *Understanding the Voices and Educational Experiences of Autistic Young People: From Research to Practice.* Oxon: Routledge.

Happé, F., & Frith, U. (2020). Annual Research Review: Looking back to look forward - changes in the concept of autism and implications for future research. *Journal of Child Psychology and Psychiatry*, 61: 218–232.

Kapp, S. K., Gillespie-Lynch, K., Sherman, L. E., & Hutman, T. (2013). Deficit, difference, or both? Autism and neurodiversity. *Developmental Psychology*, 49 (1): 59–71.

Kapp, S. K., Steward, R., Crane, L., Elliott, D., Elphick, C., Pellicano, E., & Russell, G. (2019). 'People should be allowed to do what they like': Autistic adults' views and experiences of stimming. *Autism*, 23(7): 1782–1792.

Lawson, W. (2008). *Concepts of Normality: The Autistic and Typical Spectrum.* London: Jessica Kingsley Publishing.

Leatherland, J. (2018). *Understanding How Autistic Pupils Experience Secondary School: Autism Criteria, Theory and FAMe™.* Doctoral dissertation, Sheffield Hallam University. http://shura.shu.ac.uk/23231/1/leatherland_2018_phd_UnderstandingHowAutistic.pdf

McCarthy, M. (2019). Extreme male brain theory of autism rests on shaky ground. Available at: https://www.spectrumnews.org/opinion/viewpoint/extreme-male-brain-theory-of-autism-rests-on-shaky-ground/ (Accessed: 9 April 2021).

Milton, D. E. M. (2012). On the ontological status of autism: the 'double empathy problem'. *Disability and Society*, 27 (6): 883–887.

National Autistic Society. (2021). Breaking news: Government proposal to change mental health law. Available at: https://www.autism.org.uk/what-we-do/news/change-to-mental-health-law (Accessed: 9 April 2021).

Nuwer, R. (2020). Meet the autistic scientists redefining autism research. Available at: https://www.spectrumnews.org/features/deep-dive/meet-the-autistic-scientists-redefining-autism-research/ (Accessed: 9 April 2021).

Sasson, N. J., Faso, D. J., Nugent, J., Lovell, S., Kennedy, D. P., & Grossman, R. B. (2017). Neurotypical peers are less willing to interact with those with autism based on thin slice judgments. *Scientific Reports*, 7: 40700.

Sinclair, J. (1993). Don't mourn for us. *Autonomy: The Critical Journal of Interdisciplinary Autism Studies*, 1. Available at: http://www.larry-arnold.net/Autonomy/index.php/autonomy/article/view/8/html

Singer, J. (1998). *Odd People In: The Birth of Community Amongst People on the "Autistic Spectrum": A Personal Exploration of a New Social Movement Based on Neurological Diversity.* (Honours Thesis). University of Technology Sydney (UTS), Sydney, NSW.

Tung, J. (2019). Lack of diversity hinders genetic studies. We can change that. Available at: https://www.statnews.com/2019/03/06/lack-diversity-hinders-genetic-studies/ (Accessed: 9 April 2021).

Weitlauf, A. S., Gotham, K. O., Vehorn, A. C., & Warren, Z. E. (2014). Brief report: DSM-5 "levels of support": A comment on discrepant conceptualizations of severity in ASD. *Journal of Autism and Developmental Disorders*, 44 (2): 471–476. https://doi.org/10.1007/s10803-013-1882-z.

Wood, R. (2019). Autism, intense interests and support in school: From wasted efforts to shared understandings. *Educational Review*. https://doi.org/10.1080/00131911.2019.1566213.

Woods, R., & Waldock, K. E. (2020). Critical autism studies. In Volkmar, F. (eds), *Encyclopaedia of Autism Spectrum Disorders* (pp. 1–9). New York: Springer.

5

Exploring LGBT+ identities and their relationship to inclusive practice in the primary school

Max Biddulph and Sarah Hewitt-Clarkson

In this chapter we invite you the reader to witness a 'conversation' between Max, an academic in a UK university, and Sarah, a head teacher of a primary school located in the inner suburbs of a UK provincial city. Our focus is to bring together theory, research and practice that inform the ways in which 'difference' might be understood and addressed for children in a primary school, specifically in relation to sexual orientation and gender identity. Our conversation has taken place over many months and has been wide ranging, taking us to some optimistic and, at times, quite troubling places. A key dimension that has emerged is the role of values as manifested at multiple levels, i.e. societal, institutional and personal, and this insight has been influential in steering the direction of what we discuss here.

Beginning at the macroscale: Defining and reviewing LGBT+ identities from a global perspective

LGBT+ is an evolving acronym that stands for lesbian, gay, bisexual, trans plus other sexual and gender minorities. These communities comprise individuals who identify in ways that are outside of what are seen as societal norms when it comes to sexuality and gender. 'Trans' is an abbreviation of 'transgender', which is an umbrella term for a range of identities for individuals that see themselves as different from the gender that they were assigned at birth, and its association with LGB is symbolic of the historic, social and political movements that have united all these communities. The 'plus' represents a growing list of subcategories of LGBT that includes categories such as 'queer', 'intersex' and non-binary. We are very mindful that the potential readership of this chapter is likely to be

DOI: 10.4324/9781003137634-5

international as well as readers who may be familiar with the UK setting, so it is important to consider the sociocultural attitudes of your home location. The invitation to reflect on 'culture' is deliberate, as attitudes towards sexuality and gender are strongly related to cultural beliefs influenced by factors such as faith, understandings of masculinity and femininity, and what are seen as 'acceptable' lifestyles. For example, in some cultures the label 'LGBT+' is understood as an identity or a social movement, whereas in others it is seen more negatively as a 'disapproved-of' sexual behaviour. Consequently, across the globe there is a wide spectrum of attitudes to same-sex relations and gender variance, ranging from countries that are embarked on programmes of progressive legislation supportive of LGBT+ people to countries that criminalise individuals with laws that carry penalties in the category of 'capital offence'. It is important to note though that in all cultures and countries in the world and in all groups, the phenomenon of sexualities and gender variance will exist in multiple orientations (ILGA, 2019).

Here in the UK, successive governments have pursued a relatively progressive legislative agenda since the millennium via the Criminal Justice Act 2003, which recognises the potential role of homophobia and transphobia in incidents of hate crime, and the Gender Recognition Act 2004, which provides for the legal recognition for trans people in their acquired gender and the opportunity to acquire a new birth certificate for their new gender. The Equality Act 2010 recognises that LGBT people may face discrimination, e.g. in the workplace or via the provision of goods and services, and has put in place legal protections to deter this from happening. Despite other reforms, such as the equalising of age of consent for persons of all sexual orientations and the introduction of same-sex marriage, the effects of marginalisation are still in evidence whether it is through the effects of unconscious bias of educators or the prevalence of homophobic and transphobic hate crime on the streets of UK towns and cities (Bachmann and Gooch, 2017). The impact of this on the individual manifests itself in a number of ways ranging from underachievement at school to disproportionately high rates of mental ill-health experienced by LGBT people, as well as challenges faced when accessing wider healthcare services (Bachmann and Gooch, 2018).

Given the aforementioned observations about cultures, nations and values at the macroscale, it is important to consider how social space is configured and understood more 'locally', as the impact of globalisation and migration is also making the social/attitudinal spaces of schools and classrooms ever more complex and less predictable at the microscale.

Focusing down: Gender, sexualities and primary school environments

Historically, a tension has always existed between the concepts of 'schooling' and 'sexualities', and in the 20th century in the UK context, attempts by the state to control the messaging to children and young people about sexuality and gender is characterised by legislation such as the now infamous Section 28 of the Local Government Act 1988. It is frequently assumed that primary schools would have little or no connection with the experience of sexual orientation and gender identity formation, given the age of the young people who populate these environments. The concept of 'childhood innocence' and the need to protect it prevails, and while any concerns to safeguard the well-being of children and young people should be paramount, an approach that suppresses the discussion of sexuality and gender runs the risk of masking social processes that are actually taking place. Max can deepen and qualify this observation from experience of researching in the field:

> Some years ago, I was asked to evaluate a project that aimed to raise the issue of homophobic and transphobic bullying in the primary school curriculum. In my conversations with headteachers and project personnel in participating schools, it became increasingly clear that young children *do* acquire an understanding of sexualities and gender variance from an early age. Interviewees reported that children have a strong interest in the identities and lives of others and that the media and conversations with older siblings were typical sources of informal knowledge. While much of this comes from innocent curiosity, one participant identified instances in her school community where perceptions were voiced from a less 'benevolent place':
>
> > I had another occasion of a Year 3 child shouting out of the window at somebody who'd come to run a basketball group 'gay boy'. So, I don't truly think that they always know what they're shouting. It's just a language that they've heard from somewhere when playing out with older kids.

The same participant described how pupils in school were being bullied by other children in the same class that is an extension of harassment taking place in the school community. The children on the receiving end of the harassment have an aunt who is in a same-sex relationship and both her sister (mother of the children) and the same-sex couple have experienced verbal abuse from another family that lives in close proximity on the same street. The tension in this situation manifests itself in school in a number of ways, e.g. via the 'frosty silence' that ensues when all the adults are in a classroom simultaneously and

> the distress comes from the adults and their two children [*perpetrators*], via lots of name calling that goes on in the street and in the school playground. The abusive children in my mind are quite rude to the adults in the other family and their mum actually condones the comments, she thinks it's fine, she shouts as much as they do really.
>
> I do know one of the children [*victims*] has had lots of problems last year sleeping, which I guess it's stemming from some of this, it must be.
>
> *(As cited in Biddulph, 2008)*

This example raises a number of noteworthy points:

- A decade on from the preceding extracts, Bradlow et al. (2020) and Farrelly et al. (2017) note the continuing prevalence of homophobic and transphobic bullying in schools in the UK and Ireland. As much as some schools may wish to avoid conversations about sensitive issues such as sexuality, they are involved and implicated from the outset because, as Le Master and Hummel (2018, p. 523) observe, 'bullying is a refrain of what is pervasive, and this comes from the society'.
- Research undertaken over almost two decades (Renold, 2000; Biddulph, 2008; DePalma and Atkinson, 2010; Farrelly et al., 2017) continues to report that primary school children use homophobic and transphobic language often without really understanding its meaning or its potential impact, Le Master and Hummel (2018, p. 525) noting that their victims have to endure not just 'the short-term terror' but the 'long-term trauma' that ensues.
- Bullying needs to be understood as a 'social act' and that consequently there is an impact on all pupils who comprise the social system present in classroom spaces.

While recognising that the issue of homophobic/transphobic bullying is a significant problem, Formby (2015) points out that having this as the exclusive focus has the potential to obscure an understanding of the wider picture of LGBT+ issues in school environments. De Palma and Jennet (2010) concur with this view and draw our attention to the role of school ethos in all its formal and informal expressions as a key determinant of the social climate. A deeper examination of this may reveal a more complex system of power relations which connect with other dimensions of difference such as gender and race. Goodboy and Martin (2018) remind us that while education is the context for bullying, it is also has the potential to be part of the solution. We propose, therefore, that this is the point where it becomes important to question the qualities/characteristics of the kind of space that truly values *every* child. So how can an inclusive school ethos facilitate this outcome?

> Reflecting on the key points arising from Max's research
>
> - What is your school's response to homophobic and transphobic bullying?
> - Viewing this (or any) bullying as a 'social act', what are its implications for the everyday classroom experiences of all children?
> - What do you think are the key qualities/characteristics that support the kind of space that truly values every child?
> - What next steps might you take to develop your classroom as a space in which all children are valued?

Establishing principles for LGBT+ inclusion: Exploring the role of school ethos

The day-to-day lived experiences of being in school inevitably communicate a sense of institutional priorities and values to all members of the school community. When it comes to acquiring a sense of inclusion, the social-emotional 'climate' of the school is pivotal.

Sarah invites us to consider:

> What could be more important than making children feel safe enough and *liked* enough to ask and answer questions freely, to relish new learning, to willingly and happily have a good go at the myriad of things adults ask them to do in school, every day? Psychological safety, a strong sense of belonging and self-efficacy must be taught and invested in in the same way as we do with maths or English. Children must have meaningful, thriving lives; alive, vibrant and vital.
>
> If schools do not teach children to understand equality, equity and justice then I wonder who will. In the same way that schools are expected to teach fronted adverbials, subordinate clauses and fractions, we are also expected to ensure children learn about relationships, kindness and understand that we may believe different things to our friends and that that is ok.
>
> Schools have to be a part of protecting everyone's characteristics and play a vital role in helping society become kinder and fairer.
>
> In our school the three key values are: relationships, determination and 'the ability to sparkle'. We identified these as a whole school staff many years ago and re-visit them regularly, indeed we changed our second value from *aspirations* to *determination* a few years ago when we realised we talked about determination and perseverance far more often than we do about aspirations.

Three key values helping to shape the ethos of Sarah's school

Our number one value is relationships through which we seek to understand our part as a school in the wider local, national and global community. We talk about relationships often and these conversations can be a deciding factor in how we do something or change something. For example, throughout the UK Covid-19 lockdowns, staff called home at least once a week and built new and different relationships with families that were to do with learning, knowledge and welfare in general. We are holding on to this new aspect as the world emerges from the pandemic, as it added excellent dimensions to our relationships with families. It's the quality of our relationships that determines the quality of our lives.

Determination is exactly as the word implies. Keep going; it's the power of understanding that mistakes are an important step in 'getting there'; understanding that although you are not born smart, you get smart by developing a growth mindset as opposed to fixed mindset. This relates to all aspects of school, e.g. academic work, attitudes, behaviour, restructures, staff training, governors – everything and everyone.

The ability to sparkle (we thought long and hard about the word sparkle) means we want children to be wide-eyed, enthusiastic, curious, ask questions, be passionately active in all aspects of learning and life. We have a lolly stick approach (Dylan Wiliam, Shirley Clarke) to asking children questions to cut out the negative and often sarcastic hierarchy of who answers questions if you ask children to put their hands up. We reward children via, for example, a weekly certificate for children who have asked incredible questions; another for having a great understanding of equality; and for those who challenged stereotypes, have been kind to people and so on.

Reflecting on your own practice

- What are the key values that shape your school's ethos?
- How far do they resonate with those outlined here? How do they differ?
- How do you and your colleagues ensure that the school's values are enacted in daily classroom and school life for all children?
- What barriers are there to embedding these values in the everyday experiences of all children?
- What next steps might you take in your classroom to put these values into practice?

We also refer to *sparkle* as the 'Al effect'. Many of our children speak English as a second or third or fourth language, and we know that too often success is measured in how well they do in tests. Enabling children to speak and understand English well enough to be active in conversations and to 'pass' their SATs in English are very important.

A few years ago, a girl called 'Al' joined our Year 6 class from Switzerland. Her parents spoke Arabic and while Al spoke no English, she was fluent in French and Arabic. From November to May, approximately 17 weeks, or 85 days in school, she passed her Maths SATs and SPAG (Spelling, Punctuation and Grammar) national tests and was two marks off passing her English reading. We tried to analyse what it was about her that led to such incredible progress and achievement, so rapidly. Al had an incredible thirst for knowing new stuff. She did not stop asking questions, checking, clarifying. Even on her last day at school she came in to see me with a friend. Her friend spotted a mug on my desk and said, 'Are you having a nice cuppa, Miss?' Al's immediate reaction was, 'I don't know what the word *cuppa* means!' and so she asked. I explained, and she said 'I will use that tonight with my mum. I will say mum are you having a nice cuppa?' As she left she repeated 'cuppa cuppa cuppa' as if cementing the new word in her head. Her questioning and determination to get things right and to know more to improve her language and understanding were incredible. Thus, we named this personification of *sparkle* the 'Al effect'. When that enthusiasm, determination and sparkle is lacking we help children get it and this is only possible if the adults who are around children are also curious and full of determination.

When we observe and feedback on learning and teaching, we look for relationships, determination and sparkle in classrooms, in the environment, in voices and expressions; in staff's determination to help children flourish. Ethos should ooze out of the walls and should not just be a printed strapline on banners and posters.

We do not have a programme to talk about equality. We feel equality should be 'usual-ised' and part of everyday life; for us it should not be a series of lessons, assemblies or one-off days throughout the year. We could not possibly write down every word in a policy of how our ethos works and feels. We do not have a kindness policy for example, but we expect everyone to be kind. Having three simple values which we can return to and talk about is very powerful.

Reflections

Sarah's head teacher account of school ethos raises a number of issues which it is important to comment on at this point. The first of these relates to the multiplicity of identities which may intersect within any individual child and the example of Al is a reminder that in their short lives, children may have had to learn the skill of 'world travelling', not merely in geographical terms but also in terms of managing the social and emotional 'worlds' that they traverse on a daily basis. Building on Crenshaw's (1991) work that theorises intersectionality as an analysis of identities, power and spaces of belonging, Berry (2018, p. 505) observes that the communications transacted within them is 'part of a relational process in which identities are negotiated'. In pinning the precise mechanism at work here, Kustatscher (2017) argues that it is the *emotional* experience of peer interactions that shapes the identities that are presented by the individual. Consequently, children rapidly learn the dimensions of themselves that receive affirmation and dimensions that draw other responses.

Retrospective accounts of childhood made by LGBT+ people often refer to what is initially an intangible sense of feeling different, and DePalma and Jennet (2010) note that for some children the period between the ages of 8 and 12 is when they begin to develop an awareness of an emerging LGBT+ identity. What is said or not said in school environments becomes enormously significant, and, as Atkinson (2002, p. 125) argues, schools and teachers who adopt a position of inaction are in fact making a statement in that that every absence constitutes a particular presence:

> Whatever the gaps in policy and guidance, we *do* teach about homosexuality from children's earliest days in school: through the absence of its representation in discussion, study, inquiry or subject matter; through the policing and perpetuation of heterosexual norms and assumptions; and through the blind eye we turn, collectively, to heterosexist and homophobic practices. Caught in a tangled web between education, morality, religion and the law, we teach it through the absence of non–heterosexual role models among teachers parents and pupils – even when they may be readily available; and through the assumption of heterosexual identities for all those we encounter in 'real life' … Thus the construction of homosexuality as 'other', remains intact.

Consequently, the discourses utilised in portrayals of gender and sexuality produce a hierarchy that pushes LGBT+ people to the margins, in normatively conceptualised relations with others in which they become 'othered', being assigned 'spoiled' or stigmatised identities.

So how can education counter these negative outcomes for LGBT+ children and young people? In the next section we use the setting of primary school Relationships Education as taught in one of the UK's four countries (i.e. England) to offer some positive ways forward to ensure LGBT+ inclusion in primary school classrooms. While international readers may not be familiar with the fine detail of educational policy in this context, the key idea to grasp is that inclusive practice emerges from the interplay between teacher knowledge and awareness, school ethos and values, dialogue with parents, educational policy and legal requirements.

Into practice: A case example of integrating LGBT+ issues into primary school Relationships Education

The review of the Personal, Social, Health and Economics Education (PSHE) curriculum in England has meant that from the autumn of 2020, the teaching of Relationships Education (primary) and Relationships and Sex Education and Health Education (secondary) has become a legal requirement which schools are now mandated to teach. Primary schools will of course continue to teach elements of sex education contained within the science curriculum and may choose, in consultation with parents, to teach additional aspects that they consider relevant to the needs of the children in their school community. These additional variations aside, it is important for the reader to note that for our discussion here relating to LGBT+ inclusion, we are considering the Relationships

Education curriculum only. Using our experience in this context, we now consider the practical steps in the form of four key domains, namely:

1. Establishing a foundation: Developing a Relationships Education policy
2. Developing a strategy for inclusion
3. Identifying curricular and pastoral opportunities
4. Professional development: enhancing educator understanding and awareness

---

Reflecting on the four key domains

As you read the further details about each of the four domains, reflect on the materials referred to here and the kinds of practical steps your school could take to integrate LGBT+issues into Relationships Education (or equivalent in your setting).

Establishing a foundation: Developing a Relationships Education policy

The development of a school policy is seen as a key document in marshalling all the influences that shape teaching into one place. In the case of Relationships Education, this may consist of statements about the relation of institutional values to inclusion and diversity, aims of the programme, as well as legal imperatives from government and clear statements on the challenge of 'holding' the complexity of identities, faith and beliefs in a school community. The policy can be summarised as the platform for practice. In our conversation we identified a number of sources educators may wish to research in preparing a policy:

UK government guidance, statutory requirements and advice

- Department for Education (DfE). 2019. *Relationships Education, Relationships and Sex Education (RSE) and Health Education Statutory guidance for governing bodies, proprietors, head teachers, principals, senior leadership teams, teachers.* London: DfE.
- Department for Education (DfE). 2014. *The Equality Act 2010 and schools. Departmental advice for school leaders, school staff, governing bodies and local authorities.* London: DfE.

Wider discussions about sexualities and gender diversity

- Equality and Human Rights Commission, https://www.equalityhumanrights.com/en

- Stonewall (2020). *LGBT inclusion: What Primary School Governors should know*, https://www.stonewall.org.uk/education-resources/what-school-governors-and-trustees-should-know-about-lgbtq-inclusion
- Educate Against Hate, https://educateagainsthate.com/
- Diversity Role Models, https://www.diversityrolemodels.org/
- Gendered Intelligence, https://genderedintelligence.co.uk/

Organisations advocating and sharing good practice
- PSHE Association
- National Children's Bureau, Sex Education Forum
- National Association for Pastoral Care in Education (NAPCE)

In its 2019 guidance to schools, the Department for Education emphasised the importance of developing a Relationships Education policy in consultation with parents that reflects the characteristics of the school community (DfE, 2019). An example of the expectation that schools will 'hold diversity' is communicated through the following extracts from DfE (2019):

> 20. In all schools, when teaching these subjects, the religious background of all pupils must be taken into account when planning teaching, so that the topics that are included in the core content in this guidance are appropriately handled. Schools must ensure they comply with the relevant provisions of the Equality Act 2010, under which religion or belief are amongst the protected characteristics.
>
> *(p. 12–13)*

> 36. In teaching Relationships Education and RSE, schools should ensure that the needs of all pupils are appropriately met, and that all pupils understand the importance of equality and respect. Schools must ensure that they comply with the relevant provisions of the Equality Act 2010 (please see The Equality Act 2010 and schools: Departmental advice), under which sexual orientation and gender reassignment are amongst the protected characteristics.
>
> *(p. 15)*

Perhaps inevitably in navigating a way through these competing influences, disagreement comes to the surface. Nottingham (2020) reports on the legal case between Birmingham City Council and Afsar, which followed months of protest at the school gates at two primary schools in the city, regarding their stance on LGBT+ inclusion. Nottingham (2020) notes that the ruling by Justice Warby, who found in favour of the city council, drew on both the UK Equality Act 2010 and the European Convention on Human Rights. This is an important judgement for two reasons:

- It sets a precedent in the legal acceptance of Relationships Education to be taught in an inclusive way, i.e. 'that sex and relationships education can be capable of reflecting various relationship types whilst respecting the values and cultures and religions that advocate heterosexual relationships' (Nottingham, 2020, p. 245).

- It shines a light of the extraordinarily complex territory that education has to navigate in terms of culture, values and what constitutes 'age-appropriate knowledge'.

In terms of being age-appropriate, the DfE guidance is explicit when it states in its guidance:

> 37. Schools should ensure that all of their teaching is sensitive and age appropriate in approach and content. At the point at which schools consider it appropriate to teach their pupils about LGBT, they should ensure that this content is fully integrated into their programmes of study for this area of the curriculum rather than delivered as a standalone unit or lesson. Schools are free to determine how they do this, and we expect all pupils to have been taught LGBT content at a timely point as part of this area of the curriculum.
>
> *(DfE, 2019, p. 15)*

The key to determining the focus and scope of LGBT content lies in the creativity and insight of the practitioner, responding to the explicit themes that the DfE guidance has helpfully mapped into five key domains, which are

- Families and people who care for me
- Caring friendships
- Respectful relationships
- Online relationships
- Being safe

Developing a strategy for LGBT+ inclusion

In its conceptualisation of the aims of Relationships Education, the DfE (2019, p. 20) states:

> 60. A growing ability to form strong and positive relationships with others depends on the deliberate cultivation of character traits and positive personal attributes, (sometimes referred to as 'virtues') in the individual. Alongside understanding the importance of self-respect and self-worth, pupils should develop personal attributes including honesty, integrity, courage, humility, kindness, generosity, trustworthiness and a sense of justice.

In many respects the above statements go to the heart of what has traditionally been understood as the essence of good PSHE and this requires educators to be mindful of both the holistic nature of the curriculum and vigilant to the moment-by-moment opportunities that present themselves in interactions with pupils. Sarah qualifies this by observing that:

> Most aspects of Relationships Education will be being taught already in almost all schools. What Relationships Education is doing is to bring a more consistent and uniform approach for all of our children in England and should give our young people quality, thoughtful and positive education that has been lacking for decades. No school had empty periods in their timetables waiting for a new curriculum, so we have all had to find ways of re-focussing our teaching by adapting our PSHE curriculum, adding in new aspects. We use a thematic approach by exploring an overriding theme for each half term and have a day for that half term to ensure children are taught everything they need.
>
> There are so many aspects of Relationships Education that will simply ooze out of the walls and will be part of your ethos, values and culture. In this way many aspects will be talked about informally, in corridor conversations, in assemblies, in workshops with families, in the wording of your newsletters and on your website for example. Behaviour policies and practices will also show schools' commitment to promoting and teaching about good and positive relationships. It is so important that Relationships Education understanding comes from the top − from governors, from the head teacher and all senior leaders. This is more than a separate subject that is only taught at a specific time on a specific day.
>
> All adults in school must be role models for what is stated in the relationships education policy. We cannot expect children to have positive meaningful relationships if the adults around them do not.

Identifying specific curricular and pastoral opportunities

Literacy has always offered many rich opportunities for developing empathy in our understanding of the experience of others, and we both have examples in which LGBT+ content can be used in the context of Relationships Education objectives.

For example, in meeting the need for understanding the importance of self-respect and self-worth, Sarah shares:

> There is a brilliant series of books called *Little People, Big Dreams* written by Maria Isabel Sanchez Vegara. Each celebrates a person's struggles, determination and success in life. They are beautifully written and illustrated books that give children a huge variety of role models they may or may not have heard of before. They show lives in a very inclusive way, for example in the book about Elton John, it says, 'He started eating healthily getting a good night's sleep and looking

after himself and then came David, the husband had always wanted. They built their own family and are the proud fathers of two children.'

In the book about Megan Rapinoe it says, 'While Megan was at college she realised she was attracted to women. Before she went to the London Olympics she told the world she was gay. She wanted to be an example for other gay athletes.'

In the David Bowie book it says, 'David studied art, music and design at school. Sometimes his teachers were not sure if he was a boy or a girl, but David was just delighted to be himself.'

In developing an understanding of justice and kindness, Max quotes his experience of listening to a teacher (Gavin) who told him about his use of a soap opera script, 'Moor Top', as a vehicle for exploring the social and emotional impact of a fictious instance of homophobic bullying experienced by a Year 6 pupil on a visit to their new secondary school. The materials were part of the project referred to earlier in this chapter that employed a resident writer to generate materials to resonate with the LGBT+ experience in a variety of literary genres. Gavin takes up the story:

> As a school we've started trying to integrate work on a more theme basis so when we've been looking at PSHE we've been linking that with literacy as well. We used the Moor Top soap opera because we felt that it would have more relevance to kids in a (Year 6) year group really at the time before they went to do their SATs on script writing. We found the theme of that quite frank, but one which was very useful to the kids because they found it was a real-life situation, one they may come across in secondary school.
>
> I was quite intrigued as to how the kids would respond to it. I think the children were more taken aback with how rude some of the kids can be and how the situations can arise so easily when you are at secondary school. I think it was that kind of a shock that really made them get into it. … there were a couple of Y6 lads to whom it was apparent what it was about and the subjects being touched on, and the girls within this group sort of spotted what it was about. I think the subject was made very clear to them as it came out in the language. They knew exactly kind of who was saying what and who the ringleaders were and what it was all about. And even some of the insults being thrown were things that they had heard. I questioned them about it, have you ever heard that? So, to them it was very much, this is going on, this is happening. I think it was the injustice, the bluntness of the language and if I'm honest I think they could identify that there are probably children in this class who represent some of the characters, probably more for the victims than anything else.
>
> *(Biddulph, 2008)*

An insight that Gavin and other teachers in the project shared was the richness of the conversations that arise from the stimuli like 'Moor Top' when these discussions are pupil-led, where the role of the teacher becomes more facilitative than directive. Sarah concurs with this and observes:

> We rarely have a situation that floors us and we really mean what we say about relationships, determination and sparkle being our three main values. Therefore, relationships thrive when people listen to each other and learn from each other. Sometimes in a class discussion children will say, 'oh I can't do that in my religion' or 'that's not allowed in my religion' and sometimes teachers may not even comment on it because it is fine – we all have cultures, beliefs and things that we've been brought up with that we do or don't do or have never questioned. Sometimes these things give us a good opportunity to reflect on what it means to be a human being and pull out the positives and the things we share. We have the quote from Jo Cox in our library, 'We have more in common than that which divides us', and that is a really good starting and finishing point to any of these discussions.

> We find parallels and connections throughout our curriculum and encourage children to articulate these verbally and in writing, and this really helps with what could be tricky conversations. Children are used to saying 'I am making a connection – what I've just read here reminds me of something I've read in another book' or 'I remember when we talked about … which is similar to what we talking about now.'

Professional development: Enhancing educator understanding and awareness

Our final consideration of the influences that enable LGBT+ inclusion relates to the professional development of educators themselves. The first dimension we want to highlight here relates to understanding professional responsibilities. In the Teachers' Standards (Part Two) (DfE, 2021), the requirements of the role of 'teacher' are expressed in terms of personal and professional conduct. For the many thousands of committed, dedicated teachers for whom the role is a vocation rather than a job, this code will sit comfortably in their interpretation of the role of educator. The requirements to show respect and understanding of 'difference' as encountered in school environments goes to the heart of inclusive practice, even if this means putting personally held opinions aside. Similarly, having regard to the ethos, policies and practices of the school will be something they want to enact as part of a team.

The second dimension relates to the challenge of becoming a reflective practitioner, specifically in relation to their own values position in relation to concepts such as equality and justice. Sarah observes:

> The word 'equality' doesn't feature in our values or vision, but it is implicit in them all. Children and adults cannot sparkle and thrive if they are not taught about and, more importantly, feel a sense of equality, equity and justice. This

is an important concept for education and for staff, families and children to grasp in itself. In school, we must embrace the fact that children will need to be treated differently and that that is still fair and the right thing to do. When everyone truly understand this, cries of 'it's not fair' will lessen and we will be heading towards fairer, kinder and more just schools.

It is also hugely important to revisit these important concepts, read articles, listen to others and be open enough to challenge your own thinking.

A third dimension relates to acquiring knowledge and awareness of LGBT+ issues, especially in the ways in which communities and identities are understood by practitioners, and this is particularly the case when it comes to understanding trans identities. An unsettling dimension of the legal case referred to in this chapter is the fact that the issues cut across sensitive domains of race, culture, faith, ethnicity and sexuality. It would be easy to stereotype individuals based on these dimensions, and the problem with this is that it leads to blind spots which obscure the complexity of intersectionality. With a more open mind it is possible to see how, for example, a young person *could* find themselves curious or questioning their sexual orientation, irrespective of their heritage or background. Fifty years of narratives of LGBT+ experience has taught us what a potentially lonely and difficult place this is, emotionally. Having an identity acknowledged or affirmed, albeit in the form of a passing reference, could be crucial to the longer-term experience of self-esteem.

Concluding observations

The introduction of mandatory Relationships Education in primary schools in England has opened the way for more inclusive practice when it comes to providing children with an age-appropriate, contemporary understanding of sexuality and gender variance. It takes us into a new era that punctures the unhelpful silence that has characterised the response from education in the past. Significantly, there is a benefit for all children and young people in that inclusive curricula provide an opportunity in which one of core purposes of education can be enacted. Humanistic educators have always acknowledged that 'the development of the person' is one of education's key projects via the construction of an affirmative sense of self for every child, from which a lifelong understanding of 'the self in relationship' can begin.

References

Atkinson, E. (2002). Education for diversity in a multi-sexual society: Negotiating the contradictions of contemporary discourse. *Sex Education*, 2 (2): 119–132.

Bachmann, C., & Gooch, B. (2017). *LGBT in Britain: Hate Crime and Discrimination*. London: Stonewall/YouGov.

Bachmann, C., & Gooch, B. (2018). *LGBT in Britain: Health Report*. London: Stonewall/YouGov.

Berry, K. (2018). LGBT bullying in school: A troubling relational story. *Communication Education*, 67 (4): 502–513.

Biddulph, M. (2008). *Opening Hearts: Challenging Homophobia and Homophobic Bullying in the Primary School. An Evaluation of the Pilot Study in North Derbyshire Healthy Schools*. Unpublished report.

Bradlow, J., Guasp, A., Cooke, V., Wicks, H., Bush, L., Douglas, R., Langdale, E., & Aberdeen, C. (2020). *Shut Out: The Experiences of LGBT Young People not in Education, Training or Work*. London: Stonewall/Britain First.

Crenshaw, K. (1991). Mapping the margins: Intersectionality, identity politics and violence against women of colour. *Stanford Law Review*, 43 (6): 1241–1299.

De Palma, R., & Atkinson, E. (2010). The nature of institutional heteronormativity in primary schools and practice-based responses. *Teaching and Teacher Education*, 26 (8): 1669–1676.

De Palma, R., & Jennet, M. (2010). Homophobia, transphobia and culture: Deconstructing heteronormativity in English primary schools. *Intercultural Education*, 21 (1): 15–26.

Department for Education (DfE). (2014). *The Equality Act 2010 and Schools. Departmental Advice for School Leaders, School Staff, Governing Bodies and Local Authorities*. London: DfE.

Department for Education (DfE). (2019). *Relationships Education, Relationships and Sex Education (RSE) and Health Education Statutory Guidance for Governing Bodies, Proprietors, Head Teachers, Principals, Senior Leadership Teams, Teachers*. London: DfE.

Department for Education (DfE). (2021). *Teachers' Standards Guidance for School Leaders, School Staff and Governing Bodies* (updated July 2021). London: DfE.

Farrelly, G., O'Higgins Norman, J., & O'Leary, M. (2017). Custodians of silences? School principal perspectives on the incidence and nature of homophobic bullying in primary schools in Ireland. *Irish Educational Studies*, 36 (2): 151–167.

Formby, E. (2015). Limitations of focussing on homophobic, biphobic and transphobic 'bullying' to understand and address LGBT young people's experiences within and beyond school. *Sex Education, Sexuality, Society and Learning*, 15 (6): 626–640.

Goodboy, A., & Martin, M. (2018). LGBT bullying in school: Perspectives on prevention. *Communication Education*, 67 (4): 513–520.

International Lesbian, Gay, Bisexual, Trans and Intersex Association (ILGA). (2019). *Annual Report 2019*. Geneva: ILGA World.

Kustatscher, M. (2017). The emotional geographies of belonging: Children's intersectional identities in primary school. *Children's Geographies*, 15 (1): 65–79.

Le Master, B., & Hummel, G. (2018). We, bully: On politicizing compulsory bullying. *Communication Education*, 67 (4): 520–527.

Nottingham, E. (2020). LGBT teaching in primary school: Equality, discrimination and freedom of expression. *Journal of Social Welfare and Family Law*, 42 (2): 243–245.

Renold, E. (2000). 'Coming out': Gender, (hetero)sexuality and the primary school. *Gender and Education*, 12 (3): 309–326.

6

Developing inclusive school communities through parental engagement in their children's learning

Janet Goodall and Sam Greasley

Including parents in learning

It has become a truism of much of the literature around schooling that parental engagement in learning is a vital part of narrowing the achievement gap between children from different backgrounds, and for good reasons. For the purpose of this chapter, a 'parent' is considered to be any adult with a significant caring responsibility for a child or young person. Parental engagement with children's learning can lead to a wide range of improvements, such as increases in homework return rates, reductions in absenteeism and increased outcomes for students (Boonk et al., 2018). We would also argue that supporting the engagement of parents is a vital part of any move towards inclusive education.

Booth et al. (2000) have defined inclusive education as a process that works to increase participation and reduce exclusion of children and young people from 'the cultures, activities and communities' around them, and functions through 'restructuring the cultures, policies and practices' in schooling to allow this to happen (p. 4). While much of the literature around inclusive education focuses on the classroom, we argue that this is far too limited: the cultures, activities and communities experienced by young people stretch far beyond the classroom, as does their learning. We argue here for a clear, purposeful change to the understandings of the value of parental engagement and, stemming from that renewed understanding, the inclusion of all parents and carers in the education and schooling of young people. We present a case study of chapter author Sam Greasley's school (Awel y Môr Primary School) to illustrate this.

DOI: 10.4324/9781003137634-6

What parental engagement is/is not

It is important to be clear about what is meant by 'parental engagement in children's learning'. The literature – and experience – is clear that there is often a confusion among school staff between parental involvement in school and schooling, and parental engagement in learning.

Parental involvement in school and schooling (Goodall and Montgomery, 2013) is focused on the school and remains the domain of teaching staff. Agency continues to rest with school staff, and parents are conceived as 'helping' teachers. Teachers remain the ones who are considered to be the only real authorities on learning and education (Berkowitz et al., 2017). This model of understanding parents' participation in learning is school-centric, that is, it is focused on the school rather than on learning (or indeed, on the child). Within a concentration on parental involvement with school/schooling, parents are often conceived of in a deficit mode – that is, school staff must supply what is lacking for parents and families (Baquedano-López, Alexander and Hernández, 2013). The progression from parental involvement in schooling through to the partnership working of parental engagement in learning is illustrated in Figure 6.1.

In reality, the effective elements of parental engagement take place not at school but rather in what has been called the 'home learning environment' (Sylva et al., 2004). Such engagement with learning does not require parents to deliver school-based content (Goodall, 2021b); rather, it is vested in attitudes towards learning, conversations and supportive forms of parenting. In fact, international research has shown a correlation between conversations parents have with teenagers (about general topics, not focused on schoolwork) and the engagement of those young people with literacy (OECD, 2012).

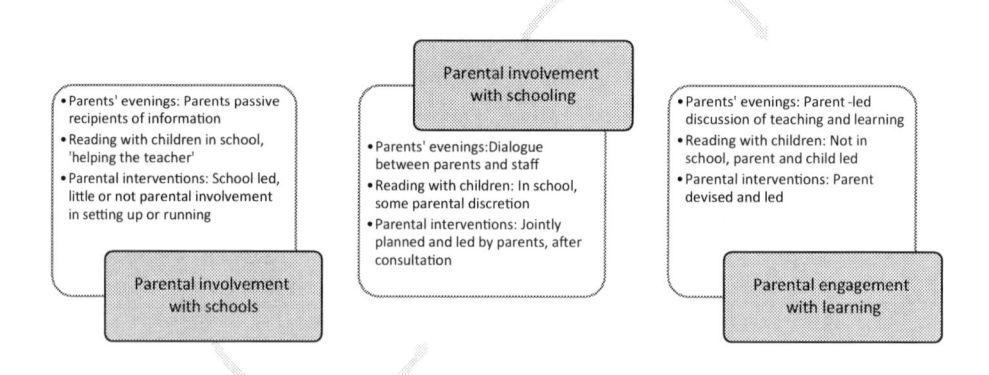

Figure 6.1 Parental involvement to parental engagement (based on Goodall and Montgomery, 2013)

Why haven't we (practitioners and society in general) got this right yet?

The move towards support for authentic parental engagement with learning is hampered in many schools, and indeed systems, by deficit modes of thought surrounding parents (Goodall, 2021a). Deficit thinking starts from a presumption of a lack of something that should be present; in relation to parents, it is often enacted as seeing parents as 'not interested' or 'not able' to be engaged in the learning of their children. The confusion around the concept of parental engagement plays a role here, because parental involvement (supporting the school, interacting with staff) is often mistaken for parental engagement with learning. Staff may assume that parents are 'not interested' when in fact we know that the vast majority of parents are interested in their children's learning and want the best for their children.

Deficit thinking relies on the use of stereotypes ('that kind' of parent) and the lack of acknowledgement of systemic factors that impact on children's lives (Gorski, 2008). Research has told us for some time that children from advantaged backgrounds do better in our current schooling system than do children from impoverished backgrounds (Chmielewski, 2019). Rather than looking to the system, however, all too often parents/families are blamed for low educational attainment (Dahlstedt and Fejes, 2014), based on assumptions about family culture (Ladson-Billings, 2017). Deficit understandings of parents and families prioritise one culture or set of cultures over others. For this reason, we would suggest a slight change to the definition of 'inclusive education' given earlier: rather than seeking just the lack of exclusion from culture and community, we would argue for the positive *valuing* of different cultures and communities within the schooling system (Pushor, 2012). As such, inclusion is, as the research holds, a process which is continually ongoing.

These issues − a deficit discourse around parents (Goodall, 2021a), and a lack of understanding of the value and nature of parental engagement among teachers and teaching staff − are disappointing but not surprising. This may, in part, be based on a further finding from the research: that teachers are often not offered enough (or indeed, any) training or support in these areas. Initial teacher training rarely seems to address the concept of support for parental engagement (Willemse et al., 2018). Many programmes preparing teachers will mention communication with parents, and many will discuss issues such as parents' evenings, and perhaps there is mention of 'difficult conversations' with parents (Flynn, 2007). This immediately sets the tone for new practitioners that dealing with parents is difficult, challenging and not important enough to warrant a great deal of their time.

In the following case study, we examine how one school, situated in an area of high deprivation and low educational attainment, faced these issues and improved relationships and outcomes for staff, pupils and parents. To accomplish this change, staff in the school, beginning with the senior leadership, changed their understandings of and relationships with the parents in the school. Parents who had felt, and had been, excluded from the life of the school have become respected members of the school community.

Moving from research into practice: The case of Awel y Môr Primary School

Awel y Môr Primary School, Neath Port Talbot, provides education for children between the ages of 3 and 11. There are currently 340 pupils on roll and a further 19 pupils who attend the pupil assessment centre (these are pupils from other schools in Neath Port Talbot who are awaiting diagnosis of social, emotional and behavioural difficulties, SEBD, as this is termed in Wales).

The school is situated in one of the most deprived areas of Wales (rank 76, decile 1; WIMD, 2019). Fifty-nine percent of the school population is eligible for free school meals, while a large proportion of the remaining children are living just above the threshold for poverty. Research conducted by the Child Poverty Action Group has shown that family income impacts on children's lives and development in a variety of ways. Living on a low-income increases parents' stress levels, in turn affecting relationships and family dynamics. It is important that this set of circumstances is considered when studying this example. All schools serve a different community: it is important to understand a community and its needs before deciding on an approach to parental engagement. This will ultimately lead to inclusion and not exclusion.

Reflecting on your school's and your community's needs

- What do you already know about the community of your school?
- What else could you find out?
- How could you do this? What data are available? Who could you talk to?

A new school leadership team took up position in September 2017, including Sam as head teacher. At this time, parent engagement was minimal, parent relationships with the school were strained, confrontations between parents and staff were frequent, complaints to the governing body were a regular occurrence, and pupil exclusions were at an all-time high (24 days of fixed term exclusion in the previous academic year, much higher than the Neath and Port Talbot average). A blame culture was firmly established where teachers perceived parents as taking little responsibility for their children's behaviour or attitude in school, and having very little input into their child's learning. Teaching staff saw little chance of improving the situation. Parents on the other hand blamed the school's approach to behaviour management, often citing that they perceived the school to be too strict and quick to provide consequences, without acknowledging why their children were behaving the way they were in class. Parents felt unable to discuss their children's behaviours with staff, finding these interactions stressful, unhelpful and sometimes intimidating. This instilled a greater sense of exclusion for the families.

The new school leadership team identified improving parent relations as a catalyst for improving pupil standards and school development. We believed that if we could develop a school community where everyone felt welcomed and trusted and that they had a role to play in developing the whole child, then we would not only see an improvement in standards but also in the well-being of our pupils.

Initially the school leadership team had to reset the culture and ethos that would support school change. Staff needed to be convinced and assured that that the learning environment we were aiming to create was the right one for our community – achievable for staff and, most importantly, met the needs of our pupils.

Starting out: Understanding our families

School staff began by exploring what life for a child living in poverty looked like. To assist us, we used information published by the Welsh government, Child Poverty Action Group, The Children's Society Action for Children. The majority of our school staff did not come from the same economic group as our families; it was important that our staff understood some of the challenges our families faced and therefore the potential challenges the school could face. Next, we explored adverse childhood experiences (ACEs; Public Health Wales) and how these were potentially influencing the behaviours we were seeing in school. It was important for us to do this because we wanted the staff to realise that the children were not choosing to behave in a certain way, but quite often it was their response to home environments and early childhood experiences that were the cause of difficult behaviour in school. This led to us forming our new behaviour policy that was heavily centred on positive relationships, both with the pupils and their families.

As with all new initiatives, it was important that the Senior Leadership Team (SLT) led by example and were visibly seen to be embracing the new approach. Over time, we were able to identify good practice among our staff that we highlighted in staff meetings, for example:

- Inviting parents into class to join structured reading sessions
- Strong communication that celebrated pupil achievements
- Home visits to new pupils

> ## Reflecting on first steps your school could take to strengthen engagement with its parent community
>
> - Looking at the three examples provided, what first steps could your school take to engage with its parent community?
> - How could you find out what might work well? Who could you talk to?

This process simultaneously encouraged other staff members to try initiatives and supported them with examples on how to forge stronger partnerships with parents. During this phase of change, there were staff members who needed more support than others to understand that we needed to approach our challenges in a different way. Some colleagues were initially concerned that we were taking a 'soft approach' and believed that the only way to deal with poor behaviour was to exclude the children involved and challenge the parents directly about their children's behaviour. It appeared that there were some deep-rooted assumptions held by some about the area our families lived in. It was also fair to notice and acknowledge that some colleagues had previously experienced negative communication with parents after discussing behaviour with them. Staff meetings were used to have challenging conversations to explore this. The Senior Leadership Team welcomed staff members' questions and views on the new direction the school was to take. The key message for senior leaders was consistency. As a leadership group, we were confident that if we got all teaching staff on board with the changes, then we would quickly see success. We found some staff members had to be supported more than others.

Building bridges to work together: Family Engagement Officer

The defining action for developing parental involvement and eventually parental engagement at our school was the appointment of a full-time Family Engagement Officer (FEO). The Education Endowment Foundation website and many case studies from across the UK provided the Senior Leadership Team with enough evidence to demonstrate the impact that the role of a Family Engagement Officer would have and therefore would be an effective use of our Pupil Deprivation Grant (PDG). This grant is provided by the Welsh government and provides targeted support to families who are eligible for free school meals or who are looked after to overcome the barriers that may prevent them reaching their academic potential. The SLT and governing body believed that this was an important appointment not only because it removed the initial workload from the teaching staff but also offered an opportunity to appoint somebody who could better relate to the parents and the community, providing a bridge to greater inclusion of parents, and therefore children, in the school. We identified a current member of staff who possessed excellent local knowledge, concerning both the layout of the estate the school served and also family dynamics. This member of staff was already effective in communicating with our families and could often navigate conversations with our parents on topics that a number of other staff found difficult to broach.

The SLT worked alongside the FEO to identify the aims of the role and came up with the following key areas:

1. To offer families support in a non-judgemental way
2. To increase the involvement of parents and family members in school life
3. To create community links

We were aware from the work of Goodall and Montgomery (2013) that the process we were embarking on would need to travel a continuum from parental involvement to parental engagement, ensuring that the foundations for effective partnership working were laid; therefore we began our project with the smallest steps. The movement from parental involvement with schooling, in which parents are passive and schools active, to parental involvement with schooling, in which activity is dictated by schools but parents take a greater role, through to partnership working in parental engagement in learning, was illustrated by our work at Awel y Môr (see Figure 6.1).

Initially senior members of staff became a frequent presence on the schoolyard during mornings and afternoons, engaging with parents and chatting to the pupils outside of the school environment. Gradually, the families began to get to know us and started chatting to us about the school and their expectations. During this time, the presence of our Family Engagement Officer was crucial. As a member of the same community, she was able to introduce us to people and to lay the foundations of our early relationships and to support some of the less confident staff members by providing ideas for parental involvement and accompanying staff during conversations with parents.

Reflecting on first steps you could take in your classroom to strengthen engagement with parents

- How might you approach a parent to begin a conversation?
- Has there been a time when you engaged well with a parent?
- What was this like and what made it so successful?

Consulting with parents/carers

The next step was to consult our parents on what they wanted from the school. We decided early on that we could never and should never predict what support or changes our families needed. Information and ideas had to come from them. Initially a small group of parents identified that methods of communication needed improving: they were unhappy that the only time they spoke to a teacher was when their child was in trouble. They were embarrassed that these conversations took place on the schoolyard, in front of other parents. The SLT introduced a text message service that tied in with the way the parents preferred to communicate. Key messages and links to our school website were sent via this service and this enabled parents to access information in a more convenient way. Class-based staff were encouraged by the SLT to use the text message service as a way to share good news or success in the classroom. The rationale behind this being that the more good news parents received, the more likely they would be to engage in difficult conversations about behaviour and progress when they arose. This helped staff put 'credit' into their parent relationships to be used in the future. Staff were also directed to no longer hold conversations regarding a child on the playground. Instead phone calls were to be made prior to the end of the school day. These small steps immediately changed the dynamics between parents and school staff. Parents were very appreciative that we had listened to their concerns and acted on them. This allowed us to move forward with our plans to develop parental engagement.

Still acknowledging that even more small steps were needed, we focused on the light-touch aspects of parental involvement: inviting parents into school to work alongside their children on craft projects and attending assemblies. The parents seemed to thoroughly enjoy being able to access school and to be involved in school life; initially a small number took part in these sessions, but over the course of the term the number of parents accessing the activities with their children soon reached 30. Throughout these sessions the FEO continued to gather information from our parents and took the opportunity to talk to them about school. From these simple activities we were able to identify a group of parents that were struggling with the behaviour of their children at home. With the assistance of Save the Children, we were able to run a programme called Families First and take our first step into parental engagement.

The Families First programme

The Families First programme consisted of eight sessions and focused on providing parents with the confidence and strategies to support their children with their social, emotional, literacy and numeracy development. The course was not only successful in supporting our targeted group of parents but also in generating support for our projects through the most powerful tool in parental engagement – word of mouth on the playground. Both the course and the FEO received glowing reports from the parent attendees. This encouraged a number of other parents to approach us and request the training. The development of the parent-to-school relationship also enabled a number of parents to request specific training requests such as understanding ADHD, child brain development, child development level 2 and British sign language, which we were able to provide thanks to links within the community. This development especially pleased us, as we had parents who were starting to direct parental engagement rather than the school control it.

Embedding inclusive changes

At this point in our development we experienced an increase in targeted pupil attendance, a reduction in behavioural issues thanks to greater support from parents and a reduction in the number of referrals to social services. This we attributed to the fact that parents were now more likely to approach us themselves with concerns, giving us the details we needed to contact the right agencies to support them, rather than us referring them to social services without all of the relevant information.

It was important that we acknowledged the effort of the parents in engaging with their child's learning. The activities they were completing asked for far more than an involvement in their child's school life. They were actively making changes to their routines and home environment to help their children. We worked closely with the community to identify rewards that celebrated these achievements This included meal vouchers to local restaurants, cinema tickets and vouchers that could be used at the local leisure centre.

A snapshot of a recent week in school, in the following list, shows the wide variety of activities taking place designed to engage and support our families:

- Each morning an online cookery class takes place. Parents are provided with a slow cooker and enough ingredients to cook ten meals. The course focuses on cooking on a budget and preparing food in advance so that parents can have quality time with their children at the end of the school day either to support them with their learning or to engage in play and talk.
- On Wednesday mornings several parents join our FEO on our regular walk and talk. Several parents have approached us following the Covid lockdowns to explain that they are struggling with their mental health and general well-being, and would welcome the opportunity to meet more parents and to participate in exercise.
- Home visits. Both the nursery teacher and the FEO have been visiting new families joining our school in September 2021. During these meetings we have shared information about the school but more importantly formed those early bonds for successful partnership working.
- Attendance checks. Our FEO is currently supporting three families with their children's attendance. This may involve phone calls, home visits or collecting pupils to bring them to school.
- Referrals to outside agencies. A large number of parents have approached us for help at home in regard to routines and behaviour strategies. Our FEO works with the families to find the right outside agency to support them.

What we've learned so far

It was extremely important that we did not have the mindset that poor families equal poor parents who have little interest in their children's education. We are mindful that some of our parents may have had bad experiences themselves at school. Arguably, this is true for all schools. We are aware that our families may not be able to provide the opportunities that better-off families might, but they can still offer the parenting their children need.

We also learned that we had to be mindful of our parents' lives: working parents might not be able to attend sessions during the school day, for example. It was important that we offered opportunities for parents to engage outside of school hours.

Covid-19 and the enforced school closures (2020 and 2021) have reminded us how important parents are in their role as teachers. During remote learning sessions the school had to rely on the parents to encourage ambition and confidence in their children, and they did a terrific job. Across a four-week period the school averaged 76% engagement with online teaching activities, a figure we never dreamed possible. This was made achievable through the work the school completed in forging those parental links and encouraging parents to take a role in their children's learning. It is testament to the parents and the school staff that during the third lockdown, children's reading ages on the whole went up, demonstrating that when working together we can achieve positive results for our pupils.

We learned that our initial intuition – that we had to work from the ground up and work with, not on, parents – was not only the respectful choice but the right one. Parents had voiced their approval of this approach through practice reviews, stating that they felt included as part of the school and its development.

And, we learned that the role of the FEO was vital to our continued success with parents. Over time, the role has changed and developed depending on the needs of our community.

Developing the role of a Family Engagement Officer in your school

Currently our FEO's responsibilities include:

- To develop and implement a family engagement and learning pro-gramme, including parent/carer forums and support groups, and ensure that targeted families access these opportunities. This may include cooking, physical exercise and activities to improve literacy/numeracy.
- To work with targeted families to engage in the learning process and life of the school. Strengthening links with parents/carers and the wider community to reduce the impact of poverty and disadvantage on educational attainment.
- To work and liaise with a range of professional agencies – social services, educational psychologists, welfare services etc. – to facilitate integrated working and improve long-term outcomes for children, young people and their families.
- To prevent relapse and disengagements by tracking and monitoring of attendance, undertaking regular reviews and implementing appropriate actions when necessary.

- To ensure that all activities undertaken are monitored/evaluated to meet grant-funding requirements and performance measures.
- To undertake home visits where required to support new nursery families and to tackle attendance issues.
- To work closely with external organisations (Flying Start, Save the Children, Team Around the Family etc.) to facilitate intervention and strategies to support and to develop personal skills.
- To contribute to the work carried out by the school and carry out other duties required to mitigate the effects of child poverty on educational attainment.

Reflective questions

- Which of these roles and responsibilities would you prioritise to support the development of parental engagement in your school?
- Are there others that would be especially important for your school and community?

Where are we going next?

Home visits have been crucial in developing those early relationships; research has shown the value of home visits, particularly for children in poverty (Bierman et al., 2017). Parents seem far more settled and comfortable to discuss their children in their own environment; the power is with the parents and this is important in an information-sharing exchange. Parents also complete a one-page profile that is then shared with school-based staff, allowing the parents to share vital information on their children, valuing the role of the parent as a teacher.

We are aware that our work will never be complete. Each year new parents join our community and bring new challenges and opportunities with them; we will have to adapt our strategies and not rely on what worked in the past. Our next steps are to shift our focus, and the majority of our time and energy to the parents of our nursery and reception pupils, instilling our three main aims:

1. Developing and maintaining effective communication with families
2. Developing reading habits
3. Sharing our high academic aspirations for their children

Our next project will hopefully allow us to achieve all three of these objectives. Our Routine for 15 initiative is a book gifting programme devoted to inspiring a love of reading in children. Each month pupils will receive a high-quality, age-appropriate book. We aim to use this resource as a vehicle for engaging parents right at the beginning of their child's education, highlighting the importance of creating a routine in the home to foster academic aspirations and to develop early reading habits. School staff will support parents when each new book is delivered, providing parents with activities that can be used to create a calm learning environment and giving advice on developing the content found within the book.

Our early aim was to provide the right support at the right time for our families. Greater parental engagement has had a large and positive impact on the learning and well-being of pupils at Awel y Môr Primary School. Having a Family Engagement Officer meant that we had the time to get to know our families and tailor our support for them, creating a project that they chose to engage with. This ultimately provided, and continues to provide, support for our parents when they need it through the development of a more inclusive community.

Bringing the research and practice together: Strengthening our inclusive school community

The work at Awel y Môr School shows that research *can* be translated into practice, but also that it is not a simple, straightforward process. Rather, it is an *embedded* process – one which begins not by seeing how the research can be applied to a specific context, but rather what parts of the context are open to the research; the process *starts* with the context and moves on to the research.

This is an extension of good teaching practice: teaching staff know that no two children are exactly alike, and good leaders know that picking up policy and research from one context does not mean it will be directly applicable or workable in another.

At Awel y Môr, this has meant starting with the community, and creating the post of Family Engagement Officer. Research has shown the importance of such posts (Lindsay et al., 2007; Lindsay et al., 2008; Lindsay et al., 2009), but having just anyone in this role would not have sufficed. In the context of Awel y Môr School, it was important that the FEO was already known to parents. This staff member formed a bridge between the community of parents and the community of staff by building up the relationships between the two groups. Research has shown the value of such relationships (Barbour et al., 2018; Goodall, 2018), and again, this builds on what teaching staff already know – relationships are fundamental to supporting learning and building inclusive communities to support that learning.

This process of relationship building, however, took time, effort and good will, on both sides. Parents and carers had to overcome years of distrust (perhaps decades, in some cases). Teaching staff had to overcome not only difficult relationships with families but an underlying blame culture, founded on a deficit view of parents and families, as previously discussed. Staff also had to come to a much greater understanding of what life was actually like for not only the children in their school but the families in their community (Mazzoli Smith and Todd, 2016, 2019).

To understand and properly support children and young people, the entire system around the child must be taken into account. This is what has happened at Awel y Môr Primary: the two previously disparate communities of parents and staff have merged into one supportive system around the child, with all the benefits described.

The journey to this outcome was not always an easy one, but importantly, it was one which was 'led from the top'; senior leaders in the school began the process not only by employing a member of staff in a new role but by (literally) putting themselves 'out there' – being on the playground, interacting with parents. This was another case of what might be called 'the enactment of research', taking the findings from previous research (Goodall and Vorhaus, 2011) and applying them to a specific context.

As the case study shows, this is never a fait accompli, the work is never completely finished – but of course the same could be said of the entire concept of a school; there are always new students, and those students come enmeshed in family and community situations. However, as the case study also shows, history is not destiny. Change for the better is possible, when practice and research are used together to support the entire learning community in ways that value and include all members.

References

Baquedano-López, P., Alexander, R. A. & Hernández, S. J. (2013). "Equity issues in parental and community involvement in schools what teacher educators need to know." *Review of Research in Education* 37 (1): 149–182.

Barbour, L., Eisenstadt, N., Goodall, J., Jelley, F. & Sylva, K. (2018). *Parental Engagement Fund*. London: The Sutton Trust.

Berkowitz, R., Astor, R. A., Pineda, D., DePedro, K. T., Weiss, E. L. & Benbenishty, R. (2017). "Parental involvement and perceptions of school climate in California." *Urban Education* 56 (3): 0042085916685764.

Bierman, K. L., Heinrichs, B. S., Welsh, J. A., Nix, R. L. & Gest, S. D. (2017). "Enriching preschool classrooms and home visits with evidence-based programming: Sustained benefits for low-income children." *Journal of Child Psychology and Psychiatry* 58 (2): 129–137.

Boonk, L., Gijselaers, H. J., Ritzen, H. & Brand-Gruwel, S. (2018). "A review of the relationship between parental involvement indicators and academic achievement." *Educational Research Review* 24: 10–30.

Booth, T., Ainscow, M., Black-Hawkins, K., Vaughan, M. & Shaw, L. (2000). *The Index for Inclusion: Developing Learning and Participation in Schools*. Bristol: CSIE.

Chmielewski, A. K. (2019). "The global increase in the socioeconomic achievement gap, 1964 to 2015." *American Sociological Review* 84 (3): 517–544.

Dahlstedt, M. & Fejes, A. (2014). "Family makeover: Coaching, confession and parental responsibilisation." *Pedagogy, Culture & Society* 22 (2): 169–188.

Flynn, G.V. (2007). "Increasing parental involvement in our schools: The need to overcome obstacles, promote critical behaviors, and provide teacher training." *Journal of College Teaching & Learning (TLC)* 4 (2): 23–30.

Goodall, J. (2018). *Analysis of the Parent Engagement Fund (PEF) Programme: The REAL and Parental Engagement Network Projects.* Bath: University of Bath, Sutton Trust.

Goodall, J. (2021a). "Parental engagement and deficit discourses: Absolving the system and solving parents." *Educational Review* 73 (1): 98–110.

Goodall, J. (2021b). "Scaffolding homework for mastery: Engaging parents." *Educational Review* 73 (6): 669–689.

Goodall, J. & Montgomery, C. (2013). "Parental involvement to parental engagement: A continuum." *Educational Review* 66 (4): 399–410.

Goodall, J. & Vorhaus, J. (2011). *Review of Best Practice in Parental Engagement.* London: Department of Education.

Gorski, P. (2008). "The myth of the "Culture of Poverty". *Educational Leadership* 65 (7): 32.

Ladson-Billings, G. (2017). "'Makes me wanna holler': Refuting the 'culture of poverty' discourse in urban schooling." *The ANNALS of the American Academy of Political and Social Science* 673 (1): 80–90.

Lindsay, G., Band, S., Cullen, M.A., Cullen, S., Davis, L., Davis, H., Evans, R., Stewart-Brown, S., Strand, S. & Hasluck, C. (2007). *Parent Support Adviser Pilot: First Interim Report from the Evaluation DCSF-RW020.* London: DCSF. http://www.dcsf. gov.uk/research/data /uploadfiles/DCSF-RW020.pdf.

Lindsay, G., Cullen, M. A., Band, S., Cullen, S., Davis, S. & Davis, H. (2008). *Parent Support Advisor Pilot Evaluation: 2nd Interim Report.* DCSF-RR037. London: DCSF. http://www .dcsf.gov.uk/research/data/uploadfiles/DCSF-RR037.pdf.

Lindsay, G., Davis, H., Strand, S., Cullen, M. A., Band, S., Cullen, S., Davis, L., Hasluck, C., Evans, R. & Stewart-Brown, S. (2009). *Parent Support Advisor Pilot Evaluation Final Report.* London: DCSF.

Mazzoli Smith, L. & Todd, L. (2016). *Poverty Proofing the School Day: Evaluation and Development Report.* Newcastle Upon Tyne: Research Centre for Learning and Teaching.

Mazzoli Smith, L. & Todd, L. (2019). "Conceptualising poverty as a barrier to learning through 'Poverty proofing the school day': The genesis and impacts of stigmatisation." *British Educational Research Journal* 45(2): 356–371.

OECD (2012). *PISA – Let's Read Them a Story! The Parent Factor in Education.* Paris: OECD Publishing.

Pushor, D. (2012). "Tracing my research on parent engagement: Working to interrupt the story of school as protectorate." *Action in Teacher Education* 34 (5–6): 464–479.

Sylva, K., Melhuish, E. C., Sammons, P., Siraj-Blatchford, I. & Taggart, B. (2004). *The Effective Provision of Pre-School Education (EPPE) Project: Technical Paper 12 – The Final Report: Effective Pre-School Education.* London: DfES/Institute of Education, University of London.

Willemse, T. M., Thompson, I., Vanderlinde, R. & Mutton, T. (2018). "Family-school partnerships: A challenge for teacher education." *Journal of Education for Teaching* 44 (3): 252–257.

7

Doing art, (un) colonised bodies: immersing curricula in our acts of living

John Baldacchino and Faisal Abdu'Allah

Introduction

Listening to the diversities of stories requires attention to the storytellers, to hear their joys and empathise with their pain; in order to be tinted by the experience of listening we must be prepared to rethink our own position/character/part in the wider themes of the human story. In this chapter, authors John Baldacchino and Faisal Abdu'Allah (see Figure 7.1) document a conversation that weaves their personal stories to explore ways in which influences of colonial curricula impacted on their understanding of self, the world and their place within it.

The central theme of the chapter is colonisation and more specifically how *de*colonising needs to move to *un*colonising the curriculum. What does this mean for teachers and school leaders? What is the difference between decolonising and uncolonising? 'De-' when applied to a verb denotes the removal or reversal of the action; decolonising means to reverse the colonisation of knowledge – to go back and remove. 'Un-' means giving the opposite force, i.e. a restart or a fresh review of the assumptions so long held about knowledge, culture, power and history. Uncolonising formalises educational spaces in which colonisation is problematised and addressed. It is a nuanced difference, but one that raises questions about the process of rethinking, confronting and reimagining how the curriculum, in whichever country or context, presents its 'truths' about the world, about people, about power and about democracy – inclusion, liberty and social imagination.

Personal experiences of colonisation

John Baldacchino: We do share a degree of common experience – albeit different in nature – in how we relate to the idea of 'decolonising the curriculum'.

DOI: 10.4324/9781003137634-7

Figure 7.1 John and Faisal

To begin with, we have and continue to experience this legacy and the need to *uncolonise* it in terms of our work in British and American universities. Also, both of us have worked with younger people in schools and other educational spaces, where, through our own experience as young children, we tend to be more than just aware of the fact that the curriculum – in how we conceptualise, design and *live* it – needs to change. More than simply decolonised, the curriculum needs to begin to inhabit an uncolonised space of thinking and being. (See Baldacchino, 2018a.)

I am also thinking of your own experience as the son of Jamaican immigrants growing up in Britain. We both share this colonial experience in terms of how we engage with the history of British colonialism and how it affected us. But we also relate to it from a set of different perspectives, amongst which is race, which in my case becomes rather challenging as notwithstanding their history, as Maltese we belong to diverse populations from the Mediterranean which mostly consider themselves as being 'White' – a narrative which also reflects the colonial period of that region.

Given the British schooling that we had there, when it came to my knowledge of school systems I could only connect with Britain (which might explain why I decided to do my graduate studies in England). But on the other hand, there were certain things which I could not fully understand when I moved to Britain as a student and then as an academic. There I found myself confronted by other perspectives, which initially shook me because the vision of the 'mother country' (as Britain was often referred to) was very different from my formerly colonised 'motherland'. But in your case, the colonial experience came from within Britain itself, which means that we both experienced a colonial schooling but from a rather different dynamic.

Faisal Abdu'Allah: For me it was quite interesting when you talk about one's education. Growing up as a kid you don't realise it's a colonised education. You think 'this is the education'. I do recall when I was 14 or 13, a friend in my class said to our teacher, 'Miss, when are we going to learn about slavery?' For some strange reason she just kept ignoring his question. And for some of the people in the class they were not interested. But this one kid – I will never forget him, Gregory – was so adamant that we needed to learn about it, and when it did happen it was almost like 45 minutes, and that was the big breath of the education that we got to talk about the black body in history.

When you are learning about – you know, Richard the Lionheart, Henry VIII and the Battle of Hastings – and you realise that there are all these wonderful figures, on whom one could vent, with whom you can align yourself with, and see your own life in an aspirational way … even if it's not based on martyrdom or slaying or taking over people's lands, you can see a sense of an aspiration. But there was none!

It's funny because a few years after that, when I began to get curious about art, in my art lessons … because that was the way in which I could visualise, create things and access these portals of escapism through colour and light. Then, my art teacher, Mr May, took us to the National Portrait Gallery in the back of his Ford Capri. Three students that were studying O level art. He took us in the back of his Ford Capri. This is in the late '80s. You couldn't get somebody who was more forward thinking than Mr May, and he was an artist. We walked into the National Portrait Gallery and he told us, 'It's OK guys. Just walk around. We'll meet again in an hour!'

I will never forget, for the first time, feeling the sense of familiarity. Some people might feel 'Oh I don't belong in this place.' We were looking at these same paintings in our art lesson. I was copying these paintings to understand rendering, colour, proportions. I developed good techniques by copying these Old Masters. But one thing troubled me. I remember asking my teacher Mr May, 'Why is it that anyone in the painting that looks like me is in a subservient position – like holding a tray or being impaled on something?'

He couldn't really give me an answer and addressed the work through the lens of being a painter but didn't give me what I would classify in this day and time as an 'informed answer'. Now in retrospect, maybe Mr May was doing that to protect me.

JB: Was he a White guy?

FAA: Yeah, he was. He was one of the great supporters of my practice. We did classes after school, where he played selections from his vinyl collection: Miles Davis, Ella Fitzgerald and Coltrane. Those were his people. While painting, I would ask Mr May, 'Is this what being an artist is like?' and he said 'Yeah.' Listening to Coltrane and Davis, at 15 years of age! Painting abstract forms without regard for the world – it was assuring.

> ## Box 7.1 Reflections on experiences
>
> John and Faisal's experiences bring to light the tensions children experience as they try to 'fit in' to an education system and where they 'stick out', as bell hooks described in Teaching to Transgress (1994). Biddulph and Burnard (2022) encourage journaling as a process to deepen reflection and assessment of practice. Possible questions in relation to John and Faisal's personal storying of their educational experiences could be:
>
> - How do children experience the curriculum in your class or in your school?
> - How are diversities experienced and represented? How are they misrepresented?
> - Whose voices are loudest? How could you amplify more diverse voices?
> - Where could children have a feeling of sticking out and not being included? What could be done to change this at an individual and school system level?
> - Imagine the day in the life of one child in your class; invite them to take an iPad or camera and to document their day; then invite them to share their photographs with you. What disrupted your view? What surprised you? What made you curious? What do you need to change/keep the same/do more of?

Unlearning and performing uncolonising acts: Conversations with the world

In this section, the conversation moves to ways in which learners' voices can become heard; where identity (the freedom to choose, the desire for inclusion, the spirit of social imagination to consider what needs to change) becomes a process of unlearning and relearning. Faisal focuses on the importance of teachers, teacher motivation and moral purpose, and the importance of professional critique.

FAA: That was when my conversation with the world began. With me as a young person being led to a doorway that could define my life in ways I could not imagine. Being the first to attend university, the one who my parents felt was full of promise and be the example of what attending to your studies could reap. There were a lot of eyes on me as a young person.

With Mr May's classes you begin to realise how, what you often say about the need for one to unlearn, is true. The more I read up when you

> Following World War I, Tulsa boasted one of the most affluent African American communities in the country, known as the Greenwood District. This thriving business district and surrounding residential area was referred to as **Black Wall Street.** In June of 1921, a series of events destroyed the entire Greenwood area. On the morning of May 30, 1921, a young black man named **Dick Rowland** was riding in the elevator in the Drexel Building at Third and Main with a woman named **Sarah Page** - they were alleged to be romantically involved. Tulsa police arrested Rowland the following day and began an investigation. An inflammatory report in the May 31 edition of the **Tulsa Tribune** reported that Rowland 'tore her clothes off and scratched her' if he was accused of attempted rape, he would be lynched regardless of his innocence. After his arrest, a confrontation between black and white armed mobs quickly assembled around the courthouse where the sheriff and his men had barricaded the top floor to protect Rowland. Shots were fired and the outnumbered blacks began retreating to the Greenwood Avenue business district. In the early morning hours of June 1, 1921, Black Tulsa was looted burned and fire bombed by airplanes. Governor Robertson declared martial law, and National Guard troops arrived in Tulsa. Twenty-four hours after the violence erupted, it ceased. In the wake of the violence, 35 city blocks lay in charred ruins, over 800 people were treated for injuries and contemporary reports of deaths began at 36. In 2001, the Tulsa Race Riot Commission released a report indicating that historians how believe close to 300 people died in the riot.

Figure 7.2 Tulsa Chalkboard 2018

talk about unlearning (see Baldacchino, 2018b), and the older I get, I realise how much of that high school education had to be unlearned; how much of that education was actually inaccurate.

When I made that screen-printed chalkboard (*Tulsa Chalkboard*, 2018; see Figure 7.2). I was trying to convey blackboards – or chalkboard – as a metaphor for my education. And I was asked: 'What do you mean?' I said, 'Well, in most schools now you have a whiteboard, which is connected to the Internet and there is another doorway in which knowledge is acquired, compared and critiqued. Whereas my blackboard only had my teacher.' And my teacher with the colonised mind would come in and they would dictate what would go on that chalkboard and into our heads. And what they would write on that chalkboard would be gospel; something I would believe. Whereas on the whiteboard someone would say something and someone else would cross-reference it.

JB: It's interesting how as you talk about 'the teacher with the colonised mind'. It reminds me of my own experience in primary and secondary schools in Malta, even though when we speak of a colonial context to learning, Malta has a set of different scenarios. You also mention social class, in terms of you coming from a migrant family. I experienced a similar situation in terms of coming from a working-class family. It turns out that I was the first graduate in my family.

I remember the books you mention. I also remember the books which featured the history of Malta. One of the things which I keep talking about when it comes to my experience of a colonial curriculum is that in my schooling, I had to unlearn and relearn at least two versions of Maltese history. It was a strange exchange of who were the friends and the foes according to how educational policy was decided. In my childhood, even Maltese language books were actually printed by Oxford University Press. There the narrative was similar to your recollection of the great figures of British history, but when it came to Maltese history, this was also framed within that imperial history, with the British being the good guys, while the French were the bad guys; similarly, the Arabs were the bad guys, but the Normans and the Knights of St John were the good guys. The whole idea of an uninterrupted Christian history was also a myth which we were fed, where 200 years of Islamic and Arab settlement – still reflected in our own Semitic language – were obliterated or taught in a bad light.

How knowledge is presented needs to be critiqued by school leaders and teachers. For example, there is a topic in the English curriculum about the discovery of South America. Christopher Columbus is portrayed as a hero who brought the New World to view. Without critique, there is propagation of the White European version of history. Obviously, we know that the Americas existed before the European boats landed. The adaptation to this curricula topic is not to remove it from the syllabus, to decolonise it, but rather to add a lens of criticality, to uncolonise it. A topic can start with a question: 'Did Christopher Columbus discover South America?' In Box 7.2, some ways of uncolonising the curriculum are shared, although there will be countless more ideas.

> ## Box 7.2 Reviewing resources in uncolonising the curriculum: Rewriting histories
>
> History, it is said, is written by the successors, not by those defeated. To uncolonise the curriculum, schools could start by (a) reviewing the books/ resources in their schools, (b) commit to investing in books that show diverse accounts of history and (c) creating curriculum opportunities to critically discuss these accounts. For example, The Windrush Child (2020) by Benjamin Zephaniah is a novel about the period of UK history after the Second World War. It tells the tale of Leonard, a child who arrived in England from Jamaica. Zephaniah pulls no punches in his telling of racism and the powerful experience of sticking out, despite trying to fit in.

> The story could be used in the following ways:
>
> 1. People living in Britain's colonies had been brought up to think of Britain as their 'mother country' and felt she would always treat them as part of her family. What does this mean? Who held the power or decisions? Why was it difficult to be accepted or to accept?
> 2. Create a poster to invite people to your classroom. What would you say? What would happen if someone accepts the invitation but doesn't behave in the usual ways of the classroom?
> 3. Choose a game that you all know, football for example. Split the teaching team into two. One group plays the accepted rules. A second group decides on new rules. Group two doesn't tell group one the new rules of the game. Play the game and afterwards discuss what happened. How did each group feel? What would have made it better?
> 4. Develop a resource bank similar to https://www.britishcouncil.org/sites/default/files/migration_education_pack.pdf.

JB: I'm trying to think about this by going back into a context of schooling. You mentioned your teacher, Mr May, who actually came from a White background, and you felt that though he knew his history of slavery and was more than just aware of racial discrimination, he chose to approach this in a way that protected your 'young eyes' – as you beautifully put it. (See Abdu'Allah and Martínez-Ruiz, 2010.) Then I was thinking about the young student in your class who actually decided to ask a question about slavery, which your other teacher took a while to answer, only to do so briefly, and unlike Mr May, decided to formally address the issue.

These two scenarios raise questions on what would really challenge the curriculum. Given that we talked a lot about our own experiences, I can't help thinking whether to *challenge* – let alone *decolonise* – the curriculum. It needs to come from educators, who, like us, have been through the colonial experience. And if not, then how would educators perceive or approach this challenge?

Other questions might invariably emerge from people who would say, 'If I didn't have that experience, how do you expect me to understand what you're talking about?' I don't mean this as an 'excuse', because some people genuinely feel that they might not be experientially equipped to face this challenge. As a man who is broadly considered as being White – though I often dispute that definition for myself, because I am not always considered as being 'White' by other White people – I often pose that question. Also, I would admit that I often feel that I miss several perspectives that concern specific issues, even when, because of my own colonial experience, I actively engage with these questions.

If I were to put it another way: I often wonder if individuals on their own could face such challenges without having experienced what you experienced as a son of Jamaican immigrants in London. I say this because even as someone who grew up in a former colony, I am painfully aware that the colonial mind, as you call it, impedes me from fully understanding the context by which I can, as an educator, confront the colonialised curriculum.

FAA: This is slightly abstract, but I hope they give you some insight into how my mind is thinking.

To start with there is the moral purpose of teachers. For a few years in London, I was invited by the Institute of Education to talk to first-year students who want to become teachers. They invite me in as an artist to speak to them about what it's like to teach art to young people. As I start my lecture, I ask them: 'Hands up anybody here who wants to teach young people to make art.' They will all put their hands up. But then I ask: 'Hands up all of you who are *still* making art.' One of them puts their hand up. My reaction is 'I want to be very honest and be transparent with you. I have to remind you that you have to teach through research, and knowledge, and body knowledge, and if you're not making work, you're not in a position to teach somebody how to make work.'

One of the things that I'm really concerned by is that to receive a good education, you need good educators. I always say to students, 'When you take a class you look at the professor who is teaching that class and research how current they are, and then decide if they should be teaching you.' It is about a mindset that is willing to step back – be the stranger as Maxine Greene (1973) says – and look afresh at the children, their lives, the journeys of their families and the knowledge around them, around us all.

For example, I was having a discussion with my daughter's school after an incident. They called the parents online and were talking about Black History Month as a tool for educating. I said, 'Look. I'll be honest with you. I'd rather you didn't teach my daughter Black History in Black History Month, because I find it very insulting. Because I think this school does not understand the contribution of black history to history and it is just better to "integrate" it into the general curriculum. Now if you want to acquiesce and give 1 month out of 12 to the history about what people from my part of the globe have achieved, then quite frankly you don't need to do that.' I said, 'I'll teach my daughter 12 months out of the year about the achievements that everyone has contributed. But you're not going to seriously include me in one month and then leave the other 11, that is not how you teach your history.'

The students by their very nature are going to ask the question, we should afford them teachers who are proficient in their respective fields to give them well-informed answers. Having a broad knowledge is good but specialist knowledge is the key.

Artistic acts of uncolonising: Renaming and seeing afresh

How can schools move beyond the compartmentalising of knowledge or people? Rather, how can they work to reconsider, reconceptualise and reimagine an educational experience that allows diversities to co-exist as an essential part of being a democratic uncolonising force? In this section Faisal and John talk about the value of the arts in expanding awareness of bringing people to new spaces of understanding of the issues inherent in the colonised mindset and practices that this evokes.

JB: Your artistic experience also reminds me of how art played an important part of my education. I was good at art – I came from a family of painters and sculptors on my father's side – and so for me art was central to whatever I did. But the colonial narrative was also present there. As a child I was fascinated by British figures in history, including Richard the Lionheart and Walter Raleigh. For example, I read a lot of Ladybird books, and I was fascinated by images of Lord Nelson, who, according to our history, 'delivered' us from Napoleonic oppression. Nelson was one of those heroes who came to Malta to 'liberate us from the French' (even though at some point the shift went the other way and suddenly the French became the good guys who 'were misunderstood'). But still, I was mostly fascinated by the visual narrative of these stories.

This is why here I want to focus our conversation on art, because it played a major role for both of us in our education. How the arts find themselves placed, or 'practised', in education also serves as a model in terms of how one could potentially begin to think of uncolonised minds and bodies. Your story of Mr May's approach to your visit to the National Portrait Gallery, and then his teaching strategies used with you in response to your questions and your increasing realisation, is itself a great example. This also highlights issues with how people see each other. How our imagination is formed.

FAA: To your point about education … for me it can only start with the point of my own arts education. I was 18 years old. I got a place at Central St Martins. It was an important step as I embraced new ways of seeing and existing.

I don't think then there was a duty, a duty for me to speak to issues on diversity and race. It didn't feel like that then. The university kept the emphasis on me being an artist, and I was going to have the time of my life in the three years I was there. I only began to understand the relationship between student and professor several years after I graduated, realising the amount of influence they should have had and could have had. I had three amazing professors, but the others were just teaching from a position of how they were taught.

I guess one of the turning points was in my first year. I was doing a lot of abstract drawings and process-based lithographs, based on the artists that I was being exposed to. I was looking at the people they were showing me: the Kandinskys, the Degases, the Monets, Rothkos … so I was looking at all those artists who didn't – culturally, or within the lineage of their life – have any correlation with me living in London, parents coming from the Caribbean. There wasn't any of those associations. I wasn't being exposed to artists who were creating through that lens.

Then in September 1989 I travelled to the United States as an exchange student for one semester. I'm there for probably a week, and then I began to realise this notion of difference when they would tell you: 'You're the guy from London!' and I'd reply 'Yeah.' 'You're sure?' and I say 'Yes!' 'Then say something … Oh you are from London!' I was a novelty. But I kept asking myself: How can I be a novelty in 1989 in Boston, United States? One of the most, educated cities. My peers could not comprehend that there was a large black presence in Europe.

Then came another turning point, just being called over to the dining table one day: 'English! Come here!' and this student says, 'Have you read this book?' I said 'What book is that?' She gave me a book on the Harlem Renaissance. I said, 'What is that?' She said, 'Well it's a really amazing movement.' I said 'The movement of what?' 'Well, there are artists, musicians, poets, theorists …' 'Really?' So, I took the book and I read it from cover to cover. It was a heavy book. It was probably around 400 pages. But I just didn't believe, John, this rich history of poets, musicians, scholars and artists, from Billie Holliday, Norman Lewis to Langston Hughes. Those scholars, practitioners would have a profound influence in my early year to form the basis of who I am now, in terms of comprehending there were musicians creating music through a body knowledge, through African language, or mathematics, or coding. … It was fascinating, and I began to think: 'What have I been doing for the last year in university?'

That's when I began to then make this search. I arrived in the United States as Paul Anthony Duffus, that was my name, a Scottish surname name. I found out there was a Duffus Castle in Scotland. After questioning my own name and being, I was reading autobiographies of individuals who had made transitions after relinquishing their birth names and adopting more Afrocentric names. That is when the journey started for me as I began to utilise the artwork as that vehicle for healing. When I came back to the UK, the first work I ever did (remember that anything I did before was abstract) was a series of screen prints from *Malcolm X No Sell Out*, 1990 (see Figure 7.3).

I was incorporating contemporary rappers as modern-day Black nationalists. I had the Malcolm X images opposite images of Ice Cube and tracks from Lakim Shabazz and people who I considered as modern-day orators

Figure 7.3 Malcolm X No Sell Out, 1990

of Black consciousness. That was the way I began to launch myself. I came back with a different name. I came back as Faisal.

I will always be the gadfly and that person in the room posing that question, just like my school friend did when I was 13, asking the teacher, 'When are we going to learn about slavery?'

JB: But my question is this. Let's imagine that everyone agrees that a colonial curriculum also implies a state of affairs where knowledge becomes compartmentalised. Let's also insist that in order to engage with teaching, one has to practise the arts, the histories and all that comes with the need to challenge the colonial mind. While we would agree with all of that as the basis of our argument, and adopt it, does that mean that the precondition for an uncolonised curriculum is more than just a commitment to it? How does that happen?

I was recently using bell hooks's book *Teaching to Transgress* (1994), and there she recounts how when she was in an all-Black segregated school as a student, they used to talk a lot about empowerment, the teachers were all into emancipation, and there was widespread consciousness in terms of race, gender and social class. Then, when education was desegregated, she recalls how she felt being in a *White* rather than an integrated school. She recalls how '[t]hat shift from beloved, all-black schools to white schools where black students were always seen as interlopers, as not really belonging, taught me the difference between education as the practice of freedom and education that merely strives to reinforce domination' (hooks, 1994, p. 4).

I think that bell hooks captures a very important dilemma. It's a compelling paradox and I don't know whether we are having a similar situation here. And it becomes extremely difficult to think about an uncolonised curriculum when you think of a situation like that.

FAA: I have to say that when people talk about diversity, I think sometimes it's a diversity in name, and it is lip service. Diversity is a White word, I have heard it been said. I get a little bit annoyed by it when people say, 'Oh yeah, London is such a diverse city!' I say, 'Really? When was it ever diverse in banking? Where is it diverse in education, the arts, I could go on … It is diversity in name only.' So, I think you raise a very good point. It's about diverse diversities not just a thing called diversity (Biddulph and Burnard, 2022).

JB: When I am faced with these paradoxes – and we come across them all the time – one of the things which I find very effective in terms of how I would handle them is through arts practice. I always find that effective because as artists we do things, set up scenarios, where our practice allows us to deal with them. The art classroom is a place that is safe enough, whereas if we take these scenarios out, probably one would get arrested, or will be mercilessly criticised. And that's because in the space of our artistic practice we try out things, like we're doing now in this conversation. Others reading or listening to such a conversation might think that we are advocating some kind of segregation, though actually what we are doing is the opposite.

With art practice it is interesting because that's how experiments with scenarios and then suddenly the paradox within the art practice allows you to embrace it and move on. Also, it allows you to continuously unlearn some of the things which we have received and can't grapple with – or perhaps we try to grapple with them, but we cannot resolve.

I know that your artwork is characterised with such a value, and here I want to explore that with you. I find that in my own theoretical work the only way that I can try to resolve issues, paradoxes, is when I approach these situations through my own art. How would I resolve this in the studio? Sometimes I just go and do sketches. In themselves the sketches are not going to tell me how to resolve problems, but as you know there is that kind of practice in art – in this case the sketching itself – which, because it is different from language and other skills that we have as human beings, it allows us to have a different take. It's nothing special. It is just a different way of looking at the problem.

You mentioned the *Tulsa Chalkboard* (Figure 7.2), which was a great example of how conversations that are difficult could be started and expanded (see Popke, 2016). I'm thinking of other works of yours.

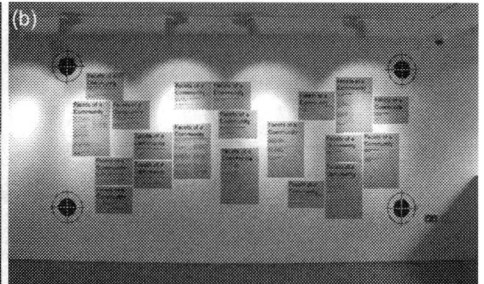

Figure 7.4 Facets of a Community, 2018

Figure 7.5 Adeve Installation, 2012

You did tapestries based on photographs of people (Figure 7.4, *Facets of a Community*, 2018; and Figure 7.5, *Adeve Installation*, 2012) who have inspired you because the sitters were normal common people. I'm just thinking if we take the discussion of an uncolonial mind and body directly into the context of art, these big questions start making sense. In fact, I would go as far as arguing that if a teacher will ask me, 'How am I going to engage with a colonialised state of affairs? How can I even begin to imagine it?' I would just say, 'Get your students to throw in paint. Get them to engage with paint and then suddenly something happens. Don't ask me what it is because I don't know, but I'm sure that there would be a conversation which suddenly begins to crack this dilemma.'

Creating new spaces for uncolonising

Creating spaces for the arts is valuable to allow for new ideas and possibilities to arise. John and Faisal advocate for these opportunities. In this section, Faisal describes one of his art pieces, an installation, that provoked responses from the viewers (who were actually participators in the experience of the art).

FAA: Spaces for uncolonising the colonised mind are important and schools have a real opportunity to co-create these spaces. One of the pieces that explored this space making in particular is *The Garden of Eden* (Figure 7.6), the piece that I made with Sir David Adjaye. It is an architectural construction. There are no images and it is an immersive space. When you arrive at the gallery, the attendants look at you and ask, 'What colour are your eyes?' So that you don't feel conscious that someone is looking at you, attendants are only looking at the colour of your eyes. If your eyes are blue, grey or green, they will ask you to turn right, and if your eyes are brown, hazel-red, they ask you to turn left. And if you ask, 'Why do I have to go right because mine are grey?' the answer would be 'Because the artist would like you to go that way.'

What happens in the *Garden of Eden* (Figure 7.6) is this glass construction that has two entrances. It has an internal central structure and an external structure. As a blue-, grey-, green-eyed person, you walk down the corridor, turn right and you walk inside a glass box. This glass box has a metal floor and a metal ceiling. In it one is surrounded by mirrors, and you see your total reflection; you see yourself in multiple faces. On the floor there is the text from *The Matrix* about the blue pill and the red pill.

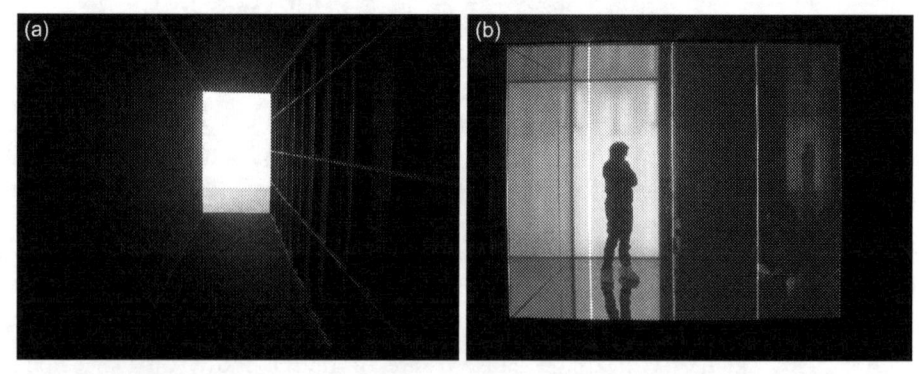

Figure 7.6 (a) The Garden of Eden, Corridor Light, 2013, (b) The Garden of Eden, Full Front, 2013

(See Kornish and Reeves, 2019.) You then read this text on the floor, but you're also being consumed by the beauty of this interior's glowing red box and the multiplicity of self.

When you go into the brown-eyed space you turn right, you walk down a dark corridor, where you can't see anything. As you get to the end of the corridor you see a shaft of light. As you turn left, you walk into a big room and you see this glass box. You can see the glass box that these people are in. The box is made of spyglass. It's a two-way mirror that the people on the outside in the brown-eyed space can see the people in the blue-eyed space. They can see them inside the box. But the blue-eyed people inside the box are not aware that someone is looking at them. They are in this totally reflective space (Figure 7.6).

People are divided by their eye colour because it's very clear to me that in society we live in the same world, but we live in different worlds. Some of the factors that determine the world that we live in partially are determined by eye colour. We know that people with grey, blue and green eyes are of a certain ethnic type, and their experience of the world is very insular; meaning that they have no idea what's going on around them. What you find is that people who have brown eyes generally are more informed because we are generally taught to code-switch early, going into a meeting with two sets of notes, and always see what's going on. The brown-eyed will be able to look into the glass box and they always know what's going on.

The Garden of Eden is looking at the idea of perception, identity, race and history. (See Abdu' Allah and Martínez-Ruiz, 2010.) Also, it's looking at the issue around physiology, different eye-colour types are determined by different levels of melanin. Everyone's eye colour has varying degrees of melanin that give you permission to enter the spaces of the work. If you had over a certain amount of melanin in your DNA, that would allow you to go into the brown-eyed space and see everything. But if you have grey, green or blue eyes, this puts you at a disadvantage and as the subject, consumed in the reflected interior with your own reflection, one is in awe in the space of infinite beauty and isolated wonder. But actually, it actually conveys the dangers of an ignorant existence, protected in a safe and vulnerable material (glass).

JB: If you reflect on how we can think about this in terms of the spaces of learning, I am always wondering how through making art – and indeed inhabiting it, as in the case of your work – we could begin to decolonise the curriculum. In fact, I often think that such immersive experiences tend to make it relatively easier to understand such concepts of spaces that one could regard as being colonised, decolonised or uncolonised.

FAA: I can see how the works can be used as a doorway to perception, well-being and other aspects of understanding. This is how a mind can unlearn; a mind that was colonised through a country's education system, online platforms, and through their daily lived experience. I hope my use of material, space, light, magic, creates images and installations that makes one think reflexively about what it means to exist. I would hope the way in which we can craft the language around art is as you said … it could be a really beautiful and creative way for people accessing higher forms of consciousness.

Towards uncolonising the curriculum

Rather than articulate an elaborate theory of an uncolonial space of learning, bringing art, educators, teachers, students and artists to create and partake in immersive situations is a powerful step to start conversations about colonial mindsets. The artistic work of Faisal brings to view the uncolonised space where one begins to understand what such a possibility looks like. Working with teachers, teaching assistants and school leaders in the arts reveals a pattern of engagement which seems liberating and where teachers become wide-awake, as Maxine Greene (1978) would say.

To uncolonise the experience is to be immersed in an experience – of naming, renaming, being wide-awake, seeing the inequalities, being ruptured by the patterns of colonial thinking. Once the artform and artwork become the normal way in which we engage, then the space is ripe to become uncolonised. This is because through the art we can be candid about the colonised spaces because the participants would simply identify and directly engage with it. Through this, it is probably at that particular stage they will come to terms with it and identify strategies about how to remove it.

Whether the arts change the world is still a matter of contention. However, as Maxine Greene suggests, the world may not be changed by the arts, but the arts may change people who may then have the voices to change the world. In this conversation between John and Faisal, the 'truths' about the world, about people, about power and about democracy were discussed and challenged. The uncolonising educator looks to new ways of inclusion, liberty and social imagination in the educational experience they co-create. Through the arts, and the spaces that can be created that are immersive and provide new experiences, becoming aware of colonised practices can be seen in a more wide-awakened state.

References

Abdu'Allah, F., and Martínez-Ruiz, B. (2010). *Chasing Mirrors Project. Faisal Abdu'Allah was Interviewed by Bárbaro Martínez-Ruiz*. London: National Portrait Gallery. https://www.npg.org.uk/learning/access/chasing-mirrors-year-3/chasing-mirrors-year1/ (accessed March 30, 2021).

Baldacchino, J. (2018a). Resemblance, choice and the hidden: Mediterranean aesthetics and the political "logics" of an uncolonial subjective economy. In Yasser Elhariry and

Edwige Tamalet Talbayev (eds), *Critically Mediterranean: Aesthetics, Theory, Hermeneutics, Culture*, 163–178. London: Palgrave Macmillan.

Baldacchino, J. (2018b). *Art as Unlearning: Towards a Mannerist Pedagogy*. London and New York: Routledge.

Biddulph, J., and Burnard, P. (2022). Storying the journey to new spaces of intercultural creative learning. In Pam Burnard and Michelle Loughrey (eds), *Unlocking Researching: Sculpting New Creativities for Primary Education*, 45–61. Oxon: Routledge.

Cornish, A., and Reeves, K. (2019). Red pill or blue pill? 20 years ago the matrix built our reality-denying world. *National Public Radio*, February 15. https://www.npr.org/2019/02/15/695270928/red-pill-or-blue-pill-20-years-ago-the-matrix-built-our-reality-denying-world (accessed March 30, 2021).

Greene, M. (1973). *Teacher as Stranger. Educational Philosophy for the Modern Age*. Belmont, CA: Wadsworth Publishing.

Greene, M. (1978). *Landscapes of Learning*. New York: Teachers College Press.

hooks, b. (1994). *Teaching to Transgress: Education as the Practice of Freedom*. London and New York: Routledge.

Popke, M. (2016). Rising star. UW printmaking prof Faisal Abdu'Allah tackles racial politics. *Isthmus*, February 18. https://isthmus.com/arts/uw-madison-printmaking-faisal-abduallah-racial-politics/ (accessed March 30, 2021).

8

Inclusive approaches for children at risk of exclusion: supporting mental health in primary schools

Lysandra Sinclaire-Harding and Ashley Grinham-Smith

Introduction

Observation: Kiera

It is 10 am and Keira's classroom has been evacuated. Artwork has been torn from the walls. Pencils, pens and scissors are scattered across the floor and tables have been overturned. Keira is standing with a chair held over her head, screaming at the teacher. Her teacher recognises this transformation: Keira's face taut and drained of colour, her pupils dilated. He wants to run for safety but instead bravely reflects calm and compassion as he silently counts the seconds until his colleagues respond to his radio call for help. Keira is eight years old. This is not the first time her classroom has been cleared to protect other pupils whilst she vents her rage.

For many UK primary schools, this scenario is not uncommon. Education has a long history of managing children with identified behavioural difficulties through behaviourist approaches that rely on learning through reinforcement and may include systems of rewards or punitive consequences such as detentions or exclusions. School policies may advocate for zero tolerance of specific behaviours but such one-size-fits-all policies deprive practitioners from taking steps to understand the individual experiences of children. Records for school exclusions

DOI: 10.4324/9781003137634-8

in England (DfE, 2020) show that 24% of children permanently excluded from mainstream primary and secondary schools in England have mental health needs. On average, at least 70 permanent exclusions occur *each week* of the school year. Black Caribbean pupils are nearly four times more likely to receive a permanent exclusion than the school population as a whole and twice as likely to receive a suspension (Demie, 2021). The consequences of school exclusion are well reported, leading to educational disadvantage, increased family stress, social exclusion, and fewer opportunities to develop skills and qualifications (Briggs, 2010). Added to this is the detrimental impact of exclusion on mental health (Ford et al., 2018).

The Children and Families Act (2014) sets out the specific duties that schools in England have in relation to identifying and supporting children with special educational needs and disabilities (SEND), including those identified with mental health needs. The associated SEND Code of Practice (DfE, 2015) replaced outdated 'emotional and behaviour disorders' terminology with 'social, emotional and mental health' in recognition of the unmet social and emotional needs that underpin complex behaviours presented by children in schools. Understanding and supporting children's needs is a complex task, in part due to the wide range of presenting difficulties including (but not limited to) anxiety, depression and self-harm.

One in eight 5–19-year-olds are estimated to have significant mental health problems in England (Sadler et al., 2018). These numbers describe high levels of need that would be considered clinically diagnosable. The Department of Health (Sadler et al., 2018) estimates that for every child with a diagnosable condition, there is another whose emerging mental health needs may not meet the thresholds for specialist intervention, but without support are at risk of problems in later life.

An alternative (and inclusive) approach

There can be little doubt that for many children, the threat of punishment reduces their disruptive behaviour. We recognise the importance for children of knowing what is expected of them and having the opportunity to celebrate successes through appropriate rewards. However, in this chapter we argue that behaviourist interventions are limited, as they generally do not consider the emotional experiences of the children or supporting adults. Furthermore, for children who have grown up in abusive or threatening environments, behaviourist approaches may trigger feelings of powerlessness and fear, causing further distress and increasing the risk of those dysregulated behaviours associated with exclusion from school.

Encouragingly, there is evidence that timely remediation and intervention may prevent exclusion as well as future mental health disorders in children whose behaviour challenges school systems (Ford et al., 2018). In much the same way as teachers make adaptations to increase accessibility for children with physical needs, we advocate for planning specific accommodations for learners with mental health needs. In this chapter we offer a number of practical tools by which practitioners can take steps to reduce learning barriers for children identified with mental health needs through planning, assessment and analysis of response to intervention. We hope to demonstrate that supporting children at risk of exclusion will also benefit the wider school community.

We offer a number of vignettes that illustrate the histories, experiences and presenting behaviours of three children. Whilst each of the vignettes are fictitious, they represent an amalgam of several children we have encountered in our work in different schools over many years. We hope their stories provide:

1. a psychological perspective on behaviour;
2. examples of inclusive tools that can be used to understand and assess needs; and
3. differentiated strategies to reduce social and emotional barriers to learning and ultimately reduce the risk of exclusion.

Emotional development, resilience and risk factors

The risk and protective factors for childhood mental health are listed in Figure 8.1. Protective factors support the development of emotional and behavioural self-regulation, and practitioners will recognise the substantial variability in self-regulation that children present in the classroom. Proficient self-regulators can control their attention and impulses; they can plan, set goals and self-organise for learning. Competent self-regulators have the resilience to cope when obstacles or upsets are encountered; they can recover and seek out support from peers or adults (Zimmerman, 1990).

Supportive parenting, combined with appropriate cognitive challenges, are fundamental for developing resilience and self-regulation. In the 1940s, researchers began to consider the impact on development of growing up in playful and stimulating environments compared to deprived or disadvantaged conditions. Enriched, playful environments provide the basic neurobiological building blocks for learning and memory, and studies investigating particular types of play have been able to show how the developing brain adapts and learns from such experiences (Pellis and Pellis, 2009).

During their early years, children are dependent upon their caregiving relationships to develop self-regulation. Home environments that are emotionally secure and include cognitive challenges, such as sensitive handling, responsive eye-gaze, talking, singing, playing and reading, are the active ingredients that prepare young minds to manage the academic, social and emotional demands of the classroom. Where caregiving routines offer security, nurture and protection

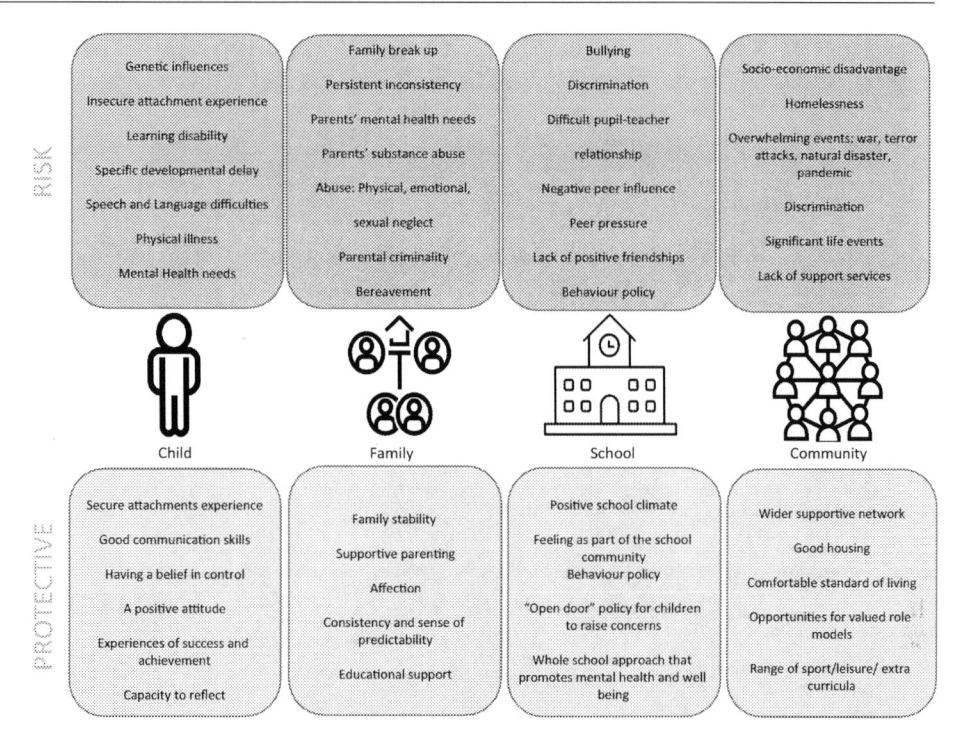

Figure 8.1 Risk and protective factors for childhood mental health (inspired by Public Health England, 2016)

from harm, we find a curious child, eager to explore and embrace learning challenges (Sinclaire-Harding et al., 2019).

Whilst the early years are a time of rapid development and growth, they are also the years of greatest vulnerability. The developing child is highly sensitive and adaptive to the social demands of the environment. Many possible negative experiences (Figure 8.1) that contribute to mental health difficulties may arise from within the child, family, school or community. Cumulative factors will increase the likelihood of the emotional and behavioural dysregulation observed in children at risk of exclusion (Ford et al., 2018).

Effects of trauma

Troy (Vignette 8.1) provides an illustration of the powerful effects of trauma, having experienced the overwhelming stress of witnessing his mother's abuse. Even more harmful for Troy was that her abuser was a man he loved and trusted. This potent combination deprived him of the opportunity to learn to trust and receive comfort from adults and left him vulnerable to a range of emotional difficulties. In order to support him in school it was necessary for the adults to understand his behaviour as a source of information about his early experiences.

Vignette 8.1 Troy

When Troy was four years old, his stepdad moved into the family home. His stepdad was kind to Troy but violent towards Troy's mother. Mostly it happened in his mother's bedroom. Troy could hear the sound of closed fists pounding her body. Sometimes Troy would stand with his hand on the door of her room, suspended in fear, guilt and helplessness. Eventually Troy became a witness to the violence – a slap across her face, a grab at her throat. One day he watched his stepdad smash his mother's face into the wall. Troy was six years old. His mother was unconscious, her nose broken and bleeding. An ambulance came for her whilst Troy was taken into emergency, temporary foster care.

For Troy, the horror of hearing and seeing his mother's abuse over many months, compounded by the trauma of being temporarily separated from her whilst she was treated for her injuries, led to a pattern of distressing behaviours in school. Separating from his mother each morning was agonising. He would frequently lash out at other adults. In class he was not able to follow instructions or play alongside other children. At times, during moments of distress he would withdraw and shut down, disconnecting himself from his surroundings and remain shut down for many minutes, or sometimes hours, before eventually recovering and re-engaging with others around him.

In situations laden with stress, behavioural and biological adaptations occur. Behavioural adaptations may be useful within the home environment (e.g. avoiding rejection or gaining attention from an unavailable caregiver) but can be unhelpful or inappropriate in school contexts. In situations of threat, our nervous systems release several hormones, including adrenaline and cortisol, important for meeting the energy demands required to respond to threat, providing resources to remain vigilant and prepare defensive responses. Over time, repeated incidents of trauma or abuse lead to chronically elevated levels of stress hormones. These have long-lasting biological effects contributing to social-emotional difficulties (Beckett et al., 2007).

Safe sanctuary

One of the behavioural adaptations or coping strategies Troy employed was to 'shut down' or disconnect from his surroundings. Dissociation can be seen along a continuum of behaviours from mild emotional numbing to uncontrollable disconnection from sensory and emotional experiences. For some children this may include loss of memory during dissociative experiences.

Whilst most children may perceive the classroom as a space in which they feel able to express their views, take risks and explore knowledge, for children like Troy the classroom feels crowded and noisy. Verbal and behavioural communications of peers and adults may be perceived as microaggressions (insults or insensitivities) that are likely to increase feelings of discomfort, anxiety or hostility. For Troy, dissociation may be understood as a strategic defence, within which he can retreat and recover from difficult emotional experiences.

A 'safe space' is a physical or relational sanctuary where a child can feel confident that they will not be judged, criticised or harassed and where they can be themselves without risk of harm. It is not always easy to help children establish a safe space from which they can learn to manage their feelings. Children may lack trust in adults and so resist adult attempts to build warm, supportive relationships.

Through careful observations and the invitation to conduct his own audit of the school building, Troy and his teachers identified a safe space within which he was able to recover from his intolerable feelings. For Troy, this quiet environment reduced the external sensory stimulation he found overwhelming and offered him the opportunity to process or express emotional experiences through a range of activities (e.g. drawing, construction toys or miniature figurines). Hypervigilant young learners may prefer to watch their peers from the safe distance of a cosy classroom book corner. Others, we have observed, may choose the crawl space beneath a teacher's desk to hide from peers, reduce sensory stimulation and increase proximity to a trusted adult who offers comfort in times of distress or fatigue.

Relational safe spaces

A safe space can be both physical and relational. Bion (1977) defines 'containment' as a dynamic process in which a child's distressing feelings are projected onto the caregiver, who in turn processes these feelings and returns them in a more tolerable form. Without containment, the child is left alone with enduring and overwhelming feelings. For adults to offer a containing function, a trusted connection between adult and child is necessary within which the adult is attuned to the emotional experience of the child. Over time, Troy built trusted relationships with two or three adults in school. From this relational safe space, Troy was able to find ways to safely explore and understand his own emotions (Winnicott, 1965).

> ## Reflections
>
> - Are there children in your class or school who would benefit from safe sanctuary?
> - How would you decide whether a physical or relational safe space (or both) is most helpful for a particular child?
> - Where in the classroom, corridors or playground does he or she feel most and least safe?

Developmental trauma

Psychology has long sought to understand the impact of developmental trauma on mental health and emotional well-being. Developmental trauma arises as a result of repeated traumatic experiences that occur in early childhood. These are relational in nature and may occur over long periods of time. The effects of such experiences are significant. Extreme stress gives rise to impairments in relationships, physiology, self-regulation, cognition and self-concept. Difficulties may extend from childhood through to adolescence and into adulthood (van der Kolk, 2017). Children exposed to maltreatment, family violence or loss of caregivers may be diagnosed with clinical disorders such as anxiety, depression, conduct, social communication, eating disorders, oppositional defiance, sleeping, post-traumatic stress and attention-deficit hyperactivity disorder (ADHD). Each of the diagnostic labels within this constellation captures a limited aspect of the traumatised child's complex self-regulatory and relational impairments, and it is likely that symptoms will be overlapping and complex. The full impact of developmental trauma is beyond the scope of this chapter; however, additional literature and resources are available to readers on the book's accompanying website (www.unlockingresearch.org).

The role of shame

One aspect of childhood behaviour that requires understanding and sensitive mitigation is the need to avoid re-invoking the child's negative self-beliefs. Children who have been severely punished, criticised, rejected or ignored learn to believe they are unwanted and unlovable (Bennet, Sullivan and Lewis, 2005). In some cases, children may continue to experience adult behaviours that are harsh, arouse fears of abandonment, or use withdrawal as a discipline strategy. These can lead to enduring messages that the child's core self is a disappointment, unlovable and fundamentally 'bad'. The secretiveness that often accompanies developmental trauma, alongside the child's recognition that such experiences reflect negatively on both self and family may perpetuate feelings of shame.

Feelings of shame act as a social warning to hide aspects of oneself from others or as a cue to change behaviour to conform to socially acceptable expectations. Children are highly motivated to terminate these painful feelings. They may seek to displace shame by blaming others or replace it with anger directed towards individuals they believe to be judging them (Bennett et al., 2005). In school, this may be towards the adults with whom they have the closest relationships. Shame can lead to intense anger and may be linked to a desire to harm witnesses of the perceived humiliation. Alternatively, some children may suppress shameful feelings, leading to sadness, withdrawal from social situations, and ultimately internalising problems such as depression or anxiety. Some maltreatment studies (e.g. Lewis, 1992) suggest that girls are more likely to develop internalising problems than boys who, by contrast, are more likely to externalise their angry feelings.

Vignette 8.2 Isaac

Following a number of different foster placements, in one of which he experienced both physical and sexual abuse, Isaac was adopted by a loving family. Isaac had no other biological family other than two younger siblings who lived in separate foster families elsewhere.

As Isaac progressed through school, his behaviour became more intimidating. In Year 6, he would damage property, throw furniture, and lash out at peers and teachers. His behaviour was worse in English lessons when he would often walk around the room, damaging or destroying the work of other children. He was eventually permanently excluded following an incident in which a teacher's nose was broken.

'Trauma-versaries'

Emotional triggers may be activated in response to someone else's behavioural cues or may be a sensory reminder of a traumatic event: a noise, smell, temperature, other physical sensation or visual scene. Triggers may arise from feeling rejected, ignored or helpless. They may also arise when a mistake has been made, leading to feelings of blame or shame. Triggers that we have termed 'trauma-versaries' are associated with a time of day, season, holiday or anniversary.

It is not always possible to identify or predict a child's internal triggers. Learning to recognise the early signs of a heightened emotional response, indicative of a trigger, is therefore a fundamental tool for educators and part of the necessary provision for supporting emotional self-regulation in children identified with mental health needs. Increasing sensitivity to heightened behaviours allows a planned response to be created. We call such plans *Emotional Support Plans* (*ESPs*).

Emotional Support Plans

Plans help to create a consistent approach for children at risk of exclusion. They are developed in collaboration with the child and family over time as practitioners increase their understanding and experience of what helps to reduce (or increase) the risk of trigger events. ESPs allow supporting adults to develop shared understanding and consistent responses. This consistency is vital for all children but particularly for those like Isaac (Vignette 8.2), who have been deprived of the opportunity to develop trust and receive comfort within early adult relationships.

The term 'differentiation' is used to describe the steps practitioners can take to reduce the risk of trigger events. By differentiating for these children, the school day becomes increasingly accessible. One indicator of Isaac's emotional dysregulation was his restlessness in English lessons, a subject area he found especially challenging. He would disengage from the task, walk around the classroom and remove items from the desks of other learners. Without intervention, his behaviour would become increasingly dysregulated. It was hypothesised that in these moments, Isaac would compare his performance to that of his peers, triggering feelings of low self-worth and shame. As the adults consistently followed the steps within Isaac's ESP, they became attuned to his distress and developed a choice of alternative activities. Over time, he developed trust in these adults who found creative ways to help him manage his negative emotions by offering positive experiences. Once calm, Isaac was later able to complete the learning task.

An editable example of an ESP is provided on the supporting website (www .unlockingresearch.org). Readers are invited to draw upon this resource to draft their own ESPs for children who may benefit from such an approach.

Supportive scripts

During times of distress, supportive scripts are found to support emotional regulation in school (Gus et al., 2017). Scripts are helpful for both adults and children. Incidents of dysregulated behaviour are daunting or even frightening for the practitioners involved and a script may reduce adult anxiety during an emotional situation. A script also offers the child consistent messaging, which can assist recovery. Consistent messaging offers a form of predictability and helps to establish trust as children recognise an expected response. This in turn can strengthen their sense of relational containment and safety.

> • Ok, I can see you are feeling .... (angry; frustrated; worried).
> • Come with me and we will... (shoot basketball hoops; chat).
> • Your safe space is there for you.
> • I am here to help.
> • I am here to keep you safe.
> • If you talk, I will listen.

Figure 8.2 Scripts to support during moments of emotional dysregulation

> • Good job, I like the way you are being a good friend/good sharing/listening/team-work.
> • Thank you, you followed instructions first time. That's great.
> • I was so impressed when you used your words to tell me how you were feeling. That showed courage.
> • I'm proud of you, I can tell you are putting effort in to this.
> • I love how safe you are being, great job.
> • Thank you for taking part in this. It's great to have you with us.
> • Thank you for making that decision, good choice.

Figure 8.3 Examples of affirmation scripts

Scripts may be included within an ESP and can be developed over time as adults learn how to reduce the risk of triggers and aid recovery from trigger events. For instance, Isaac often re-escalated if his name was used in a script, so this was avoided. Figure 8.2 provides examples of the scripts used by Isaac's trusted adults. Not only did these words help to reduce the risk of re-escalation, but they also allowed Isaac to express his feelings safely, without fear of recrimination or relational breakdown with trusted adults.

Pre-planned, affirmative statements are also powerful. Affirmative scripts (Figure 8.3) should be used frequently, as finding ways to notice and validate desirable behaviours helps the child feel valued, seen and cared for. These are prerequisites for a sense of belonging, feelings of safety and increased positive self-worth. For children at risk of exclusion, affirmative statements provide a vital message: that they are wanted. Such messaging fosters positive feelings and a sense of belonging that in turn leads to positive behaviours.

Use of PACE approach

The role of play in the development of emotional self-regulation and its impact on children cannot be underestimated. The PACE (Playful, Acceptance, Curiosity, Empathy) approach is particularly helpful for supporting primary-age children identified with mental health needs (Hughes et al., 2015). A summary of how this approach was used to support Isaac is shown in Table 8.1.

Table 8.1 Summary of PACE approach

Playful	Identifying the play preferences of a child is vital. Isaac loved to play basketball. During moments of heightened emotional distress, an attuned adult offered a well-timed invitation to go outside and play basketball. This would draw him away from potential conflict and physical harm. Tailoring playful opportunities to Isaac's interests was key to their effectiveness and, over time, new ideas were introduced to maintain his interest.
Acceptance	Perhaps one of the most challenging aspect for educators of the PACE approach is the idea of acceptance. Far from condoning unwanted behaviour, acceptance is the acknowledgement of Isaac's emotional distress. We encourage adults not to negotiate with the child during trigger events. Too much talk may lead to increased distress for a child. If an adult feels ignored, this may lead to an adult feeling offended or frustrated. It is important to acknowledge the child's feelings but to use limited language. Unwanted behaviours can only be addressed once the child has recovered from their feelings and calm is restored.
Curiosity	Adults learned that it would generally take around 15 minutes for Isaac to recover. Curious, non-judgemental 'I wonder' or 'I'm guessing' statements during this stage indicates to children that they are cared for, and their feelings are validated. For example: 'I'm guessing you were feeling angry back there? I wonder what it was that made you feel like that?' This curiosity offers a child an important opportunity to label their feelings. 'I wonder' statements also reduce the possibility of an adult assigning an inaccurate feeling to the child's experience. Identifying and labelling emotion is an important aspect of developing regulation and resilience, and can be encouraged with curiosity.
Empathy	Empathy is a central tenant of attunement. Empathetic phrases include 'I imagine that was pretty tough for you' or 'I understand that you were feeling unsafe back there, that must have been hard for you.' Showing understanding of distressing feelings does not mean that we condone unsafe behaviours. Offering empathy minimises the fear of judgement and associated shame. It provides an important model of empathic behaviour, and supports reflection and restoration following trigger events.

Biological considerations

Teachers recognise the influence that biological factors, such as hunger, fatigue or illness, have on self-regulation. Ongoing research has begun to shed light on a wide range of biological factors that underpin emotional and behavioural difficulties, including genetic factors. One area of investigation involves dopamine neuroreceptors. Dopamine has several biological functions, and irregularities of the dopamine system are associated with attention-related, neurodevelopmental disorders. For instance, children with the short version of the dopamine-transporter gene DAT1 are found to have more difficulties with attention-control and impulsivity than those with the long version (Rueda et al., 2005). Reduced availability of dopamine receptors in neural pathways is one theory for why many children with ADHD are more difficult to motivate. These findings may partially explain why children with attentional deficits have greater difficulty in focusing, following tasks through to completion, and sustaining effort and motivation.

Environmental factors are also found to influence the expression or silencing of genes. For example, children with the low activity MAOA (monoamine oxidise A) gene who also experience maltreatment and adversity are more likely to develop antisocial or aggressive behaviours than those with the high activity MAOA variant (Caspi et al., 2002). Research has still to understand fully the genetic basis of mental health, but cumulative evidence indicates that the most significant mental health disorders occur in children that experience a combination of early adversity in the presence of genetic susceptibility.

Vignette 8.3 Leah

Eight-year-old Leah is the eldest of three and lives at home with her sisters and both parents. Soon after Leah was born, her mother was unwell and had to be hospitalised for a number of weeks. At home, her mother described Leah as restless; she found it hard to settle to watch a film or eat a meal. Leah had always been impulsive, and her parents were concerned about her escalating risk-taking behaviours, such as running away or climbing.

Despite the support she received from family and school, Leah became increasingly angry and disruptive in class, especially during group activities and maths lessons. She would often appear tired, could become hugely upset and would destroy her schoolwork when she made mistakes. She was increasingly socially isolated at school.

Leah (Vignette 8.3) was eventually diagnosed with ADHD. In school, the demands of concentration, particularly in subjects that were more challenging for her, resulted in cognitive fatigue and emotional distress. These combined factors led to incidents of dysregulated behaviour for which she received a number of fixed term exclusions. An individualised plan of support was put into place which included careful tracking of incidents of dysregulation across the school day. Combined with attention training and motivational coaching, such tools can be helpful to manage the cognitive demands for children with attention-related difficulties and mental health needs.

Emotion tracking

Difficult behaviour can seem unpredictable, occurring without a recognisable trigger. Leah, for example, could throw items across the classroom or lash out at peers without apparent warning. One helpful approach is to track a child's periods of emotional dysregulation. Examples of emotion tracking for Leah are provided in Figures 8.4 and 8.5. High emotion regulation scores indicate increased emotional distress and associated dysregulated behaviours.

If helpful, emotion tracking can be undertaken to develop understanding of a child's emotional experience at different times of the day, with different adults and

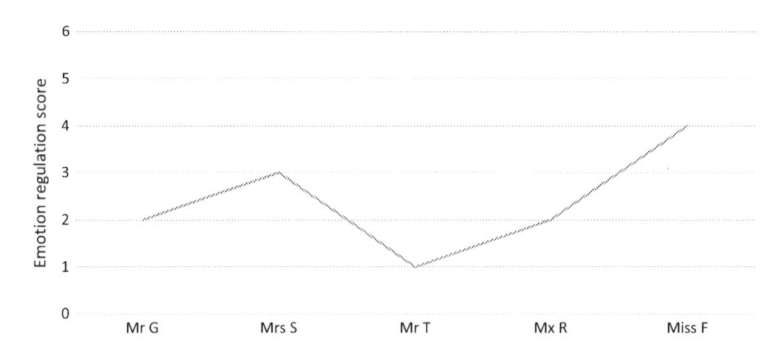

Figure 8.4 Emotion tracker for Leah (adult interactions)

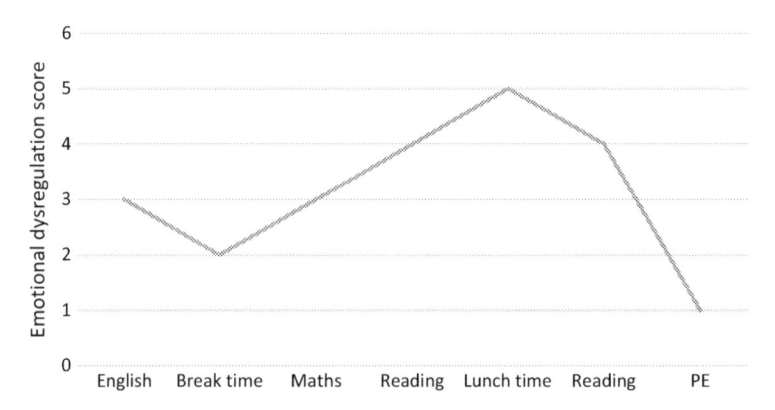

Figure 8.5 Emotion tracker for Leah (lesson subjects)

across different subjects. Informed plans can then be made in order to reduce incidents of dysregulation. Tracking and recording moments of calm and desirable behaviours is equally informative, as it allows for planning of activities to reduce Leah's stress. It was observed that Leah demonstrated an increase in dysregulated behaviours just before lunch, suggesting that she found these timetabled sessions especially challenging. Conversely, it was observed that she was particularly calm during lessons with Mr T (Figure 8.4) and after lunch, during art and especially PE (Figure 8.5).

Reflections

- Which adult does Leah seem to connect well with?
- Which subject might be the cause of frustration or distress for Leah?
- What might be happening at lunch time for Leah to increase her anxiety?
- What activities does she enjoy that might help her to manage her emotions?
- Try completing a tracker such as this for a child in your class. What do you think it reveals about their emotional experiences at school?

Putting feelings into words

We can never fully know what feelings may underpin a child's dysregulated behaviour, yet through curiosity and empathy, we can begin to imagine what they may be thinking and feeling and offer language with which to recognise and verbalise feelings of anger, worry or frustration. A number of studies have shown the positive impact of affect labelling in decreasing the subjective experience and physical symptoms of negative feelings (e.g. Torre and Lieberman, 2018). An attuned adult must be able to (a) recognise the internal thoughts and feelings of the child, and (b) treat the internal experience as equal in status to the behaviours being externalised (Fonagy and Allison, 2011).

Figure 8.6 offers examples of scripts that support affect labelling in the classroom. To support the child with affect labelling, the adult demonstrates curiosity about the child's feelings and then offers a suggestion for the emotions present within the situation. This helps the child develop their own language to describe their feelings and the reasons why such feelings may have arisen. Helping the child to recognise their own emotions supports the development of a range of emotion vocabulary necessary for developing emotion regulation. Secondly, it demonstrates to a child that an adult can tolerate their distressing emotions and continue to hold them in high positive regard. Having someone reflect positivity during emotionally charged events offers relational safety within which children can recognise, name and regulate their difficult feelings. This is a powerful learning opportunity that adults can provide to children who may be at risk of exclusion.

Supporting the adults

The challenge of supporting children who are at risk of exclusion cannot be underestimated. Whilst there is an expectation that schools reduce

> - I can see that Maeve is crying. I think that means she is upset. I imagine she is upset because…
> - I think if someone called me names, I would feel hurt and then maybe confused, especially if I thought they were my friend.
> - I notice that Simon is playing on his own over there. I wonder if he could be feeling lonely? What could we do to help him feel less lonely?
> - I know when I feel frustrated, I get a tight feeling in my chest. When I realise this, I stop, take a deep breath, and ask for a minute on my own.

Figure 8.6 Putting feelings into words

exclusionary practices, in situations where one child's behaviour puts others at risk of harm, leaders may feel they have no alternative but to suspend or exclude. In this chapter, we have discussed the notion of adults offering containment to children in distress. Yet often there are few formal arrangements in place to support the adults most directly impacted by a child's dysregulated behaviour. There can be little doubt that the strategies detailed in this chapter can place an emotional toll upon practitioners. Sturt and Rowe (2018) have called for supervision to be introduced into schools. This would provide a dedicated forum in which practitioners could receive emotional support for working with children at risk of exclusion or identified as having mental health needs. The practicalities of how to introduce supervision into school are beyond the scope of this chapter. However, it is important to recognise that in order to offer a safe space in which children can learn, adults in a school also need to feel contained and safe at work.

Reflections

- A PACE-informed approach – What playful activities would help regulate a child in your classroom?
- Scripts – Which statements might be helpful for you to plan to use both in support and for affirmation?
- Emotion tracking – How would you collect these data in your classroom? What do you think they would reveal about a child you were observing?
- Safe spaces – Where in your classroom or school would make a good safe space for a child? How could you increase the sense of safety in your classroom?
- ESPs – What might be helpful to plan for? Could any difficult behaviours be pre-empted and reduced due to a plan being put in place?

What about in your classroom?

Our aim for this chapter has been to offer suggestions for adults working with children at risk of exclusion by offering a psychological perspective of a child's behaviour in the context of their early experiences. We have also offered a number of analytical tools and practical suggestions to help develop inclusive practice, as well as reflections on how to support a child at risk of exclusion or identified with mental health needs. These approaches reassure a child that they are safe, highly regarded and, most critically, are wanted by their school community.

References

Beckett, C., Maughan, B., Rutter, M., Castle, J., Colvert, E., Groothues, C., & Sonuga-Barke, E. J. (2007). Scholastic attainment following severe early institutional deprivation: A study of children adopted from Romania. *Journal of Abnormal Child Psychology, 35*(6), 1063–1073.

Bennett, D. S., Sullivan, M. W., & Lewis, M. (2005). Young children's adjustment as a function of maltreatment, shame, and anger. *Child Maltreatment, 10*(4), 311–323.

Bion, W. R. (1977). *Seven servants: Four works by Wilfred R. Bion: Learning from experience, elements of psycho-analysis, transformations, attention and interpretation.* Lanham, MD: Jason Aronson Inc. Publishers.

Briggs, D. (2010). The world is out to get me, bruv': Life after school 'exclusion'. *Safer Communities, 9*(2), 9–19.

Caspi, A., McClay, J., Moffitt, T. E., Mill, J., Martin, J., Craig, I. W., Taylor, A., & Poulton, R. (2002). Role of genotype in the cycle of violence in maltreated children. *Science, 297*, 851–854.

Demie, F. (2021). The experience of Black Caribbean pupils in school exclusion in England. *Educational Review, 73*(1), 55–70.

DfE. (2015). *SEND code of practice 0–25 years.* London: Department for Education, Department of Health, 216–229.

DfE. (2020). *Permanent and fixed period exclusions in England: 2018 to 2019.* London: Department for Education.

Fonagy, P., & Allison, E. (2012). What is mentalization? The concept and its foundation in developmental research and social-cognitive neuroscience. In N. Midgley & I. Vrouva (Eds.), *Minding the child: Mentalization-based interventions with children, young people and their families* (pp. 11–34). London: Routledge.

Ford, T., Parker, C., Salim, J., Goodman, R., Logan, S., & Henley, W. (2018). The relationship between exclusion from school and mental health: A secondary analysis of the British Child and Adolescent Mental Health Surveys 2004 and 2007. *Psychological Medicine, 48*(4), 629–641.

Gus, L., Rose, J., Gilbert, L., & Kilby, R. (2017). The introduction of emotion coaching as a whole school approach in a primary specialist social emotional and mental health setting: Positive outcomes for all. *The Open Family Studies Journal, 9*(1), 95–110.

Hughes, D., Golding, K. S., & Hudson, J. (2015). Dyadic developmental psychotherapy (DDP): The development of the theory, practice and research base. *Adoption & Fostering, 39*, 356–365.

Lewis, M., Alessandri, S. M., & Sullivan, M. W. (1992). Differences in shame and pride as a function of children's gender and task difficulty. *Child Development, 63*(3), 630–638.

Pellis, S. M., & Pellis, V. C. (2009). *The playful brain. Venturing to the limits of neuroscience.* Oxford, UK: Oneworld Press.

Public Health England. (2016). *The mental health of children and young people in England.* London: PHE Publications.

Rueda, M. R., Rothbart, M. K., McCandliss, B. D., Saccomanno, L., & Posner, M. I. (2005). Training, maturation, and genetic influences on the development of executive attention. *Proceedings of the National Academy of Sciences of the United States of America, 102*(41), 14931–14936.

Sadler, K., Vizard, T., Ford, T., Marchesell, F., Pearce, N., Mandalia, D., Davis, J., Brodie, E., Forbes, N., & Goodman, A. (2018). Mental health of children and young people in England, 2017. Retrieved April 2020 from https://www.rcpsych.ac.uk/docs/default

-source/improving-care/nccmh/suicide-prevention/monthly-clinic/(6a)mhcyp-behaviours-lifestyles-identities-(2017).pdf.

Sinclaire-Harding, L.,Vuillier, L., & Whitebread, D. (2019). Neuroscience and early childhood education. In M. Fleer & B. van Oers (Eds.), *International handbook on early childhood education* (pp. 335–361). Dordrecht: Springer.

Sturt, P., & Rowe, J. (2018). *Using supervision in schools: A guide to building safe cultures and providing emotional support in a range of school settings.* West Sussex: Pavilion.

Torre, J. B., & Lieberman, M. D. (2018). Putting feelings into words: Affect labeling as implicit emotion regulation. *Emotion Review, 10*(2), 116–124.

Van der Kolk, B. A. (2017). Developmental trauma disorder: Toward a rational diagnosis for children with complex trauma histories. *Psychiatric Annals, 35*(5), 401–408.

Winnicott, D. W. (1965). A clinical study of the effect of a failure of the average expectable environment on a child's mental functioning. *International Journal of Psycho-Analysis, 46*, 81–87.

Zimmerman, B. J. (1990). Self-regulating academic learning and achievement: The emergence of a social cognitive perspective. *Educational Psychology Review, 2*(2), 173–201.

Maximising the work of teaching assistants: building an inclusive community of research-led practice

Paula Bosanquet and Aimee Durning

Introduction

We begin this chapter with a key question: How can we plan for high-quality inclusive teaching and learning if we do not consider the roles of all of those involved? Teaching assistants (TAs) play an integral part in the school lives of many children. They contribute to inclusive practice as both a classroom resource and through running intervention programmes. And yet, despite the rise in the number of TAs working in schools, their roles and responsibilities are sometimes not well defined, and opportunities for developing research-led practice to develop inclusive practice can be limited. This chapter will argue that TAs should be fully integrated into research-led and reflective practice processes, to develop shared beliefs and understandings that will benefit all children.

This chapter provides an insight into how *all* staff in a primary school in the East of England have engaged with research about inclusive classroom practice to improve the outcomes for all children, but especially those who have been identified as having special educational needs and/or disabilities (SEND). As a 'living case' it explores the principles and recommendations upon which opportunities for children to be included and feel included were created. We begin by examining some of the key research before moving on to exemplify the research-led practices that define the school's approach. These practices are underpinned by the following principles:

1. Consistently promoting a sense of belonging and achievement for all children.
2. Recognising the essential role of TAs in supporting high-quality teaching.
3. The use of shared professional development.

We demonstrate how all staff can and should be involved in a research-informed approach to educating all children, and share approaches and strategies that may influence thinking in other educational settings. We have witnessed the powerful effects of nurturing and encouraging children in a holistic way on their educational journey when such a collective endeavour takes place.

The role of teaching assistants in education

In England, the SEND Code of Practice (DfE/DoH, 2015) is clear that the responsibility for children identified with SEND lies with the teacher:

> Teachers are responsible and accountable for the progress and development of the pupils in their class, including where pupils access support from teaching assistants or specialist staff.
>
> *(6.36)*

> Special educational provision is underpinned by high quality teaching and is compromised by anything less.
>
> *(1.24)*

Unfortunately, research suggests that in mainstream classrooms, children identified with SEND, particularly those with greater or more complex needs, continue to be separated from their peers and their teachers (Webster, 2015; Blatchford and Webster, 2018). A key reason for this has been the use of TAs.

Over several decades, the number of TAs in schools has risen significantly. In the last 20 years, the number in mainstream schools in England has more than trebled, and this rise is reflected in education systems across the world (Webster et al., 2021). TAs have moved into highly skilled roles, supporting the most vulnerable children. There is growing evidence that TA-led structured interventions lead to children making progress (see Webster et al., 2021, for a summary). However, research into TA support inside the classroom has challenged the common-sense notion that support from additional adults should impact positively on outcomes. The large-scale Deployment and Impact of Support Staff project (Blatchford, Russell and Webster, 2012) found a *negative* relationship between the amount of TA support children received and their academic progress in English, mathematics and science. This was most marked for children with the most complex needs. The qualitative elements of the project established the Wider Pedagogical Role model to explain the reasons for these results.

Three key aspects of this model are:

1. *Deployment* – TA support was being used as a default for children identified with SEND. This led to a separation effect, where children were being taught away from both the teacher and their peers.

2. *Preparedness* – Many TAs reported working with very little direction. Teacher–TA liaison time was rarely available, and teachers had not had training in how to manage the work of additional adults.

3. *Practice* – In addition (and partly because of these issues), studies of the interactions between TAs and children showed that children were often oversupported. For example, they were given answers or too much help in completing parts of the task they could potentially carry out independently. TA–child interactions also tended to use more closed questions and close down learning conversations where new learning could have potentially taken place.

The research shone a spotlight on the inequalities and the realities that children identified as having SEND were experiencing in schools across England and Wales. The period following publication saw many headlines criticising the 'Mum's Army' of teaching assistants and the lack of academic progress of the children they were supporting. However, Webster et al. (2016) suggest that instead of vilifying TAs, their role and identity should be reframed. A key question asked in this book and throughout the Unlocking Research series is 'What is an inclusive education?' To consider inclusive education, one must think not only about the children and our vision for them, but also about the agency of the adults who support children daily. One only needs do a quick internet search to understand that the world of education is geared towards teachers. What if an educator became the Education Secretary? Would they look beyond the traditional teacher–class model? They may instead consider schools and their communities as settings where valuable TAs feature and perform a vital role; that 'TAs are the mortar in the brickwork; they hold schools together in numerous and sometimes unnoticed ways' (Webster et al., 2021, p. 2). Key questions therefore become 'What role should TAs have in developing inclusive education?' and 'How can teachers and TAs work together to ensure the best possible outcomes for all children?'

The books *Maximising the Impact of Teaching Assistants in Primary Schools* (Webster et al., 2021) and *Maximising the Impact of Teaching Assistants* (Webster, Russell and Blatchford, 2016) and the Education Endowment Foundation guidance report *Making Best Use of Teaching Assistants* (Sharples, Webster and Blatchford, 2018) set out research-based best practice principles in relation to TAs in everyday classrooms. From these works arise the following four key recommendations, which are then discussed later in the chapter:

1. TAs should not be used as informal teaching resources for low attaining pupils.
2. Use TAs to add value to what teachers do, not replace them.
3. Use TAs to help pupils develop independent learning skills and manage their own learning.
4. Ensure TAs are fully prepared for their role in the classroom.

(Sharples et al., 2018, p. 10)

The graduated approach and the teaching assistant role

The Code of Practice (DfE/DoH, 2015) sets out a graduated approach for provision for schools in England. It uses continuous Assess, Plan, Do and Review cycles to remove barriers to children's learning and review the provision put in place for children identified with SEND. The responsibility for this lies with the teacher, in consultation with the Special Educational Needs Coordinator. The graduated approach draws increasingly on research-evidenced interventions and specialist input if the strategies put in place fail to meet the needs of the child. TAs can play an important role in delivering interventions and implementing individual programmes and strategies provided by specialists (under the direction and oversight of the teacher). However, the Code of Practice (DfE/DoH, 2015) makes clear that teachers have a statutory duty to provide high-quality teaching for all children, before considering an intervention or the deployment of a TA to support an individual:

> High quality teaching, differentiated for individual pupils, is the first step in responding to pupils who have or may have SEN. Additional intervention and support cannot compensate for a lack of good quality teaching.
>
> *(6.37)*

There are clear links here to the Education Endowment Foundation recommendations that 'TAs should not be used as informal teaching resources for low attaining pupils' and 'Use TAs to add value to what teachers do, not replace them' (Sharples et al., 2018, p. 10). Whereas there is clear evidence that TA-led interventions can and do have an impact on learning, the same is not the case for classroom-based TA support (Webster et al., 2021; Blatchford, Russell and Webster, 2012). However, many TAs spend much of their time providing classroom support. We argue that TAs should be using this time to support children to access the teacher's input and help. Teachers need to plan for and manage this support effectively. This helps children to access high-quality teaching, and therefore supports the full inclusion of all children in all classroom activities. We focus for the remainder of this section on the role of the TA in supporting the provision of high-quality teaching.

What is high-quality teaching?

Although the term 'high-quality teaching' is frequently used in discussions of inclusive practice, there is little in the way of an agreed definition. We would argue that one of the key things that individual teachers and TAs (and school leaders) can do is to develop a definition of high-quality teaching that is shared and understood by all staff working around a child. Decisions can then be made about how teachers, TAs and other staff may make their unique contribution to this high-quality teaching provision. One starting point is Coe et al. (2014), who, based on extensive research, set out six components of 'great teaching' (or 'effective pedagogy').

Components of effective pedagogy

1. Pedagogical (content) knowledge – the teacher has a strong understanding of the material and can recognise and address misconceptions.
2. Quality of instruction – including effective questioning, modelling and scaffolding.
3. Classroom climate – including quality interactions and high expectations.
4. Classroom management – including good use of time, space and resources, and effective and consistent management of behaviour.
5. Teacher beliefs – including theories about learning and the role of the teacher in this.
6. Professional behaviours – including engaging with professional development and reflection on practice.

(Coe et al., 2014)

The reader will notice that these components apply to teaching all children, not just those identified with SEND: high-quality teaching requires teachers to consider all these aspects in relation to inclusive education. For example, a teacher may need to extend their subject knowledge to include how different barriers to learning may affect understanding and this then requires them to make modifications to their pedagogy in response to individual needs. Values and attitudes to inclusion need to be examined and challenged in relation to components 3, 4, 5 and 6. This is every teacher's responsibility. Consideration can then be made by the teacher as to how to utilise any within-class TA support available.

These points raise another important question: 'To what extent are these components applicable to TAs?' We would argue that all of these six areas are relevant to TAs, but that they need to be considered in relation to their role descriptors and responsibilities (i.e. they will not be the same as for teachers). A set of (non-mandatory and non-statutory) *Professional Standards for Teaching Assistants* was published by UNISON et al. in 2016 and provides a useful starting point for considering ways to professionalise the TA role and develop TAs in the aforementioned components. Much can be developed and shared across the teacher–TA workforce by building opportunities for joint professional development. Developing shared beliefs and professional behaviours around inclusion and utilising consistent approaches for components 2 to 4 would seem essential, as would supporting TAs' subject knowledge development. Together with clearly articulated roles and responsibilities, this suggests a positive way forward for schools that want to build effective teacher–TA partnerships in relation to inclusion. The Education Endowment Foundation recommendation 'Ensure TAs are fully prepared for their role in the classroom' (Sharples et al., 2018, p. 10) should include both professional development and opportunities for teachers and TAs to liaise about children's needs and progress.

Although research into the graduated approach is limited, a useful study by Greenwood and Kelly (2017) of the similar approach Response to Intervention in the United States highlights conditions that can support or inhibit effective implementation of the strategy. They are

- Partnership and collaboration
- Continued professional development
- Clarification of roles
- Leadership and a shared commitment

We would argue that school leaders and individual teachers and TAs should be actively involved in reviewing and planning for development in each of the areas raised by Greenwood and Kelly (2017). A key consideration should be whether TAs are fully integrated into these four areas.

A focus on developing independence

Of course, there will be children who need additional support to access the high-quality teaching provided by the teacher, and the teacher will need to make decisions as to how to allocate both themselves and any TA support to these children. However, one thing to be aware of is the danger of children developing 'learned helplessness' through having adult support constantly available to them. Research has shown that TA–child interactions are characterised by oversupporting and providing answers (for a summary, see Bosanquet, Radford and Webster, 2021). This leads us to the Education Endowment Foundation recommendation to 'Use TAs to help pupils develop independent learning skills and manage their own learning' (Sharples et al., 2018, p. 10). Of course, this raises the question 'What does independence mean?'

Our starting point for this would be to consider positively what the child can already do in relation to any task. Although children may need different levels of support (from an occasional drop-in by an adult to 1:1 support), the key is to predict exactly which aspects of the task will *need* to be supported, and for a TA not to become involved in any aspects which the child could do independently. Otherwise, there is the risk of oversupporting them. At the same time, a TA needs to be proactively teaching the child strategies, including the use of resources, that will help them the next time they need to perform a similar task. So, they are not only supporting them right now but also preparing them to tackle future tasks more independently.

Therefore, the key to developing greater independence is that, when TAs play a pedagogical role, they should be one that is focused on scaffolding as an approach (Radford et al., 2015; Radford et al., 2014). A term first coined by Wood, Bruner and Ross (1976), 'scaffolding' describes the way that an adult (or more experienced peer) provides structured support towards a learning goal. At the beginning of a new task an adult will offer a higher level of support for the aspects that a child finds challenging, but they allow the child to carry out the parts that they can do and are constantly seeking ways to support them to take on responsibility for the more challenging aspects.

Drawing on scaffolding theory and linguistics, Bosanquet et al. (2021) have developed a scaffolding framework as a practical support for TAs in structuring their interactions with children in a way that maximises independence, and therefore inclusion. This forms part of an overarching set of principles and strategies for framing a pedagogical role for TAs, called Maximising the Practice of Teaching Assistants. The scaffolding framework has five levels of interaction. When a child experiences difficulty, an adult should work downwards from the top of the framework, only moving to the next level if necessary.

Scaffolding for independence framework

Self-scaffolding – The child uses the resources available and the strategies that they have previously been taught to support themselves in solving any problems that arise. The TA's role is to observe and monitor, and to decide when to intervene.

Prompting – If a child is not self-scaffolding, the TA provides a prompt. This is best described as encouragement. Often, simply providing time and space to think is a helpful way of prompting. However, a prompt can be verbal (e.g. 'What do you think you could do?') or a gesture (e.g. pointing towards a helpful resource).

Clueing – If the child has had one or more prompts but is clearly struggling, then the TA would provide a clue. A clue is a small piece of information that will help but doesn't give away the answer.

Modelling – If the preceding steps have not supported the child to move forward, then the TA will need to model the step that they are stuck on. The expectation is that the child repeats the model straight afterwards.

Correcting – This is included in the framework for completeness, but TAs are encouraged not to correct in learning interactions unless as part of a teacher-agreed strategy. This is because modelling already corrects, but the child is expected to repeat the model. This allows them to demonstrate understanding of the learning point in a way that simply correcting does not.

(Bosanquet et al., 2021)

For further explanation of the scaffolding framework and helpful examples and activities, see *The Teaching Assistant's Guide to Effective Interaction: How to Maximise Your Practice* (Bosanquet et al., 2021).

Exemplifying research-informed practice: Grassroots development

In this section, we discuss how one school has utilised the guiding principles set out in this chapter, together with a wider focus on research-led development for all staff to support the inclusion of all children. This reframing took place at a newly opened primary school in the East of England during the summer of 2016, at the end of the school's first academic year. We explain how the case study school took a principled approach and implemented the recommendations from the literature discussed earlier in this chapter.

Introducing Aimee's story

I was employed as a TA during a time of rapid growth at the school and during the creation of the curriculum design and ways of working practices. In 2016, I attended Maximising the Impact of Teaching Assistants training, where I first met my co-author, Paula. At last I was provided with the knowledge and understanding to support vulnerable children that I had been employed to assist. This gift came via the sharing of a newly published book, The Teaching Assistant's Guide to Effective Interaction: How to Maximise Your Practice (now in second edition, Bosanquet et al., 2021). The book contained all the necessary answers to questions that had occupied my thoughts since I was first employed as a teaching assistant, over the ten years prior to its publication. Questions such as: 'How can I promote independence?', 'How do I scaffold learning?' and 'How can I provide the correct level of questioning during learning activities?' Immediately, I set about devouring the pages that threw light on the shadow I had felt existed. I was now empowered to contribute towards the construction of the bridge (Veck, 2014) linking the supported child to their peers, teacher and curriculum.

Fortunately, I was now part of a newly formed team of educators where educational research and theory was to be shared with all the team, not just teachers. I was soon to become familiar with the works of many philosophers, psychologists and educationalists. At last, I found a new language: there was an alternative way to educate children which didn't involve ability grouping and/or the segregation of individuals. These theories and ideas became the food that nourished the inclusive community and helped inform inclusive practices within the school. However, just as the phrase 'one swallow does not a summer make' suggests, one head teacher and an enthusiastic teaching assistant, both passionate about inclusion, cannot create an inclusive community alone. The school required like-minded educators to promote social justice and the principles of democratic education; to celebrate diverse diversities (Biddulph, 2017) within the school community; and to influence the educational discourse for all children everywhere via continued professional development sessions, social media and publications.

The Education Endowment Foundation's *Making Best Use of Teaching Assistants: Guidance Report* (Sharples et al., 2018) provided the first necessary concise information that could provide our whole team with an insight into the research discussed in the first half of this chapter. Instead of overwhelming the team with numerous research papers, the decision was made to share the summary poster of the recommendations. It was found that sharing the poster and devising an action plan helped to develop inclusive practice across the school. The small steps outlined within the action plan helped the development of practice become manageable and achievable. This is how we, as a team, implemented the recommendations and research within the school.

Recommendation 1: TAs should not be used as informal teaching resources for low attaining pupils

The leadership team took a bold move away from the traditional 1:1 TA role when possible (although there are some children who require an adult to supervise them all the time because of safety issues). Initially, this approach was met with some resistance from members of our team. We found that experienced TAs who had been so used to sitting or standing next to their designated charge found it difficult to step back and observe what the child could do unaided. So familiar were they with passing the child their pencil; opening their book for them; and providing the listening within each lesson and then parroting exactly what the teacher had said back to the child, it was difficult for them to change their practice. Some of our TAs experienced a sense of redundancy. It became obvious how dependent both child and adult were on the existing model, which was comfortable and familiar, constantly relying on one another to complete the required learning tasks.

However, the supporting adults in the classroom soon began to realise that when they stood back, they were able to observe the needs of all the children in the classroom. Throughout the school day, most children have a moment of struggle. Therefore, TAs need to be able to learn to read the classroom and step in to help during that moment of challenge or to provide the necessary questions to help a child understand the task at hand. Our team of supporting adults identified that their role is more dynamic and when they are deployed differently: it frees the teacher to work with all children, individual groups, or a child with an Education, Health and Care Plan.

As a result, in 2018 we resigned the title of 'teaching assistant' to the archives and chose to call our adults in supporting roles 'learning coaches'. This highlighted that our adults had a pedagogical role, educating children alongside the teachers. Our learning coaches were on a journey to becoming formal professional teaching resources with the ability and necessary skills to coach the best out of the children they worked with each day. This involved a vast array of continuing professional development, coaching and building reflective practices.

Thinking about recommendation 1:

- Take a moment to consider your classroom and how other adults work within it.
- Does everyone currently work with all children?
- What would you need to do to meet the requirements of this recommendation?

Recommendation 2: Use TAs to add value to what teachers do, not replace them

To fully meet the requirements of this recommendation, it was made clear at interview to newly employed learning coaches what would be required of them in their role. This would likely be different to what they had experienced in previous school settings. Learning coaches were encouraged during the first term to build relationships with the children they would support and then strive to promote a sense of belonging and facilitate inclusive practices.

This involved small interventions which enabled, for example, a supported child to enter the playground at exactly the same time as their peers. Learning coaches knew when to blend into the background, so peers instigated conversation with the child instead of the adult. They would ensure that a child identified with significant SEND was taught the names of his or her peers. These seem obvious examples, but sadly they do not always happen.

Learning coaches are encouraged to ensure that children stay in class as much as possible with their class teacher and can access the lessons whenever possible. This involves teamwork and a deep understanding of the child. In some cases, it may be that the child experiences only a small part of the lesson alongside their peers, but they are visible to all members of their class community. Their contribution is valued. We promote inclusion via our classroom family boards, which shine a light on the children's lived experiences outside of school. Highlighting those diverse diversities mentioned earlier, the children are a visible part of the school community in every sense, along with their siblings and parents/carers – not only for all the adults but also the children in their class.

In the school we implemented a dynamic relationship of class teacher and TA working together to complement teaching and learning (Webster, 2019). This model changes the traditional picture that one has of a classroom, with the teacher at the front and the TA sitting next to the child who has greater or more complex special educational needs. The learning coach could be supporting the whole class's independent learning from the front of the class, whilst the class teacher works with a child who would have traditionally been supported with a 1:1 TA. Or the class may be split into smaller groups with the class teacher working with a teacher focus group, whilst the learning coach works with others.

Additionally, we have ensured that all our children identified as having additional needs have a network of several adults who are able to support them without any disruption to their education. This means there is no lost learning experienced if a particular adult is not available. Children cannot afford time for new relationships to be built; they require a continuum of uninterrupted learning. This is possible because of the dynamic adult relationships in the school where information is shared with all. This constant whole-team dialogue provides the necessary jigsaw pieces of understanding so that all adults have a shared knowledge of need.

> ## Thinking about recommendation 2:
>
> *Teacher:* When was the last time you worked on a one-to-one basis with a child who has an Education, Health and Care Plan?
> *Teaching assistant:* When was the last time you supported the whole class whilst the class teacher worked with a child with additional needs?

Recommendation 3: Use TAs to help pupils develop independent learning skills and manage their own learning

Building on our learning from the Maximising the Impact of Teaching Assistants professional development, we have scheduled an annual learning coach continuing professional development cycle which includes input on scaffolding and coaching sessions via an educational coach. This has enabled our team to always attempt to provide the least help first.

Following a scaffolding professional development session, we created Assessment for Learning stickers to provide our teachers with a snapshot of the support level the children have needed during each lesson. This informs the

					TA Initials
Lesson:		Date:			

Names:	Self-Scaffolds: ✓ •	Prompting	Clueing	Modelling	Observations

Figure 9.1 Assessment for Learning sticker, part 1

teacher's planning and helps them decide whether particular children will need to be part of a teacher focus group or require more deliberate practice. Learning coaches are fortunate to receive professional development at the school, which ensures that the team is well prepared for the pedagogical challenges of a primary classroom and the many individuals within it. Examples of the Assessment for Learning stickers used by the learning coach team are provided in Figures 9.1 and 9.2. These are stuck in the Class Teacher's Responsive Teaching Journal at the end of each lesson.

Assessment for Learning	TA Initials
Observations & notes(e.g. useful resources, specific difficulties, useful prompts)	

Figure 9.2 Assessment for Learning sticker, part 2

During 2015/16 we tried to ensure that all teachers met the adults who worked in their classrooms once a week at lunchtime. However, with sharply rising pupil numbers, this was no longer possible. Consequently, we then contracted hours for our learning coaches to attend weekly planning meetings with their key stage colleagues. Other important information is shared with them as a group on a Friday during a learning coach gathering. Friday gatherings are a space for the team to celebrate individual child successes and a time to discuss difficulties. Through discussion we have often come to the conclusion that adults could reflect on how they could implement or consider an element of provision in order for the child to succeed. Then we adapt our practice to ensure a child has everything they require to be included.

Thinking about recommendation 3:

Teacher: How do the TAs you work with provide observational information which informs your teaching and planning?
Teaching assistant: How much support are you providing the children that you work with? Is it always the least amount first?

Recommendation 4: Ensure TAs are fully prepared for their role in the classroom

Effective high-quality teaching relies on staff beliefs (including theories about teaching and learning) and professional behaviours (including participation in professional development and reflection on professional practice). These form the final two components of the framework from Coe et al. (2014) that we introduced earlier. However, there is too little in the available literature that considers beliefs and professional behaviours as components shared by teachers and TAs. It is our argument that TAs and teachers need to develop shared beliefs about teaching and learning, and therefore need opportunities to co-construct these through shared professional development opportunities and through reflecting on practice together.

At the school, we developed a professional community of learners via 'network meetings'. These professional development sessions began as TA Forum sessions. TAs from the local area and our own team would come along to keynote sessions which featured a range of academic speakers. This has since developed into whole-team professional development meetings every week (see https://unlockingresearch.org). This shared professional development has strengthened the team and improved pedagogical understanding about what is necessary to educate children identified with additional educational needs. It has also been a positive shift away from a deficit narrative about children and their learning. We have forged relationships with teachers who work in special schools who have helped us to develop a shared understanding of high-quality teaching in mainstream classrooms. For example, through working with one school, we have changed our planning cycle for children who are working below the national curriculum expectations. We also worked with a school that supported the team with a playful approach to learning activities, speech and language support, and guidance on the Engagement Model. A relationship has been established with these schools and we continue to work with them.

Thinking about recommendation 4:

What professional development is available to TAs in your school?
What professional development has been run for teachers or TAs this year which could have been available as a joint teacher–TA session?

The importance of relationships

Education does not occur in a vacuum; relationships must be built: first, with the children and then with other educators and schools. Last year, colleagues spent time reflecting in a more focused way on all children in their classrooms. Each member of the learning coach team wrote a case study, whilst teachers focused on the definition of high-quality teaching. The case studies made for powerful reading and were hugely insightful. Each case study written by the learning coach provided a bridge for the teacher to enter the child's world.

Our learning coach gatherings have allowed us to step into the world of a child identified with SEND. Only then could we truly understand their needs and what we need to do as educators to meet their needs. Giangreco (2017) describes the relationship making process by using his friend's analogy of a bicycle. Giangreco's friend, whose son has Angelman syndrome, advocates a move away from the deficit model of children who have special educational needs as substandard (a broken bicycle). She prefers to think of her son as a stunning Italian bicycle (Yuan, 2003, as cited in Giangreco, 2017). It is important for all those who work with a child to take the time to understand their beauty, intricacies and fine workings. Once these elements are understood, education happens. Both educators and child become two cogs working seamlessly as the wheels of curriculum and belonging spin in unison.

Conclusion: Towards inclusive educational practice

Inclusive pedagogy and practices will never be satisfactory until TAs are not only valued but included in the debate about inclusion in schools. The authors' view is that TAs are too often excluded from this debate, and consequently they do not have a voice or platform to make their unique contribution to the discussion, and to share the impactful strategies that work for the children they learn alongside daily. Slee (2011, p. 39) suggests:

> Too frequently theorists of inclusive education commence without technical considerations of the means for achieving inclusion. Inclusive education is thus reduced to a list of policies, strategies and resources. These activities to pursue inclusive education represent a necessary and important discussion, but it must be the second order discussion. The first requirement is to establish our goals and our aspirations.

What we have aimed to achieve in this chapter is a discussion of some key considerations for school leaders, teachers and TAs, and some helpful strategies for maximising the work of TAs. However, what we hope that we have also highlighted is the need to start from a consideration of how to build shared goals and attitudes to inclusive practice through research-led practice which includes TAs as key to children's learning.

References

Biddulph, J. (2017). *The diverse diversities of creative learning at home: Three case studies of ethnic minority immigrant children.* (PhD Thesis, Cambridge University).

Blatchford, P., Russell, A., & Webster, R. (2012). *Reassessing the impact of teaching assistants: How research challenges practice and policy.* Routledge.

Blatchford, P., & Webster, R. (2018). Classroom contexts for learning at primary and secondary school: Class size, groupings, interactions and special educational needs. *British Educational Research Journal,* 44(4): 681–703.

Bosanquet, P., Radford, J., & Webster, R. (2021). *The teaching assistant's guide to effective interaction: How to maximise your practice,* second edition. Routledge.

Coe, R., Aloisi, C., Higgins, S., & Major, L.E. (2014). *What makes great teaching? Review of the underpinning research.* Project report. Sutton Trust.

Department for Education & Department of Health. (2015). *Special educational needs and disability code of practice: 0 to 25 years. Statutory guidance for organisations which work with and support children and young people who have special educational needs or disabilities.* January 2015. Available online: https://www.gov.uk/government/publications/send-code-of-practice-0-to-25.

Giangreco, M. (2017). Including students with developmental disabilities: Simple, not easy. In Danforth, S. (Ed.), *Becoming a great inclusive educator (disability studies in education)* (pp. 341–351). Peter Lang.

Greenwood, J., & Kelly, C. (2017). Implementing cycles of Assess, Plan, Do, Review: A literature review of practitioner perspectives. *British Journal of Special Education,* 44(4), 394–410.

Radford, J., Bosanquet, P., Webster, R., & Blatchford. P. (2015). Scaffolding learning for independence: Clarifying teacher and TA roles for children with SEN. *Learning and Instruction,* 36, 1–10.

Radford, J., Bosanquet, P., Webster, R., Blatchford, P., & Rubie-Davies. C. (2014). Fostering learner independence through heuristic scaffolding: A valuable role for teaching assistants. *International Journal of Educational Research,* 63(1), 116–126.

Sharples, J., Webster, R., & Blatchford, P. (2018). *Making best use of teaching assistants*. Guidance report. Education Endowment Foundation.

Slee, R. (2011). *The irregular school: Exclusion, schooling and inclusive education*. Taylor & Francis.

UNISON, NAHT, NET, LLS, MITA. (2016). *Professional standards for teaching assistants*. Available online: http://maximisingtas.co.uk/resources/professional-standards-for-teaching-assistants.php.

Veck, W. (2014). Hope, disability and inclusive participation in education. *International Journal of Inclusive Education*, 18(2), 177–195.

Webster, R. (2015). The classroom experiences of pupils with special educational needs in mainstream primary schools −1976 to 2012. What do data from systematic observation studies reveal about pupils' educational experiences over time? *British Educational Research Journal*, 41(6), 992–1009.

Webster, R. (2019). *Including children and young people with special educational needs and disabilities in learning and life: How far have we come since the Warnock enquiry, and where do we go next?* Routledge Focus.

Webster, R., Bosanquet, P., Franklin, S., & Parker, M. (2021). *Maximising the impact of teaching assistants in primary schools: A practical guide for school leaders*. Routledge.

Webster, R., Russell, A., & Blatchford, P. (2016). *Maximising the impact of teaching assistants: Guidance for school leaders and teachers*, second edition. Routledge.

Wood, D., Bruner, J. S., & Ross, G. (1976). The role of tutoring in problem solving. *Journal of Child Psychology and Child Psychiatry*, 17, 89–100.

10

Leading inclusive practice

Pete Dudley and Bavaani Nanthabalan

Article 2: The Convention applies to all children, whatever their race, religion or abilities; whatever they think or say, whatever type of family they come from. It doesn't matter where children live, what language they speak, what their parents do, whether they are boys or girls, what their culture is, whether they have a disability or whether they are rich or poor. No child should be treated unfairly on any basis.

United Nations Convention on the Rights of the Child

Introduction

As authors of this chapter we have over 70 years' experience of leading inclusive practice in a range of educational contexts. Bavaani Nanthabalan began teaching in her native Singapore and has been a school leader in London for many years. She is currently executive head of Netley Campus in a deprived area of Camden, London, comprising a primary school, a special school, a primary pupil referral unit and a unit for children with autism. Following a career leading educational improvement at school and at school-system levels, Pete Dudley now teaches and researches educational leadership at the University of Cambridge. Both authors have international educational experience and experience in England.

By 'inclusive practice' in this chapter we mean practice that directly aligns with aims of the chapter-opening United Nations Convention by enabling all children to learn with confidence, to thrive as learners whatever their backgrounds and starting points, whatever barriers or challenges they face, and

DOI: 10.4324/9781003137634-10

to do so with their peers. Ideally such practice exists at classroom and whole-school levels and involves families as well as community.

By 'leading' we refer not only to those with recognised 'positional' leadership roles, but anyone who takes a lead in a school at any level to ensure children are actively included in, and not excluded from, aspects of education.

A teacher who habitually reflects on children's learning and on how he or she can help every child to overcome barriers and succeed in learning will, over the course of a career, spend a lot of time focused on developing aspects of inclusive practice. If that practitioner believes that with the right conditions all children can learn (and, in aspects, excel) whatever stands in their way, the children he or she teaches will believe they can learn. If the school's leaders are also determined to create those 'right' learning conditions and support practitioners in sustaining them, then all children will learn. In a curriculum that inspires them, they will do so with passion.

Without such leadership expectations and determination, many children are excluded from learning. The consequences of such exclusion on a child's development, their capacity to learn later in childhood or life, and thus on their life chances, are almost always quietly catastrophic. Their likelihood of succeeding educationally, forming lasting relationships, achieving economic independence or making a contribution to society plummet. The chances they will fall into crime, substance misuse or poverty and die early increase.

Leading inclusive practice involves supporting colleagues to find ways to create the conditions in their classrooms or settings to motivate and inspire learners; to give each child confidence, security and control over their learning; and, for some with sensory, physical or learning disabilities, to carefully engineer and support their access to that learning.

In this chapter we will explore what creates barriers that exclude children from learning. Some barriers are deliberate, such as where a school denies admission to children who fail to meet an 'entry' standard. Some are physical – ensuring that a child with a visual impairment can fully access text and visual learning resources. But other barriers are much harder to discern – invisible even – unless we deliberately look for them. These are harder to overcome.

Fortunately, we now know much more than we did a generation ago about how people learn and consequently more about preventing those harder-to-discern barriers to learning from first forming, and more about how to diagnose and remove them. This research has also revealed, how, when it comes to learning, each of us is dependent on others – family, peers and community – and how without inclusive learning, future society risks fragmentation and loss of cohesion. Unfortunately, in wider society, understanding of how we learn and the relationship between learning, thought, language and society is still poor. This can sometimes require leaders of inclusive practice to be educators not only of their pupils but of their professional, parent and wider school communities.

Discourse on inclusion over the past half century has often been driven by resource-led debates, special interest groups and deficit views of children whose learning does not conform to a supposed norm. This makes it difficult for professionals to create a mental rubric for understanding inclusive practice more holistically and thus knowing how to approach inclusion in all its complexity in their classrooms.

We will therefore focus firstly on how we all learn and how the classroom climate, conditions and support for learning can be optimised by leaders at the whole-school level and underpinned by parents and community. We believe that understanding the nature of motivation, disposition to learn, and ability to harness linguistic mental tools to create new ideas and concepts will help you understand how to optimise learning. We identify 'three barriers' to learning for use as a reference point when you are working with colleagues to analyse why a child is not learning as expected and also how to design lesson sequences and curricula that will be inclusive of that child.

We will use practice-based examples to illustrate how senior and middle leaders can habitualise practices that are inclusive of children for whom one, two or all three barriers can combine to exclude them from learning optimally. We will provide tools designed to help you work with colleagues to analyse how these learners at risk of exclusion can be included, accessed and supported to learn. And we will also give practical examples of how you can help lead the development of colleagues' expert practice in inclusively educating the full range of your learner population.

To explain this we first need to examine how people learn, drawing on sociocultural learning theory now widely accepted across the world, which is empirically supported by neuroscientific imaging of structural changes in the brain as it develops new knowledge.

How learning happens – thought and language

A brief summary of how humans learn goes like this. Knowledge (to be learned) cannot simply be transmitted. It has to be constructed by developments of thought in a learner's brain. Our first knowledge about the world develops as a result of our interactions with nature: thirst, liquid, light, dark, temperature, gravity. A baby observing family members walking, wants to walk. Through trial and error (falling), she constructs hypotheses about how gravity affects her body that eventually enable her to stand, take faltering steps and ultimately walk. These processes are accelerated if adults and siblings help her accomplish different components of walking – balancing (by standing safely between an adult's knees) and taking steps (when an adult takes the baby's hands and weight). Her trial-and-error walking experiences are all part of an ongoing interaction or dialogue with the world. She learns from feedback when falling and eventually she combines the processes, defies gravity and walks.

In the 1920s Russian psychologist Lev Vygotsky proposed that learning is not an individual, receptive process but a social and constructive process (see

Vygotsky, 1986). The help the baby receives decreases her fear of pain allowing her to accelerate the 'try–feedback–rethink–retry' dialogue. Vygotsky called these help activities 'scaffolding' the baby's learning. Once this baby learns to use spoken language, a learning accelerator kicks in because talk allows increasingly complex concepts to be communicated linguistically (rather than by actions) to facilitate the baby's formulation of new knowledge.

Talk is thus both communicative and cognitive. When we consciously think, a voice in our heads speaks our thoughts to us helping us to formulate complete meanings and ideas as well as to express them through talk. Thought comes into being through talk, and talk comes into being through thought. They are dimensions of each other. Talk is so necessary for human learning that Vygotsky called 'talk' learning's tool of tools. Talk allows us not only to convey ideas to our conscious selves, it allows us to then encode these ideas in speech which is deciphered, and the thoughts are reconstructed in a listener's brain and incorporated into their own knowledge without need for a painful trial-and-error process. The try–feedback–rethink–retry process becomes entirely mental: linguistic and cognitive.

In class, a learner imagines what a teacher means and uses talk to check for understanding. Pupil and teacher thus enter a dialogue of 'sustained shared thinking' (Sylva et al., 2010) using talk to co-develop new ideas (knowledge). Mercer (1995) studied children learning through collaborative exploratory talk. When mutual trust and value are high, they use exploratory talk to 'inter-think' together creating joint knowledge collaboratively (Dawes, Mercer and Wegerif, 2004). Ground rules for talk optimise this learning.

Why being and feeling included is as necessary for learning as having the capacity to create new knowledge – and why feeling excluded prevents learning

> We know that we learn best when adults know us, make us feel safe, hold us responsible for our learning, and help us work constructively and productively together.
>
> *Members of the National Commission's Youth Commission in their Youth Call to Action, Aspen Institute (2018)*

Even education leaders can fail to grasp that learning happens through knowledge construction, following instead Bruner's 'folk pedagogy', that children just need to be told things to enable understanding. But Vygotsky identified something else just as essential as construction – motivation – the essential prerequisite for learning.

Learning is effortful and unpredictable – even scary. To contemplate engaging in learning one needs to be highly motivated by the potential outcome and reasonably confident of success. Overwhelming fear of failure prevents people of any age from engaging in learning.

Sociocultural theory suggests learning happens best in the place where the knowledge or skill is needed, and when knowers (a group of people who have the know-how) help learners (who do not know) to gradually join in by participating in the practice until the learner becomes a knower and joins the 'knower' community. Joining in by participating in a welcoming community of practice is a powerful, practical and theoretical metaphor for learning (Lave and Wenger, 1991). It is as useful for leaders in creating and sustaining a community of professional learning as it is for the teachers they are leading.

In school, problems in learning can start to happen when a community of knowers (the adults and some pupils) is not welcoming, or where the learners fear they are not welcome and so are demotivated and afraid to join in. (Teachers may not be conscious of being unwelcoming and learners may not consciously feel unwelcome or excluded. Such invisible 'tacit' feelings and beliefs can make inclusive practice complex to lead in schools.)

Problems also arise when the knowers do not understand how a learner can be supported to join in and become a knower or even that with support the learner is capable of learning. This can be because the knowers do not know how to communicate with the leaner; a physical disability is preventing the learner from joining in; or because the learner will need additional support or a different approach to enable her to join in.

Classroom conditions that support these conditions for such learning to happen are set out in Figure 10.1. There is clear reference to learners feeling that they belong, can be supported by talk with peers and adults, feel clear about what is expected of them, and feel positively supported to succeed.

What is omitted from the diagram are the barriers to these. As a leader of inclusive practice. you need to be sure that all the tools at your school's disposal for managing learning – curriculum, pedagogy, assessment and feedback – are created with a keen awareness of how they identify, address and counter the following barriers to inclusive learning.

The preceding paragraphs suggest these fall into three groups: (1) fear of failing; (2) feeling rejected, unvalued or disowned by the (knower) community; and (3) cognitive, participation or access difficulties that prevent a learner from joining in learning. We will describe each in more detail.

Barrier 1: Fear of failure

This barrier is created by a learner's fear that the object of the learning is impossible to attain (even if her peers have attained it). This fear is not just that of 'failing', it is also a fear of unacceptable loss of social standing or ridicule from

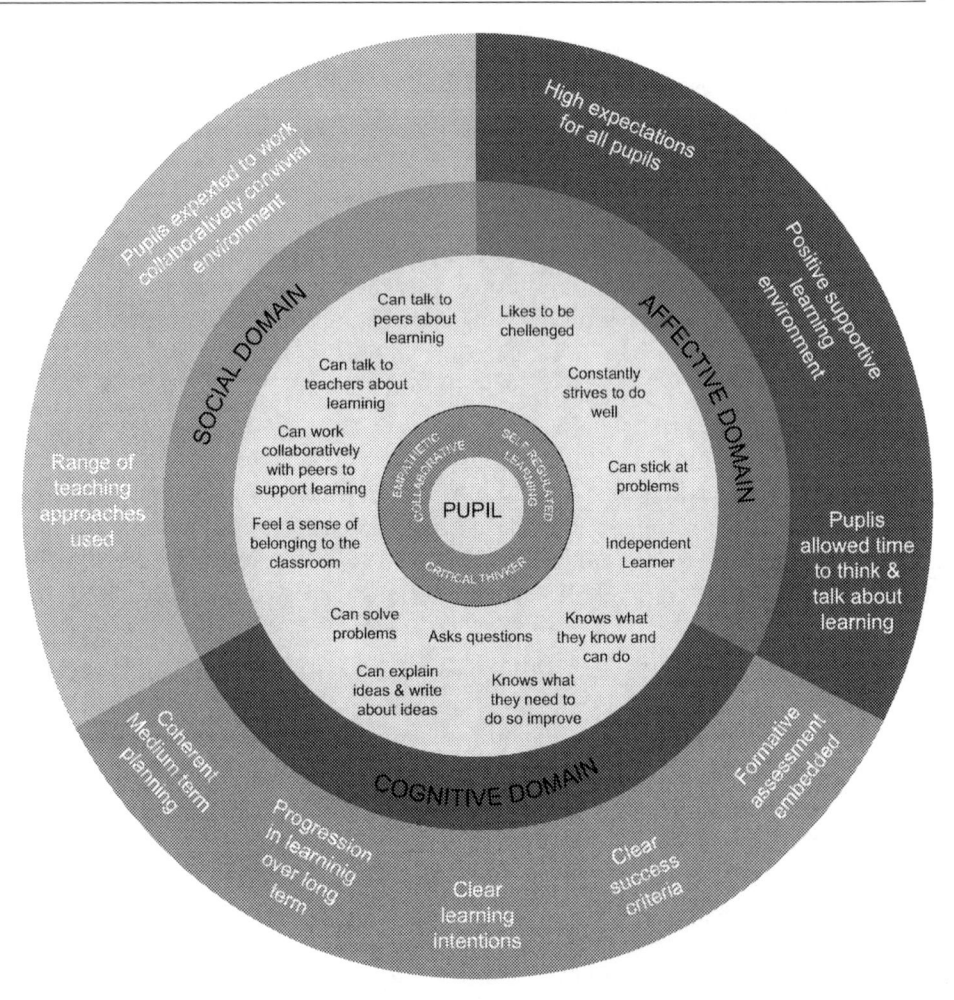

Figure 10.1 What both teachers and students do when effective teaching and learning is taking place (Wilson, 2017). Reproduced with the author's permission

members of the group who already possess the desired knowledge or who are also trying to acquire it (fellow learners).

Barrier 2: Feeling unvalued by the community and viewing the object of learning as 'not for me'

The second barrier appears when the learner perceives the object of learning as undesirable because the knower community is not one to which she sees herself belonging. She will not, therefore, go through the effort of joining in because she feels discouraged from participating in the knower group. As with barrier 1, she feels unmotivated, unsafe to take risks, and fearful of ridicule or other forms of exclusion if she fails.

Barrier 3: Being unable to participate in learning because of a cognitive, participative or access-related difficulty or disability

This happens when the learner cannot make sense of the object of learning or how it relates or may be desirable to them. This happens when there are physical, sensory, psychological or communicative barriers between the learner and those who want her to join in and gain new knowledge from them.

This third barrier also occurs when, even though the knowers value the learner, they do not know how to scaffold the ideas, component skills, or concepts that make up the object of learning in ways that will overcome the learner's barriers to seeing the object of learning as desirable or attainable. The learner may communicate in a different language or have a sensory, psychological, cognitive or other difficulty or disability that prevents such communication and motivation from forming. (See Vignette 10.1 for the strategies used to support Amir.)

Despite a common view that 'inclusion' is mainly concerned with issues of cognition, it is clear from this chapter that barriers to learning and inclusion are often not primarily cognitive. In barriers 1 and 2, learning (cognition) is suppressed by affective domain responses (emotions), such as fear of failure or of not being valued by a teacher, school or community. In barrier 3, participation is prevented by problems in communicating with the learner: because the knowers speak a different language; because a psychological condition causes the learner to perceive the world differently from the way the most others perceive it; or by physical or sensory impairments which deny a learner access to participation – sight, hearing, mobility.

In truth, many children's learning will be variously affected by all three barriers at once, as Figure 10.2 illustrates. Being in more than one group or in intersecting sets here is often referred to as intersectionality.

Use the following task 1 to map ideas you have gained from this section onto a scenario describing how inclusive approaches were researched, analysed and adopted in a complex case. You can also adapt it for use with colleagues with whom you are developing inclusive practices based on case study pupils from your school.

Task 1: Identifying affectively and access/participatorily inclusive practices and their effects on a learner

The following vignette describes how a child, identified with autism and who had previously attended special school, was supported to learn in a specialist autism unit in a mainstream school. The vignette highlights how it was possible to provide him with access to learning with peers, some in the specialist unit and others in mainstream lessons.

Read the vignette and with one colour highlight steps that were taken to strengthen the affective dimensions of Amir's learning (relating to barriers 1 and 2). In another colour, highlight ways in which the participatory dimension of his learning was strengthened. (You may feel some practices strengthened both.)

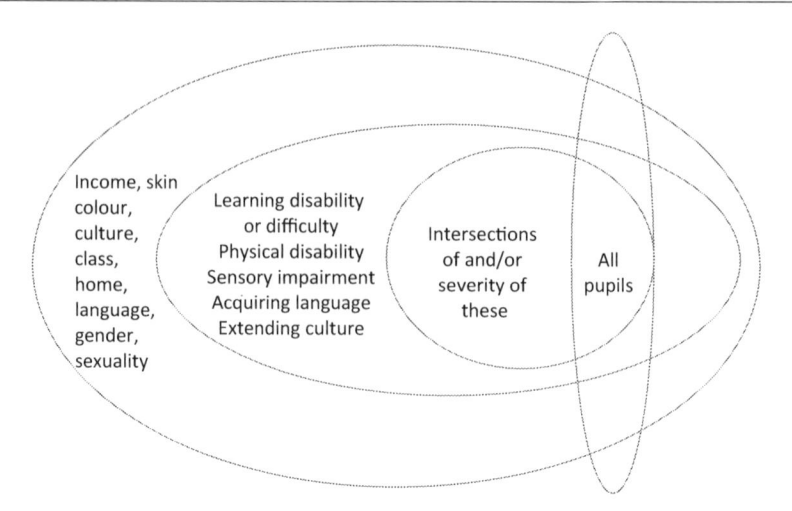

Figure 10.2 Identity, poverty, culture, communicative and access-related factors that typically give rise to degrees of exclusion from active participatory learning for groups of pupils and which, if not addressed, prevent the learning for all in the group from being optimal

Then identify which aspects of Amir's described improvements in the new setting resulted most from support in each dimension.

Vignette 10.1 A nine-year-old with a diagnosis of 'atypical autism' and learning difficulty attending Woodlands Centre for Autism

Amir transferred to Woodlands Centre for Autism from a special school. With a diagnosis of 'atypical autism', he displayed advanced verbal language but spiky social skills, extremely low self-confidence and an aversion to academic work. In his previous school, he rarely initiated interactions with peers; most socialising was with his teachers. Because his previous classmates had less well-developed language abilities, the special school recognised his opportunities to socialise with peers and develop friendships there were limited. It was agreed that he could benefit at Woodlands with more opportunities for social inclusion and peer–peer conversation in his new classroom and in the attached mainstream primary school, Netley.

Amir joined a class containing two peers with similar spoken language abilities but more developed social skills. Within his first month, we observed Amir copying their language and play, often joining in their chase games. He began using the language of 'friends' to describe these boys who had included him in their group. At the same time, Amir's low self-confidence meant he refused any work that seemed too challenging. Any redirection, even a raised teacher voice, elicited a defensive response: 'You're mad at me' or 'You hate me.' Amir withdrew himself from the classroom.

The teaching team then agreed a strategy of carefully scaffolded work, which included providing Amir with appropriate visual supports (word mats; in-task timetables; and short, focused activities). Each activity was followed-up with specific praise and time for Amir to reflect on his progress. Amir began to show increasing resilience in his academic work, and, over the year, his social interactions and initiations shifted from being mainly with adults to his friendship group.

Improvements in both his social inclusion and academic progress in Woodlands led the Autism Leader to initiate conversations with Amir's family (who are refugees) about providing additional inclusion opportunities in mainstream classroom settings. Because Amir still struggled with self-confidence related to his academic learning, he attended weekly PE and music lessons with his year group at Netley (the attached mainstream primary school). Over the term, feedback on progress from his PE and music teachers informed next steps.

Amir seemed to be watching and copying his Netley peers and took pride in the positive feedback he received. He became able to follow all instructions and was a 'model pupil'. In Woodlands, Amir would have a high level of adult support (one adult for every two pupils), yet in Netley, he engaged with the music lessons with no such support because his mainstream classmates knew his name and welcomed him into lessons. (A curriculum subject less accessible to him would have required 1:1 support.) Amir's own feedback was very positive, cheering when he saw these mainstream lessons on his visual timetable. During this time, his own resilience and persistence for work improved. He rarely refused academic tasks and much less frequently withdrew himself from the classroom.

Summary: The social inclusion opportunities offered to Amir seemed to correlate directly with an increase in his self-confidence and self-esteem. After joining peers with more developed social skills, he found opportunities to communicate and engage with children his own age and develop a friendship group. This in turn, supported his motivation, engagement and resilience for schoolwork. His family was pleased with both his academic and social progress. This was important to his school, which works in partnership with its families. The next steps were to identify further integration opportunities, but this time involving Amir in voicing his choice and interests.

Identifying children most at risk of harm from affectively exclusive practices

It is now widely accepted that all children can learn if we communicate with them, motivate them, value them; give them self-confidence to try learning, resilience to failure, and access to the right support, care and feedback. Above all if we include them.

Although teachers are frontline actors, they cannot create these conditions without active leadership support. We see a school as what Bavaani calls a superstructure for inclusive education within its community. It constructs a curriculum that reflects, celebrates and teaches diversity; and non-Eurocentric global history and contributions to science and culture from around the world – a curriculum in which all children see themselves reflected and acknowledged and thus feel valued and included. It explains the histories that gave rise to the unconscious biases and beliefs that perpetuate inequity and exclusion in our society today and how the school is countering them.

These values are used beyond school to harness and orchestrate a range of learning and family support from the community, local services, businesses and third-sector partners. This wider support for inclusivity is strengthened when schools in a locality work together to ensure inclusive learning is optimised by developing and sharing inclusion expertise and resources not only for their children but for all children in the locality.

Identifying learners at risk of harm from exclusion on the affective dimension

Brazilian educator Paulo Freire observed how many people oppressed by poverty are eventually ground down into accepting their oppression as inevitable. Freire's globally influential work Pedagogy of the Oppressed (1970) argues that the only way exclusion of the oppressed groups can be ended is through all participants in society – including oppressors – reaching a new understanding through dialogue that accepts these wrongs and injustices and seeks a new equity. He made this possible through participatory education where all are included, have choice and influence over the curriculum, and where all can achieve. Only then, he argues, can educational and societal equity and inclusion be achieved. His approach is often called emancipatory education.

Such determinism exists, often undetected, in schools. Sylva (1994) describes how, by age five, children unconsciously categorise themselves either as a failer or a succeeder in learning. Attribution theory suggests those who self-identify as 'failers' lose confidence in attempting learning because it risks exposing their 'failure' to others. This is driven by fear and low self-esteem. Too often we lose these children as learners because our practices, our curriculum – including subliminal biases in our 'hidden curriculum' – exclude them, their families and communities by omission (see barrier 2).

These ideas and behaviours result from unconsciously absorbed sexist, racist or classist ideas. Addressing them requires everyone acknowledging that we can all internalise ideas unconsciously. We must all therefore accept that we are capable of unconscious racist, sexist or otherwise biased actions. We need to be ever on the alert for these, especially, for example, people who, as White, have not personally experienced the effects of racism. Unconscious bias (a form of tacit knowledge) is professionally challenging for leaders to deal with, but preventing it is essential for an inclusive school. As a leader, one can stress that no one deliberately adopts unconscious bias. Attitudes and beliefs that cause it are picked up from wider society at a young age. No one can help acquiring their own unconscious biases, but everyone can be vigilant in identifying them and countering them when they manifest. We can certainly educate the young in ways that prevent such biases forming, and equip children to be aware of and take a stand against them as they grow up.

Evaluating risks of exclusion across a school

The conditions that encourage, and the barriers that discourage, learning and inclusion sit on two interrelated dimensions: (1) affective (how we feel when learning; related to barriers 1 and 2); and (2) cognitive–participative–access (how we think, participate and communicate when learning; barrier 3). Figure 10.3

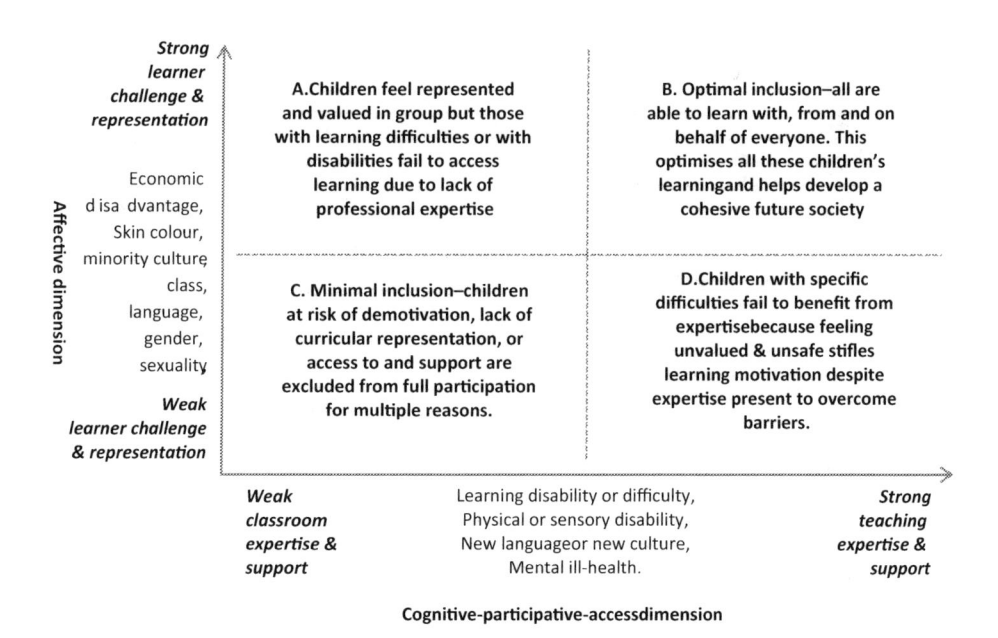

Figure 10.3 Affective and access-participation inclusion matrix

groups contributing factors along these dimensional axes. As a leader you can use this as a discussion tool when working with colleagues to evaluate inclusion in any aspect of your school's provision.

Leading and developing an inclusive curriculum

The curriculum should not only reflect and value all people equally, it should also equip children themselves to identify and challenge exclusion, racism and inequity and to act against them. So the curriculum needs to take an ethical position. Bavaani has used UNICEF's Rights Respecting Schools resources (https://www.unicef.org.uk/rights-respecting-schools/) to frame a set of curricular values, principles and learning behaviours for children, teachers and the communities of her schools. These can only be upheld if all groups have agency and responsibility for doing so: children and adults; in classrooms and on the playground; at school and at home.

Orchestrating an inclusive school that optimises learning for all involves knowing which children are likely to be at intersectional risk of exclusion from factors along each axis of the matrix in Figure 10.3. However, all children benefit from an inclusive curriculum that values all learner groups and cultures, abilities and that celebrates multilingualism.

Carole Dweck (2008) has stressed the importance of developing 'growth mindsets' in children who face explicit or subliminal exclusion from the curriculum or classroom learning community, in order to increase their self-belief as learners. She points to the 'self-efficacy' theory as a means to overcome the catastrophic self-doubt inflicted by attribution theory.

> The power of the social brain has been totally underestimated. It's the driving force in cognition; it's the gateway to learning.
>   Patricia Kuhl, co-director of the University of Washington Institute for Learning and Brain Sciences
>
> *(Aspen, 2018)*

Analysing barriers to learning in order to design inclusive learning

We first examine inclusion in terms of the affective dimension. We then examine the cognitive–participation–access dimension.

The aims of the Black Curriculum (https://theblackcurriculum.com) are an excellent starting point for anyone reviewing their school's curriculum. Netley Campus discussed the displacement of families in the community, the impact of knife crime and the disproportionate effects of the Covid-19 pandemic on

Black and minority ethnic communities, reaffirming the need for the explicit and hidden curriculum to value children's identities, heritage and environment, for the school to remain an inclusive and equal society. While the big question for the school remained 'Who do I want to be?', the issue of identity evolved through a thematic curricular agenda called 'Someone Like Me'. This builds children's confidence and engages them in their learning, connecting community and classroom.

Task 2: Curriculum development to strengthen the affective learning dimension for all learners

Read Vignette 10.2, and using Figure 10.2, highlight steps taken in the curriculum development that strengthen the affective learning dimension for learners who have historically been excluded in curricula in many English schools and whose achievements and learning are likely to have been damaged as a result.

Vignette 10.2 Developing an inclusive, relevant and connected curriculum

Our whole-school big question is 'Who do I want to be?' It resonated with our core values of respect, equality and resilience and with the vision of empowering children to become responsible global citizens. The curriculum is key to raising aspirations and the achievement of all children, and reflects our commitment to the UN Rights of the Child.

Teachers can adapt curricular study units to reflect the multiple identities of our children, and changes and issues that may affect our local community and the wider world. In the autumn we showcase the work of the children through a focus theme which is celebrated with friends and families. Pupils act as guides sharing the process of their learning to its end outcomes. The spring term has an emphasis on inclusion and autism, giving children the opportunity to participate in reverse integration, i.e. mainstream children spending time in classes in the Centre for Autism and interacting with and learning to understand the children's needs. 'Future You' is our summer project where children explore careers and the importance of financial responsibility.

The theme 'Pioneers' in autumn 2019, for instance, gave children the opportunity to learn more about people who were perhaps among the first to explore new frontiers; bring social change or innovate, create and lead in a new field. Year 4 focused on the Windrush generation as their topic question was 'Who are the people of Britain?' leading to a history study unit on invaders and settlers. The Windrush topic focused on an under-represented ethnic group in the school and community. There was media attention on

> this subject at the time, making it relevant and enabling children to make links with their own heritage. Netley serves a diverse population (over 30 languages are spoken) and it was important for children to make connections and think beyond their own community.
>
> A cross-curricular approach was also taken; Floella Benjamin's *Coming to England* was a core text; contemporary newspaper articles, films and interviews supported children to identify and understand reasons for social, economic and cultural change through historical events. Teachers shared data gained from different sources; in mathematics children collated information and presented bar graphs showing the range of places that people on the Windrush had travelled from. Equipped with such facts, children were able to engage in rich discussion and debate on the rights of migrants and refugees asking the question, 'Who had the right to remain in Britain?' The experiences and legacy of this group of pioneers were celebrated and communicated by the children through quality outcomes.

Creating inclusive practices in the cognitive–participation–access (CPA) dimension

To bring this about in our second dimension of learning – CPA – we need to be sure (1) we have the expertise and resources to deliver this (or that we can source specialist expertise); (2) we create conditions that support those with specific difficulties to overcome barriers; and finally (3) we help those with physical disabilities, psychological, cognitive or sensory impairments to access and participate in learning activities, conversations and curriculum.

Children for whom communicative development is restricted (as a result of sensory or more severe or profound learning disabilities) need opportunities to experience and interact with nature; with other people (family, teachers, peers); and, when possible, with technology that helps channel sensory or other experiential means of communication and response. Such interactions can be viewed as facilitating experiential dialogue.

Children who are at an early stage of learning through English as an additional language can, through involvement in mainstream learning practices, be supported by pre-teaching of some key vocabulary; design of activities that use visual and 'concrete' referents that make meanings easier to grasp; and by engineering collaborative discussion where the combination of resources, interaction and negotiation of meaning with more fluent peers results in 'comprehensible input' for bilingual/multilingual learners. (See NALDIC link provided later.) Prior to this, a careful analysis of specific language demands made by learning tasks can critically inform learning designs and support. This brings us to our final section.

How to lead sustained and deepening inclusive learning

We can maximise learning for pupils affected by any of the three barriers by harnessing our two dimensions – affective and CAP – in two stages. As stated, we first need to apply principles for how we organise learning in these two dimensions so we create a climate, conditions, curriculum and culture that counter such ideas and instead promote motivational feelings of being valued and included, through careful choice of curriculum, resources, collaborative and communicative pedagogical approaches and support.

Second, we need to personalise these to the specific learners in our school, identifying how each may be affected intersectionally (by more than one barrier in more than one way at once) causing children to be excluded differentially; and also by identifying any specific causes of cognitive, linguistic or access-related barriers to learning for each child. For some children several of these will apply.

This second approach requires regular analysis by teachers and middle 'phase' or subject leaders of the cognitive and language demands of learning tasks calibrated against both the known capabilities and knowledge of the learner and the intersectional barriers she faces to inclusive learning. This is so that learning tasks are sufficiently motivating, challenging and successfully communicated and accessible to the leaner to enable her engagement and participation. Such analyses cannot be carried out for every child all the time. However, there are classroom approaches in use in many schools which allow us to study children's learning in the curriculum, to understand how barriers may interact to prevent learning and to explore ways of supporting learners and teachers to overcome them. We can then build this new knowledge into the school's practice and curriculum for future use.

This requires leaders to create opportunities and support to enable teachers to become collaborative researchers of their children's learning and build cross-school systems for ensuring the outcomes of this research inform future learning and curriculum development.

Collaborative analysis of curricular demands and barriers to learning to orchestrate inclusive practice

Regular exploration of how to design, integrate and orchestrate classroom curriculum and pedagogy that addresses learning on both affective and CAP dimensions requires determined leadership, but in doing so you become a strong leader of inclusion. It requires regular, careful analysis and imagination to put into practice. But with time, such an approach can become a professionally fulfilling element of everyone's professional practice (the joy of discovering new ways of unlocking learning for successive children is never diminished by familiarity). Most inclusive, reflective leaders and practitioners are also excited and motivated to solve the next problem. Such professional reflection and revision is best done collaboratively.

One approach to achieving this is Lesson Study, originating in Japan in the 1870s, where groups of teachers collaboratively research, plan, then teach 'research lessons' (sometimes with local experts and teachers from neighbouring schools present). They also collaborate in analysing the lessons, invariably discovering knowledge about how pupils are learning and mislearning that changes subsequent practice. Lesson Study is carried out routinely in many UK schools, inlcuding the University of Cambridge Primary School (see Seleznyov and Rolls, 2021).

Becoming a researcher of your children's learning demands inclusive scaffolded support for your teachers' learning

Following a study visit to Shanghai, Netley Primary leaders introduced a Chinese variation of Lesson Study called Teacher Research Groups (TRGs) to create regular opportunities for teachers to collaboratively study how pupils were learning mathematics.

Task 3: Key opportunities for understanding and overcoming barriers to pupils' learning

Read Vignette 10.3 and identify the key opportunities for understanding and overcoming barriers to pupils' learning. Also identify how leaders ensure this form of lesson analysis is viewed as a 'safe inclusive space' in which teachers learn without fear and see benefits.

Vignette 10.3 Teacher Research Groups (TRGs)

Many teachers in England view observations as high-risk performance management designed to judge them. Some experienced teachers had not observed teaching for years and we wanted to break that cycle, and ensure it was not seen as a threat but as something that people valued as regular coaching and feedback designed to improve pedagogy.

Initially the deputy head taught mathematics content to a Key Stage 1 (KS1) class on Monday mornings attended by all KS1 teachers, each seated at a child's table with their 'reflective journal'. They observed the lesson and discussed the learning with the children. During morning assembly the TRGs held a 20-minute post-lesson discussion about how the mathematics observed was learned.

Every teacher then taught an open lesson for staff to observe. To encourage investment in the process so it could become self-sustaining, we introduced a discussion ground rule: observers used the sentence stem 'I liked how you …' in turn when making their contribution to the collaborative unpicking of the pupils' learning.

It worked! Using sentence stems enabled teachers to reflect on the positive, allowing the mathematics leader to elicit deeper insights into the observed pupil learning, lesson plan rationale, pedagogy, subject knowledge and next steps. Teachers focused on aspects they were struggling with or seeking to develop. Experienced teachers often reconfigured or reminded themselves of techniques, asking more detailed questions about the structure of the mathematics. Newer teachers focused more on early subject knowledge, pace and lesson design. TRGs enabled teachers at all stages of their careers to learn with and from each other and to evaluate their practice. This has established a self-sustaining, supportive learning network for refining inclusive practice. They all agree: the more you observe and analyse children learning and teaching, the better your teaching and children's learning becomes.

View the final report of the study visit at https://assets.publishing .service.gov.uk/government/uploads/system/uploads/attachment_data/file /773320/MTE_main_report.pdf.

By focusing on pupils together in a lesson and discussing it with them before analysing their learning, teachers gained deep insights into barriers to learning and enjoyed designing 'next steps' support.

Two other variants of Lesson Study – Research Lesson Study (RLS) and Learning Study – help teachers understand and develop inclusive practices. RLS (Goel, Norwich and Dudley, 2021; Norwich, 2018; Dudley and Lang, 2020) is used across the UK and Europe harnessing dialogic teacher learning and study of case pupils. Learning Study is increasingly used with children identified with moderate, severe or multiple learning difficulties.

Conclusion

In this chapter we have explored barriers that exclude many children from learning well, examined three vignettes of leadership practices designed to overcome these barriers at school and classroom levels, and presented tools to help in the leadership of all these. Further resources are suggested in the following websites to help you lead inclusive practice.

We began by making reference to the human right to learn of all children. We have tried to make a clear case that inclusive teaching is not only an ethical imperative, but that there are also strong scientific reasons why inclusive approaches are essential for learning for all. We hope that thinking about leading inclusion while reading this has helped you also to reflect on how dependent the future world is on a population educated to understand and respect each other's differences and to value all humanity as a result of learning together in committed, inclusive schools and settings.

Useful websites for further information

- UNICEF Rights Respecting Schools, https://www.unicef.org.uk/rights-respecting-schools/
- The Black Curriculum, https://theblackcurriculum.com
- National Association for Language Development in the Curriculum (NALDIC), https://naldic.org.uk
- National Association for Special Educational Needs (NASEN), https://nasen.org.uk
- Thinking Together, https://thinkingtogether.educ.cam.ac.uk/publications/journals/
- Lesson Study UK, https://lessonstudy.co.uk
- World Association of Lesson Studies (WALS), https://www.walsnet.org

References

Aspen Institute National Commission on Social, Emotional, & Academic Development. (2018). From a nation at risk to a nation at hope. Retrieved from http://nationathope.org/wp-content/uploads/2018_aspen_final-report_full_webversion.pdf.

Dawes, L., Mercer, N., & Wegerif, R. (2004). Thinking together: A programme of activities for developing speaking, listening and thinking skills. Birmingham: Imaginative Minds Ltd.

Dudley, P., & Lang, J. (2020). How using case pupils, pupil interviews and sequences of research lessons gives teachers insights into how to improve subsequent learning for all pupils. In Aki Murata and Christine Lee (Eds.), Stepping up lesson study (pp. 14–26). Abingdon: Routledge.

Dweck, C. (2008). Mindset: The new psychology of success. New York: Ballantine.

Goel, S. L., Norwich, B., & Dudley, P. (Eds.). (2021). Lesson study in inclusive educational settings. London: Routledge.

Lave, J., & Wenger, E. (1991). Situated learning: Legitimate peripheral participation. Cambridge: Cambridge University Press.

Norwich, B. (2018). Inter-professional lesson study as an approach to close-to-practice research. Research Intelligence 3. British Educational Research Association. Retrieved from https://www.bera.ac.uk/publication/autumn-2018.

Seleznyov, S., & Rolls, L. (2021). Easily lost in translation: Introducing Japanese lesson study in a UK school. In Eleanore Hargreaves and Luke Rolls (Eds.), Re-imagining professional development in schools (pp. 49–63). Abingdon: Routledge.

Sylva, K., Melhuish, E., Sammons, P., Siraj-Blatchford, I., & Taggart, B. (2010). Early childhood matters: Evidence from the effective pre-school and primary education project. Oxford: Routledge.

UNICEF Rights Respecting Schools. Accessed at https://www.unicef.org.uk/rights
-respecting-schools/.

Vygotsky, L. S. (1986). Thought and language. Massachusetts: Massachusetts Institute of
Technology.

Wilson, E. (2017). Impact study of the Centre of Excellence Programme: Technical report.
МОНИТОРИНГ И ЭВАЛЮАЦИЯ ПРОГРАММЦЕНТРА ПЕДАГОГИЧЕСКОГО
МАСТЕРСТВА. https://doi.org/10.17863/CAM.12373.

11

Promoting inclusion and equity in schools through practitioner– researcher partnerships

Mel Ainscow

In this chapter I draw on my own experiences to consider how partnerships between practitioners and researchers can facilitate inclusive developments in schools. As I will explain, this involves an engagement with evidence generated through a range of methods, much of which requires listening to the voices of those involved in the process of education. Such evidence can make the familiar unfamiliar in ways that challenge assumptions, encourage the sharing of ideas and stimulate joint efforts to develop more inclusive practices.

It is important to note, however, that none of this provides a simple way forward. To gain the potential benefits, it is necessary to address the challenges involved in using processes of collaborative inquiry within the busy contexts of schools.

The research programme

My interest in the idea of teacher–researcher partnerships began in the 1990s as a result of my involvement in the Improving the Quality of Education for All (IQEA) project. Initially this comprised a group of us at the University of Cambridge Institute of Education working with a small network of schools in and around London (Ainscow and Hopkins, 1992). Subsequently, IQEA led to developments in other parts of the world, including Hong Kong, Iceland and Puerto Rico (see Ainscow, 2016, for more detailed accounts of some of these projects). All of these initiatives involved teams of university researchers working in partnership with staff teams drawn from networks of schools to identify ways in which the learning of all members of the school community – students, parents and staff – could be enhanced.

DOI: 10.4324/9781003137634-11

Ideas that emerged from IQEA were taken forward and developed through three further studies, all of which were carried out in policy contexts that hardly seemed conducive to the promotion of equity. The first study, 'Understanding and Developing Inclusive Practices in Schools', occurred between 2000 and 2004. It involved a network of 25 urban schools in three English local education authorities with support from teams in three partner universities. Within the network schools, the use of evidence of various forms to study teaching was seen to help foster the development of more inclusive practices (see Ainscow, Booth and Dyson, 2006).

The second study involved an equity research network that took place in the north of England between 2006 and 2011 (see Ainscow et al., 2012, for a detailed account). It was located in a district characterised by socio-economic disadvantage, and social and ethnic segregation. Once again it involved staff inquiry groups, usually consisting of five or six members representing different perspectives within their school communities.

These ideas were explored further in a very different context, that of a network of schools in the state of Queensland, Australia, where equity is a long-standing and seemingly intractable challenge (Harris, Carrington and Ainscow, 2017). The schools within the research network explored possibilities for reframing how high-stakes accountability data were used. The focus was on finding ethical ways of ensuring quality education for all students, rather than solely relying on the reduced versions of realities reflected in accountability data.

An inquiry-based approach

These studies were all guided by the principles of inclusion and equity, summed up by UNESCO (2017) as 'Every learner matters and matters equally.' Within the studies, staff inquiry teams used a variety of collaborative inquiry methods to analyse their school contexts. These included the use of mutual lesson observation, sometimes through video recordings, and comments collected from students about teaching and learning arrangements within a school. Such approaches provided 'interruptions' that stimulated self-questioning, creativity and action. In so doing, they sometimes led to a reframing of perceived problems that, in turn, drew the teacher's attention to overlooked possibilities for addressing barriers to participation and learning. In this way, differences amongst students and staff – within and between schools – became a catalyst for improvement.

Meanwhile, teams of university researchers supported, recorded and analysed the collaborative inquiries as they occurred within the networks of schools. As a result, the approach came to be defined as a process of knowledge generation that occurs when practitioner and researcher knowledge meet in particular sites, aimed at producing new knowledge about ways in which broad values might better be realised in future practice (Ainscow et al., 2009). These experiences were usually documented in the form of accounts of practice, generated through a process of collaborative writing with colleagues in schools.

Working with schools in this country and overseas, those of us participating in this research programme became increasingly aware of the social, political and cultural complexities this involves. This led to the development of an overall framework to guide the development of the collaborative inquiries, which we refer to as an 'ecology of equity' (Ainscow et al., 2012). This formulation involves three interlinked areas within which equity issues arise:

- *Within-schools* – These are issues that arise from school and teacher practices.
- *Between-schools* – These are issues that arise from the characteristics of local school systems.
- *Beyond-schools* – This far-reaching arena includes the wider policy context within which schools operate; the family processes and resources which shape how children learn and develop; the interests and understandings of the professionals working in schools; and the demographics, economics, cultures and histories of the areas served by schools.

In what follows, I use this framework to explore the potential of teacher–researcher partnerships to promote inclusion and equity in schools. In so doing, I use short accounts of practice, written in partnership with colleagues in schools, to illustrate what this involves.

An inquiring school

Our research suggests that 'schools know more than they use' (Ainscow, 2020). This means that the starting point for strengthening the work of a school is with the sharing of existing practices through collaboration amongst staff, leading to experimentation with new ways of working that will reach out to all students. The account in Box 11.1 illustrates what this entails.

Box 11.1 All different, all equal

The school, which caters to about 500 pupils in the age range 3–11, serves a multicultural community. Today there are 23 different nationalities, with 19 different languages spoken amongst the families.

An assistant head teacher worked with a group of her colleagues in coordinating efforts to strengthen the commitment to inclusion in the school. She began by holding a staff meeting to brief her colleagues. Specifically, she asked them to work in small groups to identify children they considered to be at risk of marginalisation or exclusion.

Both the head and the assistant head agreed that all of this 'was a bit scary'. For example, the discussions that took place brought to the surface potentially uncomfortable issues, such as attitudes towards immigration, 'children who smell' and feelings about a child who was considered to be odd.

Further information was gathered from parents using a questionnaire, which had to be translated for some families. Another staff meeting was devoted to discussion as to how the views of children could be gathered. This started with a consideration of existing practices in the school for listening to the voices of pupils, which led to a list of such activities.

The assistant head and her colleagues analysed the responses for each class and then for the whole school. Though this was time-consuming, they believed that it was helpful in drawing attention to issues in the school that needed addressing. They felt that it was particularly important to capture the views of new arrivals.

At a further meeting, the staff had a chance to look at the data that had been collected. As a result, it was decided to allocate a two-week period for the use of various pupil voice activities in every class. The assistant head organised a schedule for this.

As each teacher carried out the activities in their classes, a colleague would observe the process, looking specifically at the way individual children responded. In this way they were able to integrate pupil voice activities into their day-to-day teaching and learning, something that subsequently became a part of usual practice across the school.

By the end of the school year there was strong evidence that the strategies used had led to significant changes in thinking and practice. As part of this process, safety in the school became a major area of discussion, something that had not been anticipated.

At the heart of the processes in schools like this, where professional learning takes place, is the development of a common language with which colleagues can talk to one another and, indeed to themselves, about detailed aspects of their practice. Without such a language, teachers find it difficult to experiment with new possibilities (Ainscow, Booth and Dyson, 2006).

Much of what teachers do during the intensive encounters that occur every day in classrooms is carried out at an automatic, intuitive level. Furthermore, there is little time to stop and think. This is why having the opportunity to see colleagues at work is so crucial to the success of attempts to develop practice. It is through shared experiences that colleagues can help one another to articulate what they currently do and define what they might like to do. It is also the means whereby space is created within which taken-for-granted assumptions about particular groups of learners can be subjected to mutual critique.

An engagement with evidence of various kinds to study teaching within a school can help in generating such a language of practice. This, in turn, can foster the development of practices that are more effective in engaging learners who are seen as hard to reach. Specifically, it can create space for rethinking by interrupting existing discourses and questioning usual ways of working.

The starting point for such processes is often with a consideration of statistical evidence regarding student progress. However, the need to dig deeper into factors that influence learner progress usually requires an engagement with qualitative forms of evidence. Particularly powerful techniques in this respect involve the use of mutual lesson observation, sometimes through video recordings, and evidence collected from students about teaching and learning arrangements within a school (Ainscow and Messiou, 2017).

Under certain conditions such approaches help to make the familiar unfamiliar in ways that stimulate self-questioning, creativity and action. In so doing they can sometimes lead to a reframing of perceived problems that, in turn, draws the teacher's attention to overlooked possibilities for addressing barriers to participation and learning. In this way, differences amongst students, staff and schools become a catalyst for improvement.

Here, the concern with the principles of inclusion and equity means that there also has to be a focus on the thinking that lies *behind* actions and the impacts of such thinking on practices (Sadker et al., 2009). In particular, there must be a concern with the attitudes and assumptions that influence what teachers do, some of which may be unconscious, and how these can be modified through dialogues with others, especially with learners themselves (Messiou and Ainscow, 2020).

Schools learning together

The approach I have outlined so far is based on the idea of those within schools collecting and engaging with various forms of evidence in order to stimulate moves to create more inclusive practices. The research summarised earlier provides encouraging evidence of the potential of this approach. However, it has also thrown light on the difficulties in putting such thinking into practice, particularly within policy contexts that put pressure on schools to compete. This points to some of the limitations of within-school strategies, suggesting that these should be complemented with efforts to encourage greater cooperation between schools, as in the example in Box 11.2.

Box 11.2 Learning from differences

A network of primary schools worked in partnership with a local university education department to bring teachers and researchers together. The schools followed a model of collaborative inquiry that draws on teachers' professional expertise and wider research knowledge to explore new ways of supporting learners from economically disadvantaged backgrounds. Overall, the aim was to improve the learning opportunities, experiences and outcomes of all children, and particularly those experiencing barriers to learning.

Each school determined its own focus for research, starting by identifying issues that were causing concern or were puzzling in some way. They then followed a structured research programme where the teachers and university researchers collected and shared evidence about the school's practices, whilst drawing on ideas from wider research, so that they could develop a rich, deep understanding of what is happening to learners in school. This evidence was then used to stimulate new thinking and professional learning about current practices, and to identify strategies for responding to the research findings.

The schools used exchange visits to generate evidence regarding their shared focus on developing more inclusive practices. The aim of these visits was to look specifically at relative strengths and weaknesses within schools in the network, using differences to stimulate new thinking.

The most successful visits were usually characterised by a sense of mutual learning amongst hosts and visitors. It was noticeable, too, that the focus for these visits often took some time to identify and clarify. Indeed, the preliminary negotiations that took place were in themselves a key aspect of the process.

During one such visit, the visiting teachers were each invited to observe two children. A simple observation framework, designed by the staff research group in the host school, focused on children's interactions with peers and teachers.

The children to be observed were chosen by the class teacher, who was the deputy head of the school. They were nominated on the basis that they were the children he knew least about in his class. In addition to observations, the visiting teachers were asked to interview these children. Again, a loose structure was devised, but the main emphasis was on the visiting teachers following up on things that they had seen during observations.

Afterwards, one of the visiting teachers said that the day had been 'absolutely fascinating'. She added: 'There is no way in your own school you could do this.' This seemed to be borne out by some of the imagery used by students about their teacher during the interviews that day. For example, one commented: 'He's like a piranha looking round the class. He knows when I'm not listening.' And another student remarked: 'He could be a really good teacher if he could explain but he gets too frustrated.' The joking response by the class teacher to such statements was 'I want to go home! I've had enough now!'

> The personal nature of these observations, and the teacher's willingness to listen to this feedback with colleagues from his own and another school present, illustrate the extent of the challenge that was sometimes involved in this sort of collaboration.

There is considerable evidence that forms of school-to-school collaboration of this kind can strengthen improvement processes by adding to the range of expertise made available (Ainscow, 2015; Ainscow and Howes, 2007; Muijs et al., 2011). In particular, these studies indicate that collaboration between schools has an enormous potential for fostering the capacity of education systems to respond to learner diversity. More specifically, they show how such partnerships can sometimes help to reduce the polarisation of schools, to the particular benefit of those students who seem marginalised at the edges of the system, and whose progress and attitudes cause concern.

There is also evidence that when schools seek to develop more collaborative ways of working this can have an impact on how teachers perceive themselves and their work (Rosenholtz, 1989). Specifically, comparisons of practices in different schools can lead teachers to view underachieving students in a new light. In this way, learners who cannot easily be educated within a school's established routines come to be seen less as 'having problems' but as encouraging teachers to re-examine their practices in order to make them more responsive and flexible.

Beyond the school gate

Ensuring that all children receive effective support from their families and communities is essential to the promotion of equity. This in turn means ensuring that schools can build on the resources offered by families and support the extension of those resources, as illustrated in the account in Box 11.3.

Box 11.3 Crossing boundaries

The word 'boundaries' frequently comes up during a visit to this primary school, which serves a diverse, multicultural community. First, the visitor notes the metal fence with pointed spikes that stakes out the physical boundaries of the school, whilst at the same time discouraging would-be intruders. Then, there is much talk of the cultural boundaries children cross each day as they move between contexts that are influenced by different traditions, religions and languages. There is also a sense of boundaries created by the well-articulated rules and procedures that dictate the ways in which staff and children go about their business.

The account is particularly interesting in that not so long ago the behaviour of students in the school was a major problem. Nowadays, things are much improved.

The school takes particular steps to support children and families as they move between different cultures. On first arrival in the nursery, many of the children have limited language and this has to be a priority, leading to what is often rapid progress. Staff are also sensitive to the fact that some of the children attend additional lessons at the local Mosque in the late afternoon.

Considerable efforts have been made to ensure parental support for the school's efforts to foster a more cooperative working atmosphere. The head explains that she has tried to convince parents that it was necessary to 'break the cycle of violence'.

There was also a period when some parents, particularly some of the fathers, would come into school to be abusive to the head teacher and other members of staff. Sometimes the head used what she referred to as 'veiled threats', for example: 'I've told them that I would exclude their child if things don't improve.'

In fact, the head is opposed to the exclusion of pupils, although at times she has been forced to use this approach, not least in order to attract support from outside the school. Gradually, however, the views of parents have become much more positive, as reflected by their involvement in morning assemblies and support for other school events. Here the family literacy programme that the school introduced has proved to be particularly successful.

At the same time, tensions between home and school do still exist. For example, one teacher comments that a lot of the children are related and sometimes they bring family disputes with them into school. Differences in expectations also surface on some occasions. The head explains: 'For example, some mothers will dress the boys and leave the girls to dress themselves.'

One teacher, talking about her class of 11-year-olds, notes, 'Every single boy here smokes. They steal cigarettes from home.'

Nevertheless, the visitor is struck by the quiet atmosphere, and the sense of calm and order around the school. Senior staff explain how they have worked with the parents to foster this atmosphere. One explained, 'We tell them, you have to model the behaviour you want from the children.'

So what is it that has led to these striking improvements? In particular, what forms of leadership practice have been used? It seems that there have been two overlapping phases of development, each emphasising rather different approaches.

> During the first of these two phases, much of the leadership seemed to have been centred on the head teacher herself. More recently, a different approach has emerged, one that is characterised by an emphasis on collaborative inquiry approaches that involve staff, pupils, family members and, in some situations, community representatives.
>
> In explaining all of this, the head teacher seemed to be particularly sensitive to the challenges faced by her colleagues. She noted that 'there is too much pressure on everybody'. Having said that, she appears to have been successful in developing a sense of common purpose and a commitment to mutual support that stretches beyond the school building. Here, too, there is little evidence of any distinction between the roles of teaching and non-teaching staff. One support assistant commented, 'We're all involved in everything.'

My colleagues and I have seen many examples like this of what can happen when what schools do is aligned in a coherent strategy with the efforts of other local players – employers, community groups, colleges, universities and public services (Ainscow, 2016; Drever, McLean and Lowden, 2021). This does not necessarily mean schools doing more, but it does imply partnerships beyond the school gate, where partners multiply the impacts of each other's efforts. Our experience suggests that the success of such partnerships is dependent upon a common understanding of what those involved are trying to achieve and, once again, an engagement with various forms of evidence to stimulate collective effort.

Such area-based initiatives are intended to involve a wide range of partners working together in a coordinated manner. Schools are often the key to these partnerships and may be their principal drivers. However, this is not simply about enlisting other agencies and organisations in support of a school-centred agenda. Rather, they are aimed at improving a wide range of outcomes for children and young people, including but not restricted to educational outcomes – much less, narrowly conceived attainment outcomes. Health and well-being, personal and social development, thriving in the early years, and positive employment outcomes are all as important as how well children do academically in school.

None of this arises from a downgrading of the importance of attainment but from a recognition that all outcomes for children and young people are interrelated. Furthermore, the factors which promote or inhibit one outcome are very likely to be the factors which promote or inhibit outcomes as a whole.

As a result, the focus of such initiatives is the population of an area, rather than the population of schools per se, and they may be led by non-educational organisations, such as housing associations or regeneration partnerships. Moreover, they are envisaged as being long-term and are committed to acting strategically, basing their actions of a deep analysis of the local area's underlying problems and possibilities (Kerr, Dyson and Gallannaugh, 2016).

Such approaches draw on the principles underpinning the highly acclaimed Harlem Children's Zone in the USA (Whitehurst and Croft, 2010). This project involves efforts to improve outcomes for children and young people in areas of disadvantage through an approach that they characterise as being 'doubly holistic'. That is to say, they seek to develop coordinated efforts to tackle the factors that disadvantage children and enhance the factors which support them, across all aspects of their lives, and across their lifespans, from conception through to adulthood. The Harlem project has been described by researchers as 'arguably the most ambitious social experiment to alleviate poverty of our time' (Dobbie and Fryer, 2009, p. 1).

Developments such as these have implications for the various key stakeholders within education systems. In particular, teachers, especially those in senior positions, have to see themselves as having a wider responsibility for all children and young people in their local area, not just those who attend their own schools. They also have to develop patterns of working that enable them to have the flexibility to cooperate with other schools and their wider communities.

Making sense of the process

Underlying the use of collaborative inquiry to promote inclusion and equity within education systems is a common pattern. Most importantly, it involves an engagement with evidence collected by practitioners with support from university researchers. Usually, this begins with a consideration of an established set of practices that are largely taken for granted. An interruption occurs that problematises these practices and provokes consideration of why current practice is the way it is and how it might be improved. This may then lead to actual changes in practice but not always.

Given my focus on the possibilities of developing more equitable ways of working, this begs two important questions:

- What is it that provokes the problematisation of established practice?
- And why does this necessarily lead to more inclusive practices?

In addressing these questions, we have found it helpful to draw on a range of theoretical resources. One that has proved particularly powerful is the idea of 'communities of practice', as developed by Etienne Wenger (1998), focusing specifically on the way he sees learning as 'a characteristic of practice'.

Wenger explains practice in terms of those things that individuals within a community do, drawing on available resources, to further a set of shared goals. This goes beyond how practitioners complete their tasks, to include, for example, how they make it through the day, commiserating about the pressures and constraints within which they have to operate. Practices are thus ways of negotiating meaning through social action, which underlines the importance of the conversations embedded in teachers' day-to-day work, as referred to earlier in this chapter.

In explaining this process, Wenger argues that communities 'reify' their practices by producing concrete representations of them, such as tools, symbols, rules and documents (and even concepts and theories). However, these reifications have to be given meaning through a process of participation, which consists of the shared experiences and negotiations that result from social interaction within a purposive community. The implication of this is that ideas and materials generated within one context cannot simply be lifted and transferred elsewhere.

Wenger offers some helpful guidelines for judging whether a particular social collective can be considered as a community of practice. Since such a community involves mutual engagement, a negotiated enterprise and a repertoire of resources and practices, its members should be expected to

- interact more intensively with and know more about others in the group than those outside the group;

- hold their actions accountable (and be willing for others in the community to hold them accountable) more to the group's joint enterprise than to some other enterprise;

- be more able to evaluate the actions of other members of the group than the actions of those outside the group; and

- draw on locally produced resources and artefacts to negotiate meaning, more so than those that are imported from outside the group.

By these criteria the staff teams in the studies reported in this chapter can, to varying degrees, be seen as communities of practice. Much of the evidence for this assertion rests on what was witnessed of the ongoing and informal interactions between groups of teachers. So, for example, amongst staff inquiry groups, hours of meetings, shared experiences and informal discussions over hurriedly taken lunches were observed. These sometimes involved the development of particular meanings of frequently used phrases, such as 'raising standards', 'equity' and 'inclusion'. These shared meanings help to define a teacher's experience of being a teacher. In the same way it can be assumed that groups of colleagues doing similar work in another school have their own shared histories that give meaning to being a teacher in that particular context.

There is no reason to suppose that teachers are conscious of such processes for the most part, though occasionally they may be able to articulate their importance for developments in their schools. What was significant in some of the project schools, however, was not simply the high level of collaboration that was claimed by the teachers (such claims can, of course, be challenged), but the implication that 'good practice' is defined through such collaborative processes.

In these contexts, good practice is defined not by what researchers or policymakers say, or others do elsewhere, but by what 'we' think 'works here'.

Once again, the notion of communities of practice is important here in that it views practice as being intimately bound up with the norms, values, beliefs and assumptions of a group of teachers in a particular school context. The implication is that practices cannot be understood – or, more to the point, changed – without also understanding and changing those local patterns. What is needed is something that disturbs existing assumptions and provokes some sort of reformulation, both of practice and of the thinking on which it is based.

Changing practices

This relationship between practice and local meaning-making suggests that external agendas cannot simply be 'imposed' on communities of practice. Specifically, external proposals for change, however powerfully enforced, have to be endowed with meaning within local contexts before they can inform practice. This implies that schools (or, at least, the communities of practice within schools) may well negotiate local meanings for those agendas that are different from those of the formulators themselves or, indeed, of other schools.

The significance of communities of practice is usefully summed up by Wenger (1998, p. 85) when he argues:

> Communities of practice are not intrinsically beneficial or harmful. … Yet they are a force to be reckoned with, for better or for worse. As a locus of engagement in action, interpersonal relationships, shared knowledge, and negotiation of enterprises, such communities hold the key to real transformation – the kind that has real effect on people's lives … The influence of other forces (e.g. the control of an institution or the authority of an individual) are no less important, but they are mediated by the communities in which their meanings are negotiated in practice.

There is an important caveat here. Communities of practice 'are not intrinsically beneficial or harmful' precisely because the values and assumptions to which they will subscribe are determined locally. In terms of the development of practices, there is nothing inherent in even the most dynamic community of practice which predisposes it towards generating more equitable outcomes. Indeed, a dynamic community that defends the status quo or moves rapidly in a non-inclusive direction is entirely conceivable. So, for example, Yurkofsky et al. (2020) argue:

> Educators who believe in supporting equitable schools can still carry implicit biases that affect their practices, and teachers who aspire to improve their pedagogy may in practice have trouble giving up the belief that external

factors (e.g., parental and neighbourhood influence) – as opposed to their own actions as teachers – are the primary determinants of students' achievement.

(p. 415)

What, then, makes the difference between instances where collaborative meaning-making create a potential for the development of inclusive practices and those where such practices actually arise? For this, two sets of concepts from the literature on organisational development are helpful: Argyris and Schön's (1996) idea of 'single- and double-loop learning'; and Skrtic's (1991) distinction between bureaucracies and adhocracies, together with his notion of the recognition of 'anomalies' as the catalyst for the transition from one to the other.

Argyris and Schön (1996) argue that organisations are capable of learning, but to different extents and, indeed, at different levels. What they refer to as single-loop learning takes the form of what in an educational context might be called the improvement of existing practices, but without any fundamental reconsideration of the assumptions upon which those practices are based. On the other hand, double-loop learning asks questions about the underlying aims of practice and about the implicit theories which underpin it.

Skrtic (1991) also presupposes a fundamental distinction in the way organisations solve problems. He argues that bureaucratic organisations deal with such problems by creating different subunits and specialisms to contain them, leaving practice elsewhere in the organisation undisturbed. So, for example, a school may decide to establish a separate unit to deal with the problems of disruptive behaviour, such that it avoids the need to examine ways in which its own practices may have helped to generate these problems. On the other hand, what Skrtic calls adhocratic organisations see such problems as an opportunity to rethink their existing practices in fundamental ways. Moreover, he argues that bureaucratic organisations can become adhocratic if enough of their members recognise 'anomalies' in existing practice.

It seems, then, that faced with some form of disturbance – what I referred to earlier as an interruption – some schools will close down the problem and make largely technical responses. Others may open up the problem and use it as the basis for a critical interrogation and reformulation of practice, and the assumptions on which practice is based. However, as Skrtic argues, someone has to recognise a problem as an anomaly and convince others of its significance.

Final thoughts

As I have explained, successful educational change requires the coming together of different perspectives and experiences in a process of social learning and knowledge creation within particular settings. Researchers who get involved in such processes must expect to face many difficulties and dilemmas. Consequently, they have to develop new skills in creating collaborative partnerships that cross borders between actors who have different professional experiences.

Successful partnerships involve a complex social process within which colleagues with very different experiences, beliefs and methodological assumptions learn how to live with one another's differences and, even more difficult, learn how to learn from these differences. This is why it is important to be clear that, in this kind of collaborative research, academic researchers both conduct research and are themselves the subjects of research, as their thinking and practices are examined by themselves and others. In this way, as they engage with evidence about the work of practitioners, they too are constantly challenged to think through their own practices as researchers.

Meanwhile, the different roles and sociocultural contexts of practitioners and academics create a complex set of power relations, which have to be factored into the process of introducing ideas from research (Ainscow, Chapman and Hadfield, 2020). This reveals how those who work in the field derive their power from being primary actors: they can cause things to happen or to cease to happen in a way that is denied to academics. Meanwhile, researchers derive their power from standing at a distance: they can problematise the actions of practitioners and policymakers.

At their most productive, these power relationships lead to dialogue in which the academics' views are informed by the realities of practice, and practitioners' views change in response to 'outsider' critique. At their least productive, academics mistake their distant position for superiority, and claim moral and intellectual authority over practitioners; whilst practitioners dismiss academics as being unworldly and resist their critiques. Managing these relationships is crucial to the success of attempts to use collaborative research to stimulate the improvement of policy and practice in the field.

Relevant to this, Hiebert, Gallimore and Stigler (2002) suggest that fruitful forms of collaboration require a reorientation of values and goals amongst both groups. So, they argue, teachers need to move away from the dominant view that teaching is a 'personal and private activity'. Rather, teachers have to adopt the 'more risky view' that it is an activity that can be continuously improved, provided it is made public and examined openly. At the same time, they argue that researchers must stop undervaluing the knowledge teachers acquire in their own classrooms.

Acknowledgements

Lots of colleagues have contributed to the programme of research described in this chapter, too many to mention. However, the ideas of Alan Dyson were particularly important to the argument I developed.

References

Ainscow, M. (2015). *Towards self-improving school systems: Lessons from a city challenge*. London: Routledge.

Ainscow, M. (2016). *Struggles for equity in education: The selected works of Mel Ainscow*. London: Routledge World Library of Educationalists series.

Ainscow, M. (2020). Promoting inclusion and equity in education: Lessons from international experiences. *The Nordic Journal of Studies on Educational Policy*, 6(1), 7–16.

Ainscow, M., Booth, T., & Dyson, A., with Farrell, P., Frankham, J., Gallannaugh, F., Howes, A. & Smith, R. (2006). *Improving schools, developing inclusion*. London: Routledge.

Ainscow, M., Chapman, C., & Hadfield, M. (2020). *Changing education systems: A research-based approach*. London: Routledge.

Ainscow, M., Dyson, A., Goldrick, S., & Kerr, K. (2009). Using research to foster equity and inclusion within the context of new labour educational reforms. In C. Chapman & G. M. Gunter (eds.), *Radical reforms: Perspectives on an era of educational change*. London: Routledge.

Ainscow, M., Dyson, A., Goldrick, S., & West, M. (2012). *Developing equitable education systems*. London: Routledge.

Ainscow, M., & Hopkins D. (1992). Aboard the 'Moving School'. *Educational Leadership*, 50(3), 79–81.

Ainscow, M., & Howes, A. (2007). Working together to improve urban secondary schools: A study of practice in one city. *School Leadership and Management*, 27, 285–300.

Ainscow, M., & Messiou, K. (2017). Engaging with the views of students to promote inclusion in education. *Journal of Educational Change*, 19(1), 1–17.

Argyris, C., & Schon, D. (1996). *Organisational learning II: Theory, method and practice*. Reading, MA: Addison Wesley.

Dobbie, W., & Fryer, R. G. (2009). *Are high-quality schools enough to close the achievement gap? Evidence from a bold social experiment in Harlem*. Cambridge, MA: Harvard University.

Drever, A., McLean, J., & Lowden, K. (2021). Focusing on place: Working beyond the school gate. In C. Chapman & M. Ainscow (Eds.), *Educational equity: Pathways to success*. London: Routledge.

Harris, J., Carrington, S., & Ainscow, M. with Comber, B., Ehrich, L., Klenowski, V., Smeed, J. & Spina, J. (2017). *Promoting equity in schools: Collaboration, inquiry and ethical leadership*. London: Routledge.

Hiebert, J., Gallimore, R., & Stigler, J. W. (2002). A knowledge base for the teaching profession: What would it look like and how can we get one? *Educational Researcher*, 31(5), 3–15.

Kerr, K., Dyson, A., & Gallannaugh, F. (2016). Conceptualising school-community relations in disadvantaged neighbourhoods: Mapping the literature. *Educational Research*, 58(3), 265–282.

Messiou, K., & Ainscow, M. (2020). Inclusive inquiry: Student-teacher dialogue as a means of promoting inclusion in schools. *British Journal of Educational Research*, 46(3), 670–687.

Muijs, D., Ainscow, M., Chapman, C., & West, M. (2011). *Collaboration and networking in education*. London: Springer.

Rosenholtz, S. J. (1989). *Teachers' workplace: The social organization of schools*. New York: Longman.

Sadker, D. M., Sadker, M., Zittleman, K. R., & Sadker, M. (2009). *Still failing at fairness: How gender bias cheats girls and boys in school and what we can do about it*. New York: Scribner.

Skrtic, T. M. (1991). The special education paradox: Equity as the way to excellence. *Harvard Educational Review*, 61(2), 148–206.

UNESCO. (2017). *A guide for ensuring inclusion and equity in education.* Paris: UNESCO.

Wenger, E. (1998). *Communities of practice: Learning, meaning and identity.* Cambridge: Cambridge University Press.

Whitehurst, G. J., & Croft, M. (2010). *The Harlem Children's Zone, Promise Neighborhoods, and the Broader, Bolder Approach to Education.* Washington, DC: The Brookings Institution.

Yurkofsky, M. M., Peterson, A. J., Mehta, J. D., Horwitz-Willis, R., & Frumin, K. M. (2020). Research on continuous improvement: Exploring the complexities of managing educational change. *Review of Research in Education*, 44, 403–433.

Afterword: why inclusion matters beyond primary school: University ... a space for all?

Graham Virgo

When I first started teaching at a university over 30 years ago, one of my students, Nick, used a wheelchair. I was providing teaching to small groups in an elegant room in a 19th-century building on the first floor, with no lift. Nick was carried to my room by his fellow students and then returned downstairs to his wheelchair at the end. Such was the indignity of the experience, I subsequently taught him and the other students in Nick's bedroom. That should not have happened then and it would not happen now. There are legal obligations to make buildings accessible and so inclusive. But inclusion is so much more than accessibility. Nick had been included, but at the expense of his dignity.

It is not enough in education to be inclusive, whether that be at primary school, secondary school, or in further and higher education. Inclusion must be dignified. It must also not be patronising. The obligation to be inclusive, whether that obligation is legal or moral, should enable a levelling up and not a levelling down. But neither should it involve a levelling beyond; equality of opportunity is at the heart of the inclusivity agenda. And it is not just students' experiences of learning and teaching which need to be inclusive; inclusion affects the whole education community as well. And that community includes the staff who provide and support the education.

It does not, however, follow that inclusion requires all barriers to be removed. Some barriers are legitimate. For example, many universities impose entrance requirements, both as a way of managing competition for limited places and to reflect the intellectual standards required to meet the demands of a particular degree course. But in many universities, including my own, the open access agenda enables us to offer a wide variety of non-degree courses, with their own qualifications, regardless of the student's previous educational experience. And with the growth in digital education, open access enables us to offer courses

DOI: 10.4324/9781003137634-12

around the world, so making a university-delivered education even more inclusive.

At a residential university, once legitimate education barriers have been overcome, we must ensure inclusivity of educational experience regardless of the reason why a student might otherwise be excluded, whether this is due to physical or mental disability, sex, race or sexual orientation. Universities, like other institutions, are subject to legal obligations under the Equality Act 2010 to ensure that there is no discrimination against students by virtue of these and other protected characteristics. But the moral obligation to ensure inclusivity extends beyond these characteristics, requiring us to reflect on other reasons why students might be excluded or perceive that they are excluded. For example, the widening participation agenda, which ensures that universities engage with under-represented communities, should mean that, when students from these communities are admitted, they are fully included in what we provide. This may mean that universities need to do more to support such students, not necessarily because of lower academic attainment but because of reduced opportunities to develop academic skills and to be exposed to opportunities to expand their cultural capital. It may also require financial support to ensure that the educational opportunities and wider student experiences are available to them as well.

Inclusion may be achieved by adjustment, but there is also an opportunity to embed inclusivity by reviewing every aspect of what we do and how we deliver it and not accepting that just because we have done it that way for many years we cannot change – we can. This does not mean throwing out the baby with the bathwater. It does mean being conscious always of the risk of exclusionary practices and ensuring that we are willing and able to adapt accordingly.

How we examine and assess students is a very good example of how inclusionary practice can work for the benefit of all. Examinations at many universities, including my own, have traditionally been for three hours and handwritten. For a significant number of students reasonable adjustments have had to be implemented, ranging from allowing them to use a computer to giving them additional time, sometimes very significantly. In all cases they will be marked out for different treatment: having to take the exams in different locations and having gone through a sometimes tortuous process to determine what adjustment is reasonable. An alternative is to focus on diversifying assessment (through online assessment, open-book papers, extended essays and coursework) for all. This will often have other pedagogical advantages, through assessing different skills and capabilities. But diversification of assessment will often be inclusive, by removing the need for many students to have bespoke adjustment and so ensuring that they are included.

Inclusive practice at university also encompasses the way teaching is delivered. Where teaching is delivered in person, the recording of lectures (known as 'lecture capture') benefits all students. It means that individual students who by virtue of their circumstances need to use recordings to assist with their learning do not need to have bespoke provision. But it also means that the student who misses a lecture due to illness can engage with the lecture later. In addition, lecture capture enables students to revisit material which they found difficult at the time (and lecturers can have access to data enabling them to identify which parts of the lecture students revisit) and provides a significant tool in assisting in the revision of material. Recording of lectures for all is a truly inclusionary practice.

As we rebuild from the impact of the Covid pandemic, we should be in a position to ensure that inclusive teaching, learning and assessment practices are fully embedded in our universities. When the first lockdown started we needed to adapt quickly. Digital technology enabled us to assess students wherever they might be in the world, to teach asynchronously and synchronously and to expand the materials for learning significantly through digital resources. This looks truly inclusive. But we have to be careful. The risks of exclusion and marginalisation are significant. Reliance on technology has exposed digital poverty, whether it is the lack of appropriate hardware or poor broadband. Students forced to work from home are often in environments which are not conducive to their focused engagement, for example through the lack of quiet space. The learning loss suffered in primary and secondary schools will have a very significant detrimental impact on widening participation, unless there is concerted action by universities, schools, communities and government to provide concentrated and meaningful support. At universities, loneliness, arising from the reliance on impersonal digital technology, can be shown already to exclude from the benefits of a university experience. Lack of social contact will impact on mental health and well-being. As McCloskey (2020) identified, 'the mental health and psychosocial impact of restricted movement, school closures, and subsequent isolation are likely to intensify already high levels of stress, especially for vulnerable youth', leading to reduced learning and educational outcomes. If there is one thing that we have learned from the response to the pandemic, it is the importance of in-person interaction and social engagement, otherwise there is a danger that the significant advances made through inclusive education will be undermined by a new psychosocial exclusion.

Whether it is reflections on the impact of the pandemic or the research and thinking about inclusive educational practices, and whether it is at primary school or at university, what is undeniably clear is that inclusivity matters.

Reference

McCloskey, S. (2020). Development education, COVID-19 and neoliberalism. In P. Carmody, G. McCann, C. Colleran & C. O'Halloran (eds.), *COVID-19 in the Global South* (pp. 39–50). Bristol: Bristol University Press.

Index

Page numbers in *italics* represent either figures or photographs, while page numbers in **bold** mark tables.

Abdu'Allah, F. 91, *92*, 93–100, *101*, 102, *103*, 104–106
ableism 15–16, 19; and deficit language 19, *20*, 138, 142–143; and insults 19–20
abuse, and trauma 111–112
accessibility, and inclusion 177
accommodation, term use 22
activism, and disability 14
ADHD (attention deficit hyperactivity disorder) 45–46, 51, 55, 118
Adjaye, D. *104*, 105
affirmation: and ESPs *117*; language around 24–26
Ainscow, M. 160–173
anxiety, and autistic students 53
Argyris, C. 172
art education 93, 98–99; and cultural influences 99–100
Assessment for Learning stickers 135, *136*
Atkinson, E. 68
attribution theory 152
Australia, equity in 161
autism 45–54, 56–58, 147–149
Awel y Môr Primary School 77, 80; Families First programme 84–85; Family Engagement Officer (FEO) 82–83, 88; and parents 80–84, 88–89; Senior Leadership Team (SLT) 80–83

Baldacchino, J. 91, *92*, 93–106
Beardon, L. 52, 54
behavioural difficulties, impacts of 108–109
Berry, K. 67
Biddulph, J. 94
Biddulph, M. 61–76
Bion, W. R. 113

Birmingham City Council legal case 70–71
Black, Asian and minority ethnic (BAME) communities, and autism 48
Black Curriculum 152–153
Black History Month 98
blackboards, vs. whiteboards *95*
Black-Hawkins, K. 1–12
Booth, T. 77
Bosanquet, P. 125–139
boundaries 166–168
Bowie, D. 73
Bradlow, J. 64
Bruner, J. S. 131, 144
bullying: against autistic children 58; and homophobia 63–64, 73
Burnard, P. 94

Campbell, F. 15
Child Poverty Action Group 80
'childhood innocence' 63
children 150; backgrounds of 79; communication development restrictions in 154; exclusion of 142; identities of 67; on inclusive classrooms **11**, 12; lived experiences of 10; with mental health needs 109–110; parents supporting 166–167
Children and Families Act (2014) 109
Clavering, E. 22
Coe, R. 129, 137
cognition 147; *see also* learning
cognitive–participation–access (CPA) 154
Coleman-Fountain, E. 22
collaborative action research 30, 161–162, 165, 169–171, 173
colonial experiences 92–93, 97–98

Columbus, C. 96
communicative development 154
communities of practice 169–172
confidentiality 24
containment 113
COVID-19 pandemic 179; impacts on education 7, 152–153; and school emotional climates 65; and schools 65, 86
Cox, J. 74
Crenshaw, K. 67
Criminal Justice Act 2003 62
Crompton, C. J. 57
cultures: reflecting on 62; valuing different 79

De Palma, R. 64, 67
decolonisation 91, 97–98, 101; need for 95–96; of teachers *95*; through art 105–106
deficit thinking: and ableism 19, *20*, 138, 142–143; about parents 79
Department for Education (DfE): Code of Practice 128; Inclusion Statement 6, 10; materials for Relationships Education policies 69–70; on Relationships Education policies 70–71
Deployment and Impact of Support Staff project 126
desegregation 101–102
'despite' language 19, *20*
determination 66
'Developing Inclusive Classroom Communities' study **11**, 12
Diagnostic Statistical Manual (DSM5) 46
dialogues, student/teacher *32*
differentiation 116
'Differently-abled', term use 25
disability: and activism 14; as barrier to learning 147; *vs.* difference 49–50; and identity **23**; labeling **17**, 121; neurodiversity reframing 46; portrayals of 17–18; refusing to acknowledge 25; term use 21
disrespect, through language 18, 24
dissociation 112–113
diversity 102; and the DfE 70; term use 22–23
dopamine 118
double empathy model 57
double-loop learning 172
Down Syndrome 15, 21
Dudley, P. 141–158
Durning, A. 125–139
Dweck, C. 152
dyslexia 45–46, 51
dyspraxia 45–46, 51

'ecology of equity' 162
Education Endowment Foundation 82; *Making Best Use of Teaching Assistants* 127–130, 133

educational barriers 142, 146, *148*, 157, 177; breaking down 4; disability as 147; evaluating *151*, 152; fear of failure 145–146, 150; harms from 150–151; and school/school collaboration 166; and universities 177–178
educational marginalisation, and inclusive education 2
emotion tracking 119, *120*, 122
emotional support plans (ESPs) 116–117, 122
equality 67, 74–75
Equality Act (2010) 10, 62, 69–70, 178
equity, promoting 166
European Agency for Special Needs and Inclusive Education (EASNE) 5, 7–9; *Profile of Inclusive Teachers* 8–9
European Convention on Human Rights 70
exclusion *see* educational barriers
extreme male brain theory 48
eye colour *104*, 105

Facets of a Community 103
Families First programme 84–85
Family Engagement Officers (FEOs) 82–83, 86–88
family poverty 34, 80, 82, 85–86
feedback, on teacher-communication 26
Fielding, M. 31–32, 42
Fletcher-Watson, S. 50
Formby, E. 64
Freire, P. 150
friendships, peer-to-peer **11**
Frith, U. 46
function-based terminology 52

Galbally, L. 30–43
Gallimore, R. 173
The Garden of Eden 104, 105
Gender Recognition Act 2004 62
genetics, impacts of 118–119
Giangreco, M. 138
Goodall, C. 45–58
Goodall, J. 77–89
Goodboy, A. 64
Greasley, S. 77–89
Greene, M. 98, 106
Greenwood, J. 130
Grinham-Smith, A. 1–12, 108–122

Happé, F. 46, 50
Harlem Children's Zone 169
Hewitt-Clarkson, S. 61–76
Hiebert, J. 173
'high-quality teaching' 128–129
historical figures 96, 99; lack of education about 93
Hodge, N. 19–20
'home learning environments' 78

home visits 81, 85, 87
homophobia 62; and bullying 63–64, 73
hooks, b. 94, 101–102
Hopkins, A. 53
Hulbert, A. 15
Hulbert, R. 15
Hummel 64

identities, and intersection 67
identity-first language **23**, 24, 50–51
Improving the Quality of Education for All (IQEA) project 160–161
inclusion 31, 79, 178; and accessibility 177
inclusive education 31, 79, 139, 150, 152; beliefs about 8–9; developing 152–154; and high-quality teaching 129; hospitality metaphor for 22; impacts of COVID-19 on 7; personalising 155; *vs.* SEN 2; and teachers 127; variety of understandings of 2; and whole school improvement 35, 153
Inclusive Inquiry 30, *32–33*, 34, *35*; expanding 41; first lesson 36–37, *38*, 39; second lesson 39–41; and student researchers 35–37, *38*, 40–41
inclusive practices *3*, 4, 138–139, 141–142, 157; and collaborative meaning-making 172; and Inclusive Inquiry *32*; and learning 144–145
Initial Teacher Education (ITE) 5
insults 19–20
ITE programs 8–9

Jennet, M. 64, 67
journaling 94

Kapp, S. 48
Kelly, C. 130
knowledge, and learning 143
Kustatscher, M. 67

labels **17**, 49, 121
language: and ableism 16–17, 19; for affirmation 24–25; and autism 47, 49–53, 56–58; cautions about 20–23, 50; of deficits 19, *20*, 138; and disrespect 18, 24; English 66–67; and identity 20, **23**, 24; impacts of 27, 58; and inclusivity 14–15; and insults 15, 19; and learning 143–144; learning English 154; non-verbal 26; and 'othering' 15, 17–18, 22–23, 50, 56; "retarded" 14; strength-based 25–26
Lawson, W. 57
'layers of discrimination' 11; UNESCO on 6–7, 10
Le Master 64
leadership for inclusion 142–143; supporting teachers 155

learned helplessness 130
learning 143–145, *146*, 150, 169–170; double-loop 172; and inclusion 144–145; new knowledge about 142–143; single-loop 172
learning coaches 134; working with teachers 135, 137; *see also* teaching assistants (TAs)
Leatherland, J. 47
Lesson Study 156–157
Levels of Use Framework 32, *33*
LGBT+ people: bullying of 63–64; impacts of discrimination on 62; inclusion of 71–75; label 61–62; othering of 68
Little People, Big Dreams series (Sanchez Vegara) 72–73
Local Government Act (1988), Section 28 62–63
Lodge, C. 32

Malaquais, C. 20
Malta 95–96, 99
Marais, C. 14–27
Marcellino, R. 14
Martin, M. 64
Maximising the Impact of Teaching Assistants (Webster, Russell and Blatchford) 127
Maximising the Impact of Teaching Assistants in Primary Schools (Webster et al.) 127
McAnulty, D. 56
McCloskey, S. 179
McLaughlin, J. 22
Memmott, A. 47
mental health: accommodations for 110; behaviourist approaches to 109; and developmental trauma 114; risk/protective factors for 110, *111*; and school exclusions 109; and shame 114–115
Mental Health Act (1983) 47
Mercer, N. 144
Messiou, K. 30–43
Milton, D. E. M. 57
Montgomery, C. 83
'Moor Top' soap opera 73–74

Nanthabalan, B. 141–158
National Curriculum Framework 10; Inclusion Statement 10
neurodiversity 45–47, 49–50, **55**, 56, 58; and masking 52–53; *see also* autism
non-verbal communication 26
'normal': construction of 16; and perceptions of disabled people 16–17, 19
Nottingham, E. 70

observations: of lessons *33*, 36–38, 156–157, 161, 163–166; by students 30, 33–34, 36, 39–40; by TAs 133–134, *136*, 137; *see also* Inclusive Inquiry

PACE (Playful, Acceptance, Curiosity, Empathy) approach 117, **118**, 122
parental engagement 167–168; at Awel y Môr Primary school 80–81, 83–84, 88–89; defined *78*; and home visits 81, 85, 87; importance of 77; improvements from 85; reflecting on 82–83
parents: at Awel y Môr Primary school 80–83, 85, 88–89; and children's mental health 110, *111*; children's support from 166–167; consulting with 83–84; deficit thinking about 79; defined 77; and inclusive education 77; as teachers 86
Pedagogy of the Oppressed (Freire) 150
Personal, Social, Health and Economics Education (PSHE) 68, 72; *see also* Relationships and Sex Education and Health; Relationships Education
person-first language **23**, 24, 50
play dough 37–40
professional development for inclusion 9, 69, 74–75, 125–126, 129–130, 133–138; Inclusive Inquiry 43
Professional Standards for Teaching Assistants (UNISON) 129
Pupil Deprivation Grants (PDGs) 82

questions: about current practices 169; about education-related beliefs 9; about schools 80; ambiguous language 57; for children 12, 42; on children's experiences 94; on COVID-19 7; on inclusive education 3–5, 31–32; language-based 26; Leah 120; on safety 114; on school values 66; and teaching assistants (TAs) 127, 132, 134–135, 137–138; "Who do I want to be?" 153–154

racism 15, 19; *see also* colonial experiences; decolonisation; uncolonisation
Rapinoe, M. 73
relational safe spaces 113
relationship-building, by learning coaches 134
relationships 12, 65, 67, 71–72, 74, 110, 113, 116, 138; between children **11**; teachers and parents 79–81, 83–84, 87–88; teachers and students 81, 99, 134; teachers and TAs 129–130, 135
Relationships and Sex Education and Health 68
Relationships Education program 68–75
Robinson, C. 30
Rose, K. 56
Ross, G. 131
Rouse, M. 2, *3*, 4
Rowe, J. 122
Rudduck, J. 30
R-word (retarded) 14, 19, 27, 47
Ryan, F. 16

safe spaces 113–114, 122
safety 113–114; and the ability to learn **11**, 65; classrooms as 113, 122; increased discussion of 163
sand activities 37–40
scaffolding 131–132, 147, 149
Schön, D. 172
school communities, and inclusive education 2–3, 145
school exclusions 109, 119, 121–122
school leadership: and inclusive education 4–5, 142; *see also* Awel y Môr Primary School
schools: collaboration in 162–165; collaboration in/between 162–165; and COVID-19 65, 86; and learning problems 145; and parental involvement *78*; problem-solving methods of 172; social-emotional climate of 65–67, 125–126; supporting families 81, 85, 167–168
'self-efficacy' theory 152
self-regulation 110; biological influences on 118–119
SEND Code of Practice 109, 126, 128
sexism 15, 19
sexuality: and bullying 63–64; international attitudes towards 62; and schooling 62–63, 68
shame 114–115
shared values, children on **11**
Sinclair, J. 51
Sinclaire-Harding, L. 108–122
Singer, J. 45
single-loop learning 172
Skrtic, T. M. 172
slavery, lack of discussion of 93
Slee, R. 18, 139
sociocultural theory 145
sparkle 65–66
special educational needs (SEN) 16; at Awel y Môr Primary School 80; *vs.* inclusive education 2; and labels **17**, 21, 121; and school exclusions 109; term usage 21–23
Special Educational Needs Coordinator 128
Stigler, J. W. 173
stresses 112, 114
student researchers, and Inclusive Inquiry 35–37, *38*, 40–41
student voices 163; and diversity 94; and inclusion 31, 42; *see also* Inclusive Inquiry
students: assessing 178; and confidentiality 24; learning *146*; reaching out to 162–163; on teachers 165–166
Sturt, P. 122
support: individualised 148–149; term use 22–23
supportive scripts 116, *117*, *121*, 122

talking, and learning 144
Teacher Research Groups (TRGs) 156–157

teachers 150, 163, 170; attitudes of 22, 164; and
autism spectrum disorder 54; core values for 9;
and decolonisation 97–98; and the DfE 74–75;
EADSNE on 8–9; engaging with researchers
164; expanding knowledge of 4, 156–157;
and inclusive education 127, 142, *146*; and
the Inclusive Inquiry study 36; influences
of 99–100; and language-use 27; modelling
behaviours 167; moral purpose of 98; and
observations 156–157, 165; and parental
involvement *78*, 79; responsibilities of 126,
128; unlearning 94–95; working with learning
coaches 135
teachers' values, in schools 65–67
teaching assistants (TAs) 125, 127; building
relationships 134; and high-quality teaching
129; increased use of 126; negative impacts
of 126–127; professional development for
137–138; recommendations for 127–128,
133–138; student over-reliance on 130–131,
133–134
*The Teaching Assistant's Guide to Effective
Interaction: How to Maximise Your Practice*
(Bosanquet) 132
Teaching to Transgress (hooks) 94, 101
textbooks, and disability 18
Thiessen, D. 31
Thunberg, G. 53, 56
The Times 16
trans people: label 61; protections for 62; *see also*
LGBT+ people
trauma: and the classroom 113; developmental
114; impacts of 111–112; triggers for 115–116
trust 112–113
Tulsa Chalkboard 95, 102

UK National Autistic Society 47
uncolonisation 91–92, 96–97, 102, 106; and art
99–104; *vs.* decolonisation 96
'Understanding and Developing Inclusive
Practices in Schools' 161
UNESCO 6–7; on inclusion and equity 161; and
'layers of discrimination' 6–7, 10
UNICEF, Rights Respecting Schools 152
United Nations: Convention on the Rights of
the Child (1989) 30–31, 141, 153; Sustainable
Development Goals (SDGs) 5–8
United States: Harlem Children's Zone 169;
impacts of language in 27; Rosa's Law 14
universities 177–179

Virgo, G. 177–179
Vygotsky, L. 143–144

Waldock, K. E. 52
Walton, E. 14–27
Ward-Sinclair, J. 45–58
Webster, R. 127
welcome, term use 22–23
Wenger, E. 169–171
Wider Pedagogical Role model 126–127
Windrush 153–154
The Windrush Child (Zephaniah) 96–97
Wood, D. 131
Wood, R. 56
Woods, R. 52
Wordsworth Primary School 31, 33–35; *see also*
Inclusive Inquiry
World Down Syndrome Day 21

Yurkofsky, M. M. 171–172

Taylor & Francis eBooks

www.taylorfrancis.com

A single destination for eBooks from Taylor & Francis
with increased functionality and an improved user
experience to meet the needs of our customers.

90,000+ eBooks of award-winning academic content in
Humanities, Social Science, Science, Technology, Engineering,
and Medical written by a global network of editors and authors.

TAYLOR & FRANCIS EBOOKS OFFERS:

A streamlined
experience for
our library
customers

A single point
of discovery
for all of our
eBook content

Improved
search and
discovery of
content at both
book and
chapter level

REQUEST A FREE TRIAL
support@taylorfrancis.com

 Routledge
Taylor & Francis Group

 CRC Press
Taylor & Francis Group

Printed in the United States
by Baker & Taylor Publisher Services